The American Elections of

The 2012 American elections were highly competitive, with the unusually close partisan balance making the elections an opportunity for each of the two major parties. This book assembles leading political scientists and political journalists to explain the 2012 election results and their implications for America's future.

In addition to assessing election results, the book examines the consequences of the large ambitions of the Obama presidency and the political and policy risks entailed in the pursuit of those ambitions. It also explores congressional elections and policymaking since 2008 and how they affected election results in 2012. The book promises a more coherent focus than that evident in similar edited works, achieved through a limited number of chapters and clear definition of chapter content.

Janet M. Box-Steffensmeier is Vernal Riffe Professor of Political Science and Distinguished Scholar at Ohio State University, where she also serves as a professor of sociology (courtesy) and the director of the program in statistics and methodology. She has twice received the Gosnell Award for the best work in political methodology and the Emerging Scholar Award of the Elections, Public Opinion, and Voting Behavior section of the American Political Science Association. She was an inaugural fellow of the Society for Political Methodology.

Steven E. Schier is Dorothy H. and Edward C. Congdon Professor of Political Science at Carleton College in Northfield, Minnesota. He is the author or editor of 14 books, most recently *Transforming America: Barack Obama in the White House* (2011) and numerous scholarly articles. His analysis has appeared in the *New York Times*, the *Washington Post*, *USA Today*, *Atlantic Magazine*, and other publications.

The American Elections of 2012

Edited by
Janet M. Box-Steffensmeier
Steven E. Schier

Routledge
Taylor & Francis Group

NEW YORK AND LONDON

First published 2013
by Routledge
711 Third Avenue, New York, NY 10017

Simultaneously published in the UK
by Routledge
2 Park Square, Milton Park, Abingdon, Oxon OX14 4RN

*Routledge is an imprint of the Taylor & Francis Group,
an informa business*

Library of Congress Cataloging-in-Publication Data

The American elections of 2012 / Janet M. Box-Steffensmeier and
 Steven E. Schier, editors.
  pages ; cm
 1. Presidents—United States—Election, 2012. 2. Elections—
United States—History. I. Box-Steffensmeier, Janet M., 1965–
 JK19682012.A54 2013
 324.973′0932—dc23
 2012051045

ISBN: 978-0-415-80710-4 (hbk)
ISBN: 978-0-415-80711-1 (pbk)
ISBN: 978-0-203-12244-0 (ebk)

Typeset in Bembo
by Apex CoVantage, LLC

Printed and bound in the United States of America
by Edwards Brothers, Inc.

Contents

List of Tables and Figures

Tables

Figures

Preface

This work brings together some of America's top political scientists and journalists to analyze the American elections of 2012. In addition to closely fought races for the presidency and for many congressional seats, 2012 witnessed new peaks in fundraising and campaign spending and unprecedented importance of new media. To understand these issues and the many reasons for Obama's reelection and the continuation of the status quo in the congressional balance of power, we have brought together the insights of leading scholars and political journalists. Our focus here extends beyond the outcomes themselves to include extensive examination of the role of the media, public opinion, campaign money, and religious beliefs in the 2012 elections.

We intend this to be a useful volume for many undergraduate courses. It is a suitable supplementary text in American government survey courses but also can find a place in upper-level undergraduate courses on political parties, elections, political behavior, institutions, Congress, and the presidency. All the topics covered in the chapters that follow are regularly addressed in these courses, and students always respond well to seeing the abstract concepts and theories applied to the most recent election cycle, with which they will typically have some familiarity.

The coeditors' plan for an edited volume on American elections arose some years ago after a breakfast meeting of political scientists who are natives of the Iowa counties of Henry and Lee, in the southeastern corner of the state. Jan hails from near West Point, Iowa, and Steve grew up in Fort Madison, Iowa, towns about ten miles apart. Fond memories of that area led to the book's dedication to the people of southeastern Iowa.

List of Contributors

Robert G. Boatright is an associate professor of political science at Clark University in Worcester, Massachusetts.

Janet M. Box-Steffensmeier is Vernal Riffe Professor of Political Science and director of the program in statistics and methodology at Ohio State University in Columbus.

Leigh A. Bradberry is an assistant professor of political science at California State University, Northridge.

Roger H. Davidson is an emeritus professor of political science at the University of Maryland, College Park.

James L. Guth is Kenan Professor of Political Science at Furman University in Greenville, South Carolina.

John F. Harris is the founder and editor in chief of *Politico,* the Internet political news site based in Arlington, Virginia.

James Hohmann is a national political reporter at *Politico.*

Megan M. Moeller is a graduate student in the Department of Government at the University of Texas at Austin.

Barbara Norrander is a professor of political science at the University of Arizona in Tucson.

Diana Owen is an associate professor of political science and the director of American Studies at Georgetown University in Washington, DC.

Nicol C. Rae is the dean of the College of Arts and Sciences at Montana State University in Bozeman.

Steven E. Schier is the Dorothy H. and Edward C. Congdon Professor of Political Science at Carleton College in Northfield, Minnesota.

Sean M. Theriault is an associate professor in the Department of Government at the University of Texas at Austin.

Christopher Wlezien is a professor of political science at Temple University in Philadelphia, Pennsylvania.

1 Obama's Coalition

How the President Customized His Campaign and Cobbled Together His Majority

John F. Harris and James Hohmann

As the 2012 presidential election got underway, the answers to two large questions at the center of American politics were shrouded in uncertainty. Or perhaps a more precise way of putting it is that plenty of commentators and strategists—sitting at diverse places on the political spectrum, citing an abundance of evidence and theories—were plenty certain of their answers, but no solid consensus had emerged that seemed especially convincing to fair-minded people who did not have a strong personal or political stake in the argument. By the end of the 2012 election, President Barack Obama's victory over Mitt Romney—narrow in many of the most pivotal swing states but emphatic in its broad national reach—had started to provide some insight on two tantalizing questions.

The first question was, who is Barack Obama? Well into his first term, the 44th president remained an ideologically opaque figure. No one could doubt that he was a man of clear progressive instincts with ambitious goals for expanding and reforming the role of government in American life. But he had steadfastly resisted allowing himself to be defined with more precision. Was he a descendant of the "Third Way" school of politicians, like Bill Clinton in the United States or Tony Blair in the United Kingdom, both of whom saw their task as modernizing progressive parties and moderating the more liberal impulses of party activists and special interests? Or was he trying to place himself in the same lineage of presidents with more epic ideological aims—a latter-day Franklin Delano Roosevelt? At different moments and in different moods, Obama sent opposite signals. When pressed to reconcile these contradictions, he and his advisors would simply reject the premise of the inquiry, saying Obama was not interested in ideology but regarded himself solely as a "pragmatist." But this was a singularly unsatisfying answer. Pragmatic to what ends? Pragmatism is equivalent to aimlessness unless it is harnessed to a coherent vision of governance—of articulated problems and proposed remedies. What's more, the most successful pragmatists in the modern presidency—including centrist Bill Clinton and ideologue Ronald Reagan—had, by the time they sought reelection, also revealed much about the theory of their situation. That is, it was clear what they regarded as the central elements of their coalition, and they had established signature strategies and techniques for advancing their policy goals.

Obama, by contrast, by the beginning of 2012, had not established anything that could be called "Obamaism"—neither a clear ideological program nor a distinctive political style. In one sense it was odd that a president who had presided over some $800 billion of federal spending—"the New New Deal," as journalist Michael Grunwald has called it—and also passed an overhaul and expansion of the federal government's role in health care could be ideologically undefined (Grunwald 2012, 121). But so it was. On the right, Obama inspired paroxysms of rage from people who believed he had revealed himself as a leftist of unrestrained ambition. Among liberals, Obama was often viewed with disappointment—someone who had embraced more continuity than reversal of Bush-Cheney on national security policy and who on domestic policy was too timid and accommodating toward the GOP opposition. How could both critiques be true?

And yet in part because of Obama's discomfort with articulating his political philosophy—with finding clear and compelling language to harness his specific programs to a larger argument about the proper role of government—this murkiness flourished, perhaps even in Obama's own mind. On the big questions, he seemed to still be improvising, finding his opportunities in the moment. In fairness to him, an improvisational style was an understandable response to a political environment that remained uncommonly fluid.

And so there was the other great question hanging over 2012 at the outset: where lies the center of American politics? And the natural follow-up to that question: on what trajectory is that center moving? The 2012 election occurred following three consecutive disruptive elections. In 2006, Democrats dethroned a 12-year Republican majority in the House of Representatives. In 2008, Obama made history by becoming the nation's first African American president, in the process consolidating Democratic control of the House and ending eight years of Republican control of the executive branch. In 2010, Republicans reversed the tide by reclaiming control of the House and putting sharp limits on Obama's power. Indeed, the two years after the 2010 midterms were a legislative dead zone in which Obama had no power to pass large initiatives and during which he and House Speaker John Boehner failed to craft a "grand bargain" on fiscal issues. With the 2008 election pointing in one direction about the course of the country and the 2010 pointing the opposite way, it seemed reasonable to expect that 2012 might help settle the question.

The 2012 election did in fact do its job. We now have a much clearer picture of Obama the politician and also a more confident basis for understanding the character of the American electorate in a presidential context.

Who is Barack Obama? The evidence, not merely from the election but from the totality of his first term, including the critical post-election transition to a second term during which this chapter has been written, suggests we should think of him as a what-the-market-will-bear interest-group liberal.

The American electorate, meanwhile, seems to have shifted leftward—not dramatically, it seems, but decisively—in a fashion that forces us to rethink longstanding assumptions. For a generation, the most successful national leaders have tended to think of the United States as a center-right nation. For Democrats such as Bill Clinton, that meant practicing defensive politics. He believed he could push a progressive agenda most effectively by taking advantage of a contradiction: Americans liked conservative rhetoric, promoting small and modest government, but were steadfast in liking many specific big-government programs such as Social Security and Medicare and other programs aimed at education and the environment. Conservatives such as George W. Bush faced opposite circumstances. He could take the rhetorical offensive on such issues as support of traditional social values and a robust national security, so long as he steered clear of programmatic extremism—epitomized by his failed 2005 proposal to partially privatize Social Security.

The 2012 election results do not suggest that the country has moved dramatically leftward on questions about the size of government—good thing, too, given that there is hardly the money to fund such a vision. But it is equally clear that it would be hard for any Republican, much less Mitt Romney, to get elected by promising even in nonspecific terms to dramatically reduce the size of government. More broadly, Obama won reelection by going on both the rhetorical and substantive offensive in ways that Bill Clinton, who proclaimed in 1996 that "the era of big government is over," never felt that he could do. No one in 2004, when George W. Bush boosted his turnout operation with targeted appeals to social conservatives, could have imagined that eight years later it would be Democrats who would be willing to talk publicly about their support for same-sex marriage, and it would be Republicans who would just as soon avoid the subject. Even the Obama of 2008, when he clung to Bill Clinton's "safe, legal, and rare" formulation about abortion rights and generally tried to reduce the profile of this issue, would have been surprised to learn that four years later he would give starring roles to leaders of the abortion rights movement. The leaders of Planned Parenthood and NARAL/Pro-Choice America both had prime-time slots at the Democratic National Convention and played prominent surrogate roles in the general election. Democrats plainly did not feel that they were on the defensive on these or numerous other issues. By contrast, the high point of Romney's general election campaign, his strong performance in the first presidential debate in Denver, came when he sounded most like a Republican version of Bill Clinton—practicing a defensive-minded politics of reassurance, separating himself tonally and even substantively from traditional Republican politics, and presenting himself as a non-ideological creature of the center.

So what do we mean when we describe Obama as a what-the-market-will-bear liberal? An explanation of what the 44th president is not may help sharpen the definition.

He is not, first of all, a great national uniter. This was, of course, the promise of Obama the first time he sprang into national notice, with his famous keynote address to the Democratic National Convention at Boston in 2004. He made an appeal then to purge national politics of what he described as needless malice and blind partisanship, in favor of a new politics that sought sensible common ground and rejected classifying people as belonging to "red America" and "blue America." This was all the premise of his 2008 campaign—that his unique personal story and commitment to a new synthesis would transcend Washington's stale divisions and create new governing coalitions. What became of this original vision—whether it was thwarted by intransigent and vindictive Republicans or was never more than rhetorical mush in the first instance—is an imponderable. Our own instinct is that Obama was sincere in his promise, but naïve, lacking a deep understanding of Washington and how he might realistically achieve the promise. In any event, by 2012, the notion of winning on a unity message was long gone. To the contrary, Obama, like George W. Bush and his Karl Rove–run campaign of 2004, was more than willing to win by dividing the country on terms favorable to him.

Obama was also not running as a great national educator. That is, he did not view the 2012 campaign as an occasion to attempt systematically to move the electorate to some position where it did not already reside. For instance, Obama believes that climate change presents a mortal threat to the planet. But his efforts early in his first term to promote a policy remedy, with a "cap-and-trade" plan for greenhouse gases, were thwarted in large measure because of the skepticism of moderate Democrats. In 2012, Obama accepted political realities—rather than attempt to change realities through the power of presidential suasion—and rarely talked about climate change, especially in manufacturing-heavy swing states such as Ohio.

Obama is also not a Bill Clinton New Democrat. An irony here is that Clinton in 2012 did more than any other Obama surrogate, by far, to energize Democrats on behalf of the president's reelection. One can speculate that his reasons may have been at least as much about advancing Hillary Rodham Clinton's interests as about personal affection for Obama. Still, Clinton likes to be needed and likes being asked for help—and he gave it enthusiastically and effectively. Obama, who doesn't especially like asking for help, needed it badly enough to ask. The days of 2008, when Obama aides privately would speak almost as disdainfully of Clinton and his alleged brand of "small-ball politics" as they would speak of Bush and Cheney, were long gone. Significantly, however, Clinton's 2012 appeals for Obama were made on the strength of his personal appeal. They did not flow from a 1990s-era ideological message. During two elections and two terms, the essence of Clinton's "New Democrat" or "Third Way" appeal was that the party must shed the image that it was merely the sum of its constituencies and special interests. Indeed, Clinton was even willing to disappoint those constituencies and special interests—as with the 1996 signing of welfare reform—in support of the national interest. Clinton sought to move the Democratic conversation away from special-interest rights and entitlements and toward the notion of using government to create opportunity, in exchange for government beneficiaries embracing more responsibility.

Within the constraints of what he could not or would not do, Obama clearly remained an ambitious president—and thus our conclusion that he is a what-the-market-will-bear liberal. That is, he is not an ideological exotic— the evidence suggests he is a fairly conventional urban liberal, as befits his Illinois background representing urban constituents. He will promote the most vigorous interpretation of what a traditional urban liberal would support, consistent with what he thinks he can achieve within acceptable political costs. If he concludes the cost is imprudently high, he will move on to other items without great remorse. No doubt Obama has always supported same-sex marriage; he even told a local Chicago newspaper this was his position as early as the mid-1990s (Weinger 2012). Later, he insisted implausibly that this position was inaccurate, attributing the confusion to staff error. But as president, he maintained that he opposed same-sex marriage, until 2012 when a shift in public opinion allowed him to state a more forthright view, even as he continued to maintain this was a state issue. There is no doubt that Obama's views on global warming are sincere as well, but there's also little doubt that he will continue to keep his distance from this issue until the political costs of embracing it decline. One sees this same calculus at work in Obama's negotiations with House Speaker John Boehner over a fiscal grand bargain. What does Obama want? He wants tax rates to rise as high as he can reasonably get them in the current political environment. Yet he clearly also does not view the matter as a theological question—he'll get the best deal he can and move on. There is nothing novel about a president practicing political caution and the art of compromise. But Obama's penchant for making these traits the essence of his strategy—rather than tools of his strategy—is a distinctive signature.

If Clinton wanted the Democratic Party to stand for more than the sum of its parts, Obama in 2012 took on Republicans with a different message: our parts are bigger than your parts. That is, there are more people in Democratic-leaning constituency groups and special interests who benefit from having Democrats in power than there are Republican-leaning interests who fear the costs of having Democrats in power. To an extent he had not in 2008, Obama explicitly appealed to women, African Americans, Latinos, LGBT citizens, and young voters. He repeatedly used the power of the presidency to strengthen his hand with these five Democratic constituencies, knowing they would be critical to the coalition that would win him a second term. Obama saw his 2012 task not as transcending Democratic special interests but as unabashedly mobilizing them to maximum effect.

From this belief flowed a strategy with two related prongs: defining Mitt Romney in ways that would be singularly unappealing to these interests and constituencies and using technology and targeted messages to ensure that these people turned out in high numbers to back a second term. Notably not among these prongs was a clear, detailed, or memorable statement of what he hoped to achieve in a second term. It was not the most inspirational campaign, as evidenced by both lower overall turnout than 2008 and a lower percentage of the total vote for Obama (Liptak 2012). But the campaign was admirably effective, as a president facing reelection with an unemployment rate of nearly 8 percent and approval ratings that barely reached 50 percent marched his way to a second term. Republicans, who after their 2010 gains were expecting to dislodge this history-making president, instead went to battle with a weak candidate with a weak message and a weak organization. They were left in something akin to the position of the Michael Dukakis character from a *Saturday Night Live* skit in 1988; the Dukakis character paused during a presidential debate, looked incredulously into the camera, and said, "I can't believe I'm losing to this guy." But lose the Republicans did. What's more, their 2012 defeat signaled the likelihood of more defeats unless they understand and react to the political strategies—and the ideological and demographic realities—that drove Obama's victory.

One Size Does Not Fit All

Romney got into trouble the week after November's election when he told donors that the president won reelection by handing out "gifts" to core Democratic constituencies. Said Romney on a call he did not realize reporters were listening in on,

> The Obama campaign was following the old playbook of giving a lot of stuff to groups that they hoped they could get to vote for them and be motivated to go out to the polls, specifically the African American community, the Hispanic community and young people. In each case they were very generous in what they gave to those groups. . . . The president's campaign focused on giving targeted groups a big gift—so he made a big effort on small things. (Reston 2012)

Even many top Republicans quickly criticized the comment as offensive, but the sentiment hints at an underlying truth about Obama's inelegant reelection.

Although Republicans always wanted the election to be as much as possible a referendum on Obama's job performance, specifically his handling of the economy, Obama's strategists saw the election as a "block-by-block knife fight" to be decided by a small number of voters in a handful of states. "This isn't 2008," a top Obama campaign advisor told our colleagues Mike Allen and Jim VandeHei in June 2012. "We just think people are looking at the race the wrong way. . . . The expansion of the electorate is our base. It's African Americans, Hispanics, young people, and women" (Allen and VandeHei 2012a). The Obama campaign launched "Operation Vote" to focus on turning out these Democratic base groups. Separate structures targeting each of those groups in key states focused on registering new voters and keeping them motivated. It took additional programmatic offerings, along with aggressive outreach, to shore up each group.

In early 2011, top Obama advisors closely studied George W. Bush's 2004 victory over Sen. John Kerry for clues on how they could reelect a president with middling approval ratings. They decided that a key was to disqualify Mitt Romney, who they always presumed would eventually win the GOP nomination, in the minds of as many voters as possible. "Unless things change and Obama can run on accomplishments, he will have to kill Romney," a prominent Democratic strategist aligned with the White House confessed to *Politico* 15 months before Election Day (Smith and Martin 2011). But they also saw how Bush had focused as much on mobilizing his conservative base as on persuading independents. When Romney wrapped up the nomination, the Obama campaign launched an unorthodox, early-summer ad blitz that attacked Romney over his tenure at Bain Capital (Thrush and Martin 2012). The goal was to define him early while ad rates were still low. The campaign knew there was a lot of dissatisfaction with the president, but they thought they could nonetheless stop some of Obama's 2008 voters from defecting by creating fear of the alternative.

Wooing Women

The Obama campaign unveiled an interactive website in May 2012 called "The Life of Julia" that allowed voters to click through 12 stages of a fictional woman's life to see the different ways that the incumbent's policies help an average, middle-class American woman over the course of six decades—and, by contrast, to see how a President Romney might hurt her. The site noted that the first bill Obama had signed into law after being elected president was the Lilly Ledbetter Fair Pay Act. "Thanks to Obamacare, her health insurance is required to cover birth control and preventive care, letting Julia focus on her work rather than worry about her health," another infographic added. "Romney supports the Blunt Amendment—which would place Julia's health care decisions in the hands of her employer—and repealing health care reform so insurance companies could go back to charging women 50% more than men." Republicans mocked the "Julia" gimmick, and Romney joked about it on the campaign trail. They believed it epitomized paternalism and a Democratic mindset that government should protect women from cradle to grave (Slack 2012). But after the campaign ended, an Obama official called the infographic one of the campaign's greatest successes.

After downplaying social issues in 2008, Obama embraced them in 2012 as part of a plan to prevent women from bleeding to Romney. The Obama campaign used Georgetown graduate student Sandra Fluke as a prominent campaign trail surrogate after radio shock jock Rush Limbaugh demonized her for supporting the availability of birth control. Planned Parenthood chief Cecile Richards introduced Obama at a campaign rally in Northern Virginia just weeks before Election Day (Nather and Mahtesian 2012). When the Department of Health and Human Services mandated employer coverage for contraception as part of the federal health care overhaul, Republicans predicted that there would be a Catholic backlash that could cost Obama states such as Iowa (Hohmann 2012b). Howls from clergy and religious groups led to an "accommodation," but the president seemed to calculate (correctly) that there was far more upside with women than downside with religious conservatives who were unlikely to vote for him anyway.

Romney had taken a hard line on abortion during the elongated primaries, reiterating that he wanted to overturn the Supreme Court's landmark *Roe v. Wade* decision and to defund Planned Parenthood. The Obama campaign would not allow Romney to successfully distance himself from either comment as the general election approached. During the second of three debates, asked about diversity, Romney spoke of reviewing "binders full of women" while governor of Massachusetts, to make sure that there was gender equality in his cabinet. Obama pounced, ridiculing the statement on the stump for days. After Romney told the *Des Moines Register* editorial board that he did not want to change existing law on abortion, Democrats generated negative headlines and forced a Romney spokeswoman to walk back the comments (Budoff Brown 2012). In the final weeks, the Obama campaign ran a TV ad in every swing state contrasting Romney's more moderate remarks on abortion with conservative statements he had made in the primaries.

GOP missteps gave Democrats opportunities to accuse Republicans of waging a "war on women" all year long. A week before the start of the Republican National Convention, Missouri GOP Senate candidate Todd Akin, who had served as a member of the House until his run for the Senate, declared to a St. Louis Fox affiliate that victims of "legitimate rape" very rarely get pregnant because their bodies prevent them from doing so. National Republicans tried to get Akin to drop out, but he did not. "The interesting thing here is that this is an individual who sits on the House Committee on Science and Technology but somehow missed science class,"

Obama joked at a New York fundraiser two days later. "And it's representative of the desire to go backwards instead of forwards and fight fights that we thought were settled 20 or 30 years ago" (Epstein 2012). Then in late October, Republican Senate candidate Richard Mourdock of Indiana said that even in the case of rape, God always intends for women to get pregnant (Robillard 2012a). Romney publicly disagreed with Mourdock's comment, but he did not distance himself from the candidate for whom he had cut a television advertisement just one week before.

Aggressively courting women paid dividends. Exit polls showed that Obama carried them by 11 points, 55 percent to 44 percent, and they made up 53 percent of the electorate.

This led to much Republican handwringing after the election. Karen Hughes, a former top advisor to George W. Bush, said the college-age daughters of many of her friends voted for Obama because they were turned off by the suggestion that rape could somehow be "legitimate." "If another Republican man says anything about rape other than it is a horrific, violent crime," Hughes wrote, "I want to personally cut out his tongue" (Hughes 2012). Louisiana governor Bobby Jindal wrote an op-ed for the *Wall Street Journal* advocating over-the-counter sale of oral contraceptives (Jindal 2012). "As a conservative Republican," he wrote, "I believe that we have been stupid to let the Democrats demagogue the contraceptives issue and pretend, during debates about health-care insurance, that Republicans are somehow against birth control."

Holding Hispanics

Obama carried 68 percent of the Latino vote in 2008, but he did not follow through on his promise during the first campaign to push comprehensive immigration reform. He even deported more than one million undocumented immigrants. His advisors saw potentially alarming signs of disappointment among the fast-growing electorate (Romano 2012). It was no coincidence that the tide began to turn only after Obama issued an executive order in June 2012 that halted the deportation of younger illegal immigrants who enroll in college or enlist in the military.

The Obama campaign believed it needed to add more Latino voters to the rolls to win certain swing states. That required investing in a massive, costly field operation two years before the election. "We spent a year, almost a year-and-a-half, registering voters . . . in order to keep Florida on the map," Marlon Marshall, the Obama campaign's deputy national field director, said at a post-election conference (Hohmann 2012a). The campaign mainly focused on the booming Puerto Rican population around Orlando.

The incumbent's campaign also assembled an outreach team in the communications division 18 months before the election. One year before the election, a Latino vote director was hired and tasked with designing a Latino field program in every swing state—not just ones with high concentrations of Latinos. In the middle of 2011, Obama's team built a Spanish-language media list of more than 700 thought leaders—from the smallest Spanish-language paper in Iowa to talk-radio hosts who lure millions of listeners (Hohmann and Schultheis 2012). At that point, very few Hispanic media leaders were paying any attention to the election, but Obama campaign aides began aggressively working to earn free media to highlight parts of the president's health care overhaul and the administration's "Race to the Top" program that tested well with Latino voters.

Anticipating that Romney would ultimately win the nomination, Obama's operation in Chicago set out to drive up Romney's negatives very early with voters who they knew were not happy with the president's record. At the end of December, on the eve of the Iowa caucuses, Romney said that he would veto the DREAM Act as president. Largely under the radar, Obama's media shop pushed the story hard in the Spanish-language press and celebrated internally when it got covered. They also made sure word got out to the right Spanish-language media when Romney talked about "self-deportation" during a GOP debate. The campaign went on the air with Spanish-language advertisements in Nevada, Colorado, and Florida on April 17, right after Romney had effectively clinched the nomination. They ads stayed up through Election Day.

The president saw Romney's pandering to conservatives in the primary as a lucky break. Trying to get the endorsement of the editors of the *Des Moines Register* on a call that was not meant for public consumption, Obama explained, "Since this is off the record, I will just be very blunt. Should I win a second term, a big reason . . . is because the Republican nominee and the Republican Party have so alienated the fastest-growing demographic group in the country, the Latino community. And this is a relatively new phenomenon. George Bush and Karl Rove were smart enough to understand the changing nature of America" (VandeHei and Allen 2012).

Obama's website said he supported a permanent DREAM Act but gave just as much play to blaming Republicans for "standing lock-step against it." Campaign literature also stressed that Obama had made sure the government spent more money on early childhood learning programs. "Approximately 19% of the children helped by these child care programs are Latinos, as are 33% of participants in Head Start," said the campaign's Latino outreach page (BarackObama.com 2012). "The President has also made a significant investment of over $1 billion for Hispanic Serving Institutions, including a recent set of grants to nearly 100 HSI's totaling $100 million."

Romney wound up losing the Latino vote by the largest margin of any Republican presidential candidate since Bob Dole, pulling an anemic 27 percent nationwide. Obama's swing state outreach tangibly helped, evidenced by the fact that he did slightly better in targeted states than nontargeted states. In Colorado, for example, exit polls showed Obama won Hispanics by a 52 point margin. In Arizona, the margin was 49 points. Obama carried Florida by less than 80,000 votes, or 0.86 percent, making it the closest state in the election. Besides Puerto Rican registration, his advisors believe that Romney's selection of Paul Ryan helped them win the Sunshine State's 29 electoral votes in part because it allowed them to eat into Cubans' traditional support for Republicans—somewhat beneath the radar, they had emphasized the Wisconsin congressman's past opposition to the Cuban trade embargo.

The Kids Are Alright

Mitt Romney marveled that young voters turned out as a "larger share in this election even than in 2008," back when Obama's quest for the presidency felt more like a social movement than a traditional campaign. Exit polls showed the youth vote's share of the electorate increased slightly from 18 percent to 19 percent, though this is within the margin of error. When talking to donors, the failed Republican candidate chalked this up to the chance for young people to now stay on their parents' health insurance plans until they turn 26 and to legally mandated contraception coverage—which he called "a big gift to young people"—along with Obama's support for partial forgiveness of college loan interest (Reston 2012). Obama strategists would agree that each of those initiatives helped them, and they would probably add the president's support for same-sex marriage and his moves to end the war in Iraq, one of the original causes that helped catapult him to national prominence.

Obama realized that winning younger voters would be a heavier lift the second time, and he rallied regularly at college campuses throughout his presidency with this in mind. During the home stretch, from the Democratic convention until the election, the president, his wife Michelle, and Vice President Joe Biden made more than 30 stops at college towns. In April, pushing a student loans initiative, he appeared on Jimmy Fallon's late-night comedy show while visiting the University of North Carolina (Memoli 2012). Weeks before the election, he sat down with MTV to answer questions about everything from Bob Marley's music to climate change and gave an interview to comedian Jon Stewart on *The Daily Show.* First Lady Michelle Obama appeared in a skit on *Jimmy Kimmel Live!* in which she used a bullhorn to wake the host (Samuelsohn 2012). The campaign even ran an ad targeting youth on Top 40 radio in Iowa and Virginia, called "C'mon Man." With a much longer list of surrogates in entertainment than Romney had, the campaign hosted a spate of free concerts in the battlegrounds.

The president wound up winning the youth vote nationally, 67 percent to 30 percent. An analysis from the Center for Research and Information on Civic Learning and Engagement at Tufts University characterized voters under 30 as decisive in Florida, Virginia, Pennsylvania, and Ohio (Robillard 2012b). This in part resulted from the changing face of America. A report from the Pew Research Center noted that Obama actually lost white non-Hispanics under 30, a group he had won in 2008 (Pew Research Center 2012). But he carried young Hispanics by roughly the same amount as in 2008. Just 58 percent of voters under 30 were white non-Hispanic, compared to three in four over 30.

Upping African American Turnout

The first African American president always felt like he could count on nearly monolithic support from African Americans. His challenge was the number, not the share, of the vote; just like with Hispanics, polls suggested lagging enthusiasm. In 2008, Obama tried hard not to focus too much on his racial background, fearing it could drive some away. The campaign knew that others would talk about such a central part of the candidate's identity, and they saw little political upside to emphasizing it. In 2012, he seemed more willing to talk about it. His advisors also worked harder to mobilize black votes.

There were some rough patches. In September 2011, Obama upset some members of the Congressional Black Caucus after he admonished them at a gala dinner to "stop complaining, stop grumbling, [and] stop crying" (Williams 2011). The CBC had pushed Obama to more aggressively stimulate the economy.

Obama's White House and campaign touted a series of policies aimed at helping the black community, from unemployment insurance extensions to programs encouraging minority entrepreneurship. He held a summit on African American issues a year out from the election, and the White House published a 44-page report touting accomplishments for African Americans—including the health care overhaul. A "barber shop and beauty salon" program aimed to get African Americans to register fellow African Americans. The campaign signed up "congregation captains" to recruit other Obama supporters at predominantly black churches (Hennessey 2012). Another Project Vote initiative encouraged African American supporters to host block parties called "Barack the Block."

Just as with other groups, part of the push to galvanize African American turnout involved driving up Romney's negatives. The *New York Times* reported a month before the election that several voters interviewed in North Carolina

> agreed that the president has not given enough attention to issues that are important to black communities, the most pressing being anti-poverty measures . . . but many said they also remain suspicious of Mr. Romney's record on civil rights and diversity. As governor of Massachusetts, for

instance, he eliminated the Office of Affirmative Action. Mr. Romney's Mormon faith is also an issue. The Church of Jesus Christ of Latter-day Saints barred blacks from the priesthood until 1978. (Saulny 2012)

After the election, Obama officials said that Clint Eastwood's bizarre "chair" speech at the Republican National Convention had played a key role in galvanizing African Americans who perceived the monologue as disrespectful to the president.

Nationally, African Americans made up 13 percent of the electorate, and exit polls showed Obama carrying 93 percent of them. The day after the election, multiple Romney sources pointed to the share of African Americans who voted in Ohio in 2012. In 2008, the black percentage of the electorate was 11 percent. In 2012, it was 15 percent (Hohmann and Palmer 2012). In Virginia and Florida, exit polls showed that the same share of African Americans turned out as four years earlier, something that many GOP pollsters and turnout models did not fathom. Obama won Ohio by just 2 percent. "With regards to African American voters, 'Obamacare' was a huge plus—and was highly motivational to African American voters," Romney said on his post-election donor call (Reston 2012). "You can imagine for somebody making $25–, or $30–, or $35,000 a year, being told you're now going to get free healthcare—particularly if you don't have it, getting free healthcare worth, what, $10,000 a family, in perpetuity, I mean this is huge" (Reston 2012).

Paul Ryan attributed his ticket's loss to the "urban" vote. "Well, he got turnout," the vice presidential nominee told the *Milwaukee Journal Sentinel* in his first interview after the election, when asked if the result was a rejection of the Republican vision (Glauber 2012). "The president should get credit for achieving record-breaking turnout numbers from urban areas for the most part, and that did win the election for him."

Galvanizing the Gay Community

At first blush, Obama coming out in support of same-sex marriage was politically perilous. A poll taken by Gallup immediately after his May announcement showed that 40 percent said the president's stance would affect their vote—26 percent said it would make them less likely to vote for him, twice as many as said it would make them more likely to support him (Jones 2012). With the announcement prompted by Joe Biden's own announcement on NBC's *Meet the Press* that he supported gay rights, some close to the president also worried it would come across as Obama pandering (Thrush and Budoff Brown 2012). African Americans, historically opposed to gay rights, were cause for particular concern. So were conservative Democrats in places such as Iowa, where three Supreme Court justices who had ruled in favor of same-sex marriage were removed by voters in 2010, and voters in the swing state of North Carolina, where voters passed a constitutional amendment banning same-sex marriage the same week Obama announced he backed it in a nationally televised interview.

In the final analysis, the move helped Obama at the ballot box. Five percent of voters identified themselves as gay, lesbian, or bisexual in exit polling. Among that group, Obama won 76 percent, and Romney won 22 percent. Among straight voters, exit polls showed Obama and Romney tied at 49 percent. A post-election study by Gary Gates of the Williams Institute at the UCLA School of Law noted that Romney would have won Ohio and Florida if gay votes had been excluded (Cohen 2012). Taking a position in support of same-sex marriage also helped the president raise money, and Republicans never emphasized the issue because they thought it was a distraction from the economy.

Obama stopped short of supporting full marriage rights for same-sex couples, saying that he supports marriage equality personally but respects the decision each state makes. He had already repealed the "Don't Ask, Don't Tell" policy in the military. The campaign organized voter registration drives at pride festivals and saturated communities with heavy concentrations of LGBT voters. For the first time, measures legalizing same-sex marriage passed in Maine, Maryland, and Washington on Election Day, and Minnesota voters rejected a constitutional amendment that would have banned same-sex marriage.

The tide of public opinion continues to turn on what rights same-sex couples deserve. A *Politico*/George Washington University Battleground poll conducted a month after the election found a plurality of Americans supportive of same-sex marriage. Only one in four said same-sex couples should not be allowed to have any kind of legal recognition, whereas 40 percent supported full legal marriage and another 30 percent supported civil unions. Nearly half, 48 percent, approved Obama's handling of the marriage issue (Hohmann 2012c). Prominent Republicans believe that the party needs to adjust its position to appeal to younger voters going forward, even though social conservatives remain a core base for the GOP. "According to Jan van Lohuizen, a former pollster for President George W. Bush, public support for civil-marriage rights for same-sex couples increased by 1% each year from 1993 through 2009, and by 5% per year in 2010 and 2011," wrote former Republican National Committee chairman Ken Mehlman in an op-ed for the *Wall Street Journal;* Mehlman came out of the closet as gay after going into the private sector (Mehlman 2012). Although just 17 percent of Republicans supported same-sex marriage in the *Politico* poll, 40 percent backed civil unions.

Precision Kills

Obama carefully tailored his campaign, customizing his advertisements and microtargeting his appeals in a more sophisticated way than had ever been done before. It is natural for the winner of a national campaign to look brilliant and for the loser to look like a dope. The incumbent made mistakes, to be sure. But he deserves credit for running a far more refined media campaign than his Republican opponent, which allowed him to reach the different elements of his coalition with messages that would best resonate with each.

A system called "the optimizer" used data obtained from door-knockers and phone canvassers to determine which channels the campaign should advertise on and when. "The Obama team was on 60 channels during one week near the end of the campaign, compared with 18 for the Romney operation during the same period," the *Washington Post* reported after the election, based on a review of cable advertising data. "With Romney, they went after pure tonnage. With Obama, you see them capturing those niche audiences," Tim Kay, political sales director for NCC Media, a consortium of cable operators, told the paper (Farnam 2012). Until late in the campaign, Romney ran a one-size-fits-all campaign focused on making the election a referendum on Obama and touting Romney's unspecific plan to grow the economy faster than Obama could. The Republicans relied more on traditional broadcast TV, whereas Obama sought out the audience he wanted to reach more deliberately (Haberman, Burns, and Schultheis 2012). Romney national political director Rich Beeson marveled at the customization. "We were going after it with a meat cleaver, and they were going after it with a scalpel," he said (Hohmann 2012a). That meant that northwest Ohio got inundated with ads highlighting Romney's opposition to the auto bailout, and women in northern Virginia saw clips of Romney saying he wanted to defund Planned Parenthood.

The Obama campaign put a premium on variety. In June, for example, they launched Spanish-language ads in Florida to push voter registration. An Orlando version featured a Puerto Rican, whereas the Miami version showcased a Colombian (Smith 2012). In New Mexico, as another illustration of the attention to nuance, the Obama campaign was careful to say "Hispanic" instead of "Latino" in all its literature (Allen and VandeHei 2012).

The Obama campaign took better advantage of the opportunities afforded by radio as well. An unreleased Obama radio ad touted the president's support for same-sex marriage, for example. This theme was not featured in TV commercials. Documents obtained by our colleague Josh Gerstein showed that the Obama campaign had planned to ask stations to play the spot about same-sex marriage during periods of the day when 18- to 34-year-olds were most likely to be listening. "What are you going to tell them? You were just too busy? You didn't think it mattered? Is that what you're going to tell your friends who can't get married? The ones who couldn't serve openly in the military?" a young woman narrator says in the spot, which ran on Top 40 stations. "You're going to tell them they can't make decisions about their own bodies anymore because you didn't think your vote counted?" (Gerstein 2012).

Will "Obamaism" Endure?

This analysis of Obama's victory raises important questions for him and for the opposition Republicans alike.

For Obama, the main question is, what does he do with his victory? The weeks after his election were devoted largely not to preparing for a robust second term, but to closing the unfinished business of his first term—that is, averting a fall over the "fiscal cliff" and crafting a comprehensive budget deal with John Boehner. But surely there is more to the story than this. Obama's impressive victory leaves him with something Bill Clinton pined for but never enjoyed—a playing field that is ideologically and demographically tilted in his favor. He has the opportunity, if he has the creativity, to practice something more ambitious than "pragmatism" and to bridge the achievements of his first term and his second in a way that historians will say represents a genuine ideological arc. This is the only way he can create "Obamaism" that will outlast Obama.

Meanwhile, perhaps it will fall to Republicans to revive the lost philosophy known as "Clintonism." The GOP heading toward 2016 should be chastened in a way that the most ambitious and forward-thinking Democrats were chastened following their routs in 1980, 1984, and 1988. Republicans can hardly do any better among white males—62 percent—than Romney did in 2012. They can hardly do any worse than he did among Hispanics and younger voters—27 percent among Latinos and 36 percent among 18- to 24-year-olds. It is clear this is not a winning formula. And it is clear to at least some strategists that the party's overriding mission must be to find a new formula. In other words, Republicans are looking for their Bill Clinton. In 1992 he helped Democrats soften, or in some cases abandon, the parts of their ideology that had become intellectually stale and politically unsalable. Clinton's support for deficit reduction, free trade, welfare reform, anti-crime measures, and the elevation of a politics emphasizing civic obligation over individual entitlement was both pragmatic and sincere. His personal buoyancy stood in contrast to the dour personas of Jimmy Carter, Walter Mondale, and Michael Dukakis.

Republicans, who have lost the popular vote in five of the last six presidential elections, would do well to modernize their party along similar lines. The Clinton model would have them soften or abandon social positions that are out of step with younger voters and women and craft an economic agenda that emphasizes widely shared opportunity and prosperity more than protections for wealthy taxpayers. Most likely, such a model would come, as Clinton came in 1992, from the ranks of governors rather than from among Washington politicians.

Republicans also can take heart—and Democrats and political analysts should take caution—in a timeless truth about American politics: nothing stands still. And no trend continues indefinitely. Obama's current political advantage will last only so long as his policies are seen as effective. And even then, the natural rhythms of politics will come into play. The electorate's mood will change, and so will national circumstances. Ambitious Republicans will find their opportunities because that is what ambitious politicians do.

What's more, recent elections teach us that in modern politics the advantages of one party or the other tend to be perishable. After George W. Bush's victory in 2004, many analysts offered predictions that the GOP's structural lead on national security issues, combined with its superior techniques of voter identification and mobilization, would give the party a generation-long advantage in presidential politics. These predictions were demolished in just four years. After 2012, recidivists and slow-learners in the journalistic and academic communities are predicting that Democrats' demographic and turnout advantages will put them in a dominant position for the next generation, to which the only reasonable response is "we'll see." But it seems clear that the scholarly and journalistic addiction to searching for evidence of long-term shifts—as though political forces were akin to tectonic plates—is a throwback to an earlier era, when demographic and ideological advantages did indeed often last for decades. In our modern society—highly mobile, highly informed, and highly fickle in its national moods—these seismic shifts are less likely.

Obama's 2012 victory was an expression of new political realities—for the time being. We close by recalling Arthur Schlesinger Jr.'s injunction about "the inscrutability of history." The great liberal historian, who surely would have been cheered by Obama's victory, offered timeless wisdom when he wrote, "Far from offering a shortcut to clairvoyance, history teaches us that the future is full of surprises and outwits all our certitudes" (Schlesinger 2008, 473). In that spirit, let us enjoy watching the drama of Obama's second term unfold and take comfort that our understanding of American politics is fragmentary—never more than an election away from being reshaped anew.

REFERENCES

Allen, Mike, and Jim VandeHei. 2012. "Barack Obama's Group Therapy." *Politico*, June 19. http://dyn.politico.com/printstory.cfm?uuid=1B1CE16F6A8D-4137-A6EC-52ED0D002510 (accessed December 17, 2012).

BarackObama.com. 2012. "Latino Accomplishments." http://www.barackobama.com/latinos/accomplishments (accessed December 17, 2012).

Budoff Brown, Carrie. 2012. "President Obama Tries to Regain Edge with Women." *Politico*, October 26. http://dyn.politico.com/printstory.cfm?uuid=8138E73F-F12F-45E4-9FAA90E056310C3A (accessed December 17, 2012).

Cohen, Micah. 2012. "Gay Support Buoyed Obama, as the Straight Vote Split." *New York Times*, November 16, A21.

Epstein, Reid. 2012. "Obama: Todd Akin 'Somehow Missed Science Class.'" *Politico*, August 22. http://www.politico.com/politico44/2012/08/obama-todd-akin-somehow-missed-science-class-132876.html (accessed December 17, 2012).

Farnam, T. W. 2012. "Obama Campaign Took Unorthodox Approach to Ad Buying." *Washington Post,* November 14. http://www.washingtonpost.com/politics/theinfluence-industry-obama-campaign-took-unorthodox-approach-to-adbuying/2012/11/14/c3477e8c-2e87-11e2-beb2-4b4cf5087636_print.html (accessed December 17, 2012).

Gerstein, Josh. 2012. "Radio: The Other Air War." *Politico,* November 1. http://www.politico.com/news/stories/1012/83143.html (accessed December 17, 2012).

Glauber, Bill. 2012. "Paul Ryan Says Losing Race 'a Foreign Experience.'" *Milwaukee Journal Sentinel,* November 12. http://www.jsonline.com/news/wisconsin/ryan-says-losing-race-a-foreign experience-fe7k527-179000091.html (accessed December 17, 2012).

Grunwald, Michael. 2012. *The New New Deal: The Hidden Story of Change.* New York: Simon and Schuster.

Haberman, Maggie, Alexander Burns, and Emily Schultheis. 2012. "Mitt Romney's Unusual In-House Ad Strategy." *Politico,* October 9. http://www.politico.com/news/stories/1012/82217.html (accessed December 17, 2012).

Hennessey, Kathleen. 2012. "Obama Campaign Strives to Revive Black Voter Enthusiasm of 2008." *Los Angeles Times,* October 27. http://www.latimes.com/news/nationworld/nation/la-na-black-voters-20121027,0,661227.story (accessed December 17, 2012).

Hohmann, James. 2012a. "Obama, Romney Campaign Officials Dissect 2012 Election at Dole Institute." *Politico,* December 8. http://www.politico.com/story/2012/12/campaign-officials-dissect-election-cycle-84796.html (accessed December 17, 2012).

Hohmann, James. 2012b. "Paul Ryan Ramps Up Fight for Catholic Vote." *Politico,* August 12. http://www.politico.com/news/stories/0812/79653.html (accessed December 17, 2012).

Hohmann, James. 2012c. "Poll: Plurality Supports Gay Marriage." *Politico,* December 9. http://www.politico.com/story/2012/12/poll-plurality-supports-gay-marriage-84803.html (accessed December 17, 2012).

Hohmann, James, and Anna Palmer. 2012. "Romneyworld Reckoning Begins." *Politico,* November 7. http://www.politico.com/news/stories/1112/83549.html (accessed December 17, 2012).

Hohmann, James, and Emily Schultheis. 2012. "Obama's Bold Push to Win Latinos." *Politico,* November 10. http://dyn.politico.com/printstory.cfm?uuid=516CC066-14B9-4DBF-A6F1-0D15CDE6D4E0 (accessed December 17, 2012).

Hughes, Karen. 2012. "Communication Lessons from the Election." *Politico,* November 9. http://www.politico.com/news/stories/1112/83632.html (accessed December 17, 2012).

Jindal, Bobby. 2012. "The End of Birth Control Politics: Over-the-Counter Sales of Oral Contraceptives Will Cut Off a Disingenuous Attack Line." *Wall Street Journal,* December 13. http://online.wsj.com/article/SB10001424127887324640104578163120400999916.html (accessed December 17, 2012).

Jones, Jeffrey M. 2012. "Six in 10 Say Obama Same-Sex Marriage View Won't Sway Vote: More Say It Makes Them Less Likely Rather than More Likely to Vote for Obama." Gallup.com. May 11. http://www.gallup.com/poll/154628/six-say-obama-sex-marriage-view-won-sway-vote.aspx (accessed December 17, 2012).

Liptak, Kevin. 2012. "Report Shows Lower Turnout Than 2008 and 2004." CNN, November 8. http://politicalticker.blogs.cnn.com/2012/11/08/report shows-turnout-lower-than-2008-and-2004/ (accessed December 17, 2012).

Mehlman, Ken. 2012. "Making the Same-Sex Case: Legalizing Marriage for Gay Couples Will Cultivate Community Stability and Foster Family Values." *Wall Street Journal,* November 20. http://online.wsj.com/article/SB100014241278873233532 0457812891255410772.html?mod=googlenews_wsj (accessed December 17, 2012).

Memoli, Michael. 2012. "Obama on Jimmy Fallon: Top Moments with 'POTUS with the Most-est.'" *Los Angeles Times,* April 25. http://articles.latimes.com/2012/apr/25/news/la-pn-obama-on-jimmy-fallon-highlights-20120425 (accessed December 17, 2012).

Nather, David, and Charles Mahtesian. 2012. "Democrats Go All in for Abortion Rights." *Politico,* October 26. http://dyn.politico.com/printstory.cfm?uuid=5E7C88DC-90CE-4A3B-ABB4-F3748DF23349 (accessed December 17, 2012).

Pew Research Center for the People and the Press. 2012. "Young Voters Supported Obama Less, But May Have Mattered More." Washington, DC: Pew Center. http://www.people-press.org/2012/11/26/young-voters-supported-obama-less-but-may-have-mattered-more/ (accessed December 17, 2012).

Reston, Maeve. 2012. "Romney Attributes Loss to 'Gifts' Obama Gave Minorities." *Los Angeles Times,* November 15. http://articles.latimes.com/2012/nov/15/nation/la-na-romney-donors-20121115 (accessed December 17, 2012).

Robillard, Kevin. 2012a. "GOP Splits over Richard Mourdock Comment." *Politico,* October 24. http://www.politico.com/news/stories/1012/82806.html (accessed December 17, 2012).

Robillard, Kevin. 2012b. "Study: Youth Vote Was Decisive." *Politico,* November 7. http://www.politico.com/news/stories/1112/83510.html (accessed December 17, 2012).

Romano, Lois. 2012. "President Obama Moves to Lock in Latino Vote." *Politico,* October 7. http://dyn.politico.com/printstory.cfm?uuid=C03956764172-4A99-9104-67B1BACFE911 (accessed December 17, 2012).

Samuelsohn, Darren. 2012. "President Obama's Get-Out-the-Youth-Vote Push." *Politico,* October 27. http://dyn.politico.com/printstory.cfm?uuid=190CDA6C-26DE-49D1-B255-CD3AB5335E39 (accessed December 17, 2012).

Saulny, Susan. 2012. "Less Zeal for Obama in a Vital Group of Voters." *New York Times,* October 10, A12.

Schlesinger, Arthur M., Jr. 2008. *The Politics of Hope and the Bitter Heritage: American Liberalism in the 1960s.* Princeton, NJ: Princeton University Press.

Slack, Donovan. 2012. "Obama Techie Says 'Life of Julia' a Campaign Highlight." *Politico,* November 19. http://www.politico.com/politico44/2012/11/obama-techie-says-life-of-julia-a-campaign-highlight-149925.html (accessed December 17, 2012).

Smith, Adam. 2012. "Obama Launches 3 New Spanish Language Ads in Florida." *Tampa Bay Times,* June 20. http://www.tampabay.com/blogs/the-buzz-florida-politics/content/obama-launches-3-new-spanish-language-ads-fla (accessed December 17, 2012).

Smith, Ben, and Jonathan Martin. 2011. "Obama Plan: Destroy Romney." *Politico,* August 9. http://www.politico.com/news/stories/0811/60921.html (accessed December 17, 2012).

Thrush, Glenn, and Carrie Budoff Brown. 2012. "Biden Blamed; Politics Drove Timing." *Politico,* May 9. http://www.politico.com/news/stories/0512/76140. html (accessed December 17, 2012).

Thrush, Glenn, and Jonathan Martin. 2012. "Politico's New Campaign E-book: An Early Look." *Politico,* December 14. http://www.politico.com/story/2012/12/ politicos-new-campaign-e-book-an-early-look-85092.html?hp=l17 (accessed December 17, 2012).

VandeHei, Jim, and Mike Allen. 2012. "Lessons Learned from 2012." *Politico,* November 4. http://dyn.politico.com/printstory.cfm?uuid=A01BF198-18DC-4E9A-9686-C29F615E0AF3 (accessed December 17, 2012).

Weinger, Mackenzie. 2012. "Evolve: Obama Gay Marriage Quotes." *Politico,* May 9. http://www.politico.com/news/stories/0512/76109.html (accessed December 17, 2012).

Williams, Joe. 2011. "White House Makes Its Case to Black Voters." *Politico,* December 5. http://www.politico.com/news/stories/1211/69752.html (accessed December 17, 2012).

2 The Campaign and the Media

Diana Owen

The 2012 presidential election was the noisiest, nastiest contest of the new media era. Media in the campaign reflected trends established in recent presidential contests taken to extremes. The quantity of messages circulating during elections has grown radically, along with the number of media platforms. In the late 1980s, entertainment media became more politically relevant. Soon after, in the mid-1990s, the Internet debuted in elections, and campaign websites, political blogs, and basic discussion boards were established. Electoral communication reached a new phase in its development with the use of social media in the 2008 presidential campaign, which encouraged sharing information, collaborating, and networking.

The volume of campaign information reached a fever pitch in 2012, especially as activity on social media exploded. Campaign committees, political parties, consultants, and advocacy groups waged aggressive media campaigns in mainstream, entertainment, and social media. The presidential candidates and their wives made highly publicized appearances on entertainment talk shows, such as *The View.* Political advertising reached the saturation point on air and online, especially for voters in battleground states. The mainstream press sought to compensate for the fact that they had few reporters covering events live from the campaign trail by increasing the quantity of information they provided. Journalists filled space with elaborate features based on polling data and fact-checking results and filed blog posts in addition to news stories.

Average citizens contributed to the din, although their input was not nearly as momentous as it had been four years earlier when innovations in social media offered new options for meaningful electoral engagement. Social media had featured a decidedly populist bent in the previous presidential contest—voters took it upon themselves to adapt social media platforms to accommodate campaign activities and created content to get their views across on their own terms. This innovative, populist spark was not as evident in 2012. Candidates, political organizations, and journalists reasserted their command of the political media hierarchy. Citizen input was often facilitated by elites who provided the platforms, structure, and impetus for citizen media engagement.

The 2012 campaign, though not a breakout event for political media, will be remembered for a number of developments beyond the sheer volume of messages. The overall tone of campaign news stories, ads, and social media content was highly negative, nastier than media in 2008. Election news was heavily driven by events and data that overshadowed serious, in-depth discussions of issues. Candidate debates, in particular, provided a news hook that allowed for the constant assessment of candidates' personalities, performances, campaign strategies, and relative standings in the election. Fact-checking emerged as a distinct category of news, especially as candidates' speeches and debate comments were subject to constant inspection. Polling data, long a staple of coverage that focuses on the horse race between candidates, were ubiquitous. Polls were accompanied by a litany of other metrics used to underpin analyses of candidate popularity, fundraising, voter sentiments, and social media site traffic. Campaign memes proliferated and became a mechanism for initiating discussion about candidates and campaign events. The ad wars in this election were especially fierce; the amount of money invested, the number of organizations producing ads, and the platforms for distribution grew markedly. It was clear throughout the campaign that the already-blurry distinctions between professional journalism, hybrid media, and amateur content have become further obscured. Mainstream news organizations sought to emulate social media even as new media outlets, such as BuzzFeed and Huffington Post, attempted to bring election beat reporting back into the mix (Ellis 2012).

The Nominating Campaign

Media coverage of the 2012 campaign began years in advance of Election Day, as has become the norm. The 2010 midterm elections showcased the expanding role of social media platforms as tools for contesting, engaging in, and reporting on the campaign. Social media was a prominent element of mainstream media coverage of the congressional elections, which set the stage for the presidential contest. News stories about the presidential campaign had many of the typical characteristics of election coverage. Horse-race journalism focusing on who is ahead and behind in the election abounded, especially during the Republican nominating campaign, when many voters were undecided about their candidate preference (P. Blumenthal 2012). The horse race was tracked not only through an abundance of opinion poll data, but also through a variety of additional metrics such as the number of followers the candidates had on social media, the tone of conversations about Romney and Obama on Twitter, fundraising totals, and number of ad placements. The press was preoccupied with the strategic aspects of electioneering and behind-the-scenes operations of candidates' campaign committees and fundraising apparatuses. Reporters aggressively vetted the candidates' track records and personal character.

Mainstream news organizations updated their approach to reporting to more fully integrate new media into their repertoire. They employed election-specific social media for gathering information supplied by citizens as well as for reporting. They experimented with a "utility-based" approach to news reporting in which they devised new ways of presenting information that was time- or event-driven. News organization websites, such as CNN.com, MSNBC.com, FoxNews.com, washingtonpost.com, and nytimes.com, created dashboards where they supplied users with updated data on the race through dynamic, easy-to-navigate infographics (Ellis 2012). The *Washington Post* had an interactive election map where users could track the election and find the latest polling information as well as state-by-state breakdowns by demographics and issue positions. The *New York Times* featured a dynamic graphic where users could plot a path for an Obama or Romney victory. These tools allowed journalists to provide analysis in real time and offered users "war rooms in [their] own living rooms" (Smith 2012). The graphics and associated commentary brought data to life for voters and proved to be profitable. Twenty percent of traffic to the *New York Times*'s website during the last week of the election was to statistician Nate Silver's polling blog (Ellis 2012).

Events provide anchors for media coverage in a highly complex electoral environment. They allow journalists to adapt stock story lines to specific circumstances. During the Republican nominating campaign, press coverage focused heavily on twenty debates that took place over the course of ten months; the first debate was held on May 5, 2011, and the last took place on March 3, 2012. The debates included a rotating cast of candidates, including Gary Johnson, Ron Paul, Herman Cain, Tim Pawlenty, Rich Santorum, Michele Bachmann, Mitt Romney, John Huntsman, Newt Gingrich, and Rick Perry. They were sponsored by a variety of political organizations, including Tea Party factions, nonpartisan groups, media organizations such as CNN and Fox News, political leaders such as former Arkansas governor Mike Huckabee, and academic institutions. The primary debates took place across the country and employed a variety of formats. The debates became high-stakes events for candidates because their performances generated extensive media coverage that could shift momentum in favor of or against a candidate.

There was a symbiotic relationship between the amount of media coverage that a candidate received and her or his poll numbers (M. Blumenthal 2011). Ron Paul was treated favorably by the media but got very little coverage, which hurt his candidacy. The candidates' treatment in the media and position in public opinion polls often would vary by extremes from week to week. Minnesota representative Michele Bachmann climbed in the polls and media coverage in July 2011, but made an early exit from the race in January 2012. Texas governor Rick Perry surged ahead of Mitt Romney in September and then quickly disappeared from the radar screen. In October, businessman Hermann Cain made a strong showing in the debates, climbed in the polls, and fell quickly after a series of missteps. Candidates with strong debate performances earned positive coverage in the immediate aftermath, which could influence their momentum in the campaign. Newt Gingrich's lively debate performance before the South Carolina primary in January prompted positive press coverage and cut into front-runner Mitt Romney's lead in the polls. Gingrich won South Carolina handily. Winning or doing better than expected in a state primary or caucus also could prompt more positive coverage, whereas a poor performance could bring a candidate's quest for the nomination to an end. Mitt Romney's press coverage was primarily negative until his narrow victory in his home state of Michigan at the end of February. When it appeared as though his candidacy was inevitable, Romney's media coverage took a turn for the better (Project for Excellence in Journalism 2012d). President Obama, the presumptive Democratic nominee, was treated like a candidate rather than the chief executive throughout the nominating season despite the fact his active campaigning was kept to a minimum.

It took Romney fifteen weeks of state contests before he earned the Republican nomination. In a post-election rundown, he lamented the long nominating process and criticized the protracted debate series, stating that it was "absolutely nuts." He questioned the utility of debates to voters and argued that the excessive number of debates stirred infighting among Republicans, exposed the candidates to gaffes with which the media had a field day, and gave the Democrats material that could be used against the nominee in the general election (Colbert 2012).

The national nominating conventions serve as the gateway to the general election. In recent years, journalists have felt frustrated in covering conventions that were overly scripted to promote the political parties and their nominees. The national media limited its convention coverage to just a few hours, relegating gavel-to-gavel reporting to back-channel cable stations. The conventions offer candidates the opportunity to introduce themselves afresh to the public and, if necessary, to tweak their image. The Republicans and Democrats used speeches by the candidates' wives to try to humanize their husbands, who both had the reputation of being personally aloof.

The most memorable media event from the convention period was the rambling speech made by actor Clint Eastwood at the Republican National Convention. For twelve minutes in prime time, Eastwood dressed down an empty chair representing "invisible Obama." Eastwood's performance was on the same day as a stirring speech by rising Republican star and Florida senator Marco Rubio and preceded Mitt Romney's address, yet it grabbed the next day's headlines (Barbaro and Shear 2012). The speech inspired a new term, "Eastwooding," which meant talking aimlessly and angrily to an empty chair, and became the source of one of the campaign's most popular memes. Memes are slogans, images, and videos used as shortcuts to convey a message or make an argument. On social media, memes take on different meanings as they are passed from user to user (Lewandowski 2012). Many of the campaign memes in 2012 were hilarious, and the Eastwood memes were no exception. Immediately following the speech, a Twitter account with handle @InvisibleObama was set up to spread the Eastwood meme, and it had more than 40,000 followers within a few hours (Colbert 2012). Obama's social media team quickly responded by tweeting a photo of Obama presiding over a meeting at the White House in a chair labeled "The President" with the caption "This seat's taken." Social media sites encouraged people to "go ahead, make Eastwood's day and tweet your own chair pictures," and thousands did (Fitzgerald 2012). An image by an anonymous creator of a photo of Grampa Simpson under the newspaper headline "Old Man Yells at Chair," was a widely circulated meme (Itzkoff 2012).

Presidential Candidate Debates and the Shifting Media Narratives

The presidential debates can be used to illustrate media dynamics in the general election. The debates were signature events of the election and precipitated shifts in the media narrative. Presidential candidates Barack Obama and Mitt Romney faced off in three debates. The first was a discussion of domestic policy on October 3 in Denver, followed by a town meeting–style debate on foreign and domestic policy on October 16 in Hempstead, New York. The series finished with a foreign policy deliberation on October 22 in Boca Raton, Florida. The vice presidential candidates, Democrat Joe Biden and Republican Paul Ryan, met on October 11 in Danville, Kentucky. The debates employed a new format where the moderators were encouraged to give the candidates leeway in answering questions rather than cutting them off based on strict time limits.

The debate pre-event media ritual began well in advance of the mile-high face-off in Denver. Pre-debate media employed the game frame and emphasized the candidates' debate preparation strategies. The press treated the debates like a contest between competitors rather than a forum for the candidates to present their views to the public. The presidential campaigns played into the game frame by attempting to manage expectations of their candidates' performances while at the same time seeking to psych out their opponent (Reeve 2012). Journalists analyzed the candidates' pre-debate practice sessions. News reports emphasized that Romney prepared harder for the debates than Obama. They noted that he carefully studied Obama's previous debate performances. At the same time, the Romney camp sought to lower expectations by making it clear that their candidate faced a formidable opponent in Obama. Romney's campaign emphasized that he had never before participated in a presidential debate and sought to portray him as the underdog. Romney was widely quoted as saying, "The president is obviously a very eloquent, gifted speaker—he'll do just fine" (Kois 2012). Media analysis suggested that Romney needed to draw a stark contrast between himself and Barack Obama on the issues without appearing angry (Baker and Parker 2012).

The Obama campaign's pre-debate message stressed the fact that the president was focused on governing the country while Romney was "prepping like an Olympic decathlete" (Reeve 2012). Obama's representatives insisted that the president was immersed in government policymaking and did not have the time or the need to focus on debate preparation. At the same time, his advisors cautioned that the president might be underprepared for the debate because he was not used to answering questions in brief and often made speeches (Baker and Parker 2012). Obama campaign spokesperson Jen Psaki issued a press statement designed to lower expectations: "while Mitt Romney has done 20 debates in the last year, [Obama] has not done one in four years, so there's a challenge in that regard" (Kois 2012).

The horse-race frame that dominates media coverage of elections is a central element of debate stories. Debate horse-race coverage operates on two levels: (1) conveying poll results and analysis indicating the debate winner and (2) reporting on post-debate polls gauging the candidates' standings in the presidential race. The first presidential candidate debate is especially important because it can set the agenda for the evaluation of future debate performances. A candidate who has a weak debate debut or who commits a gaffe will have a lot to overcome in subsequent debates. A loser in the debates will have to contend with serious negative media as the campaign heads down the home stretch (Jamieson and Birdsell 1988; Lehrer 2011). However, a questionable performance in an early debate is not insurmountable. Republican Ronald Reagan's performance in the first presidential debate in 1984 raised concerns about his age and ability to govern. He overcame this perception with a clever sound bite in the next debate, referring to his opponent Democrat Walter Mondale's "youth and inexperience" (Schroeder 2008). A good performance in debates can help fundraising, solidify a candidate's base, and stimulate turnout among supporters. A superior performance can produce a post-debate bounce in the polls for a trailing candidate. Most often, the debate bounce is short-lived, but occasionally it can boost a candidate that the press has all but written off. Shifts in poll results from debates rarely change the outcome of the election (Erikson and Wlezien 2012). Ultimately, this was Mitt Romney's experience after a strong showing in the first debate.

With polls indicating that Romney was falling behind Obama in key battleground states, including Ohio, Florida, and Virginia, the press deemed the first debate as "do-or-die" for the Republican nominee. Romney hoped to use the debates to rejuvenate his campaign after a series of setbacks, including the well-publicized release of a video of his remarks at a private fundraising event. The left-leaning magazine *Mother Jones* released a video in which Romney stated that 47 percent of Americans are dependent on government and feel they are victims entitled to assistance. The video had been surreptitiously recorded in May at a private Romney fundraiser in Boca Raton, Florida. The story went viral and generated bad publicity that Romney failed to neutralize when he stood behind the substance of his remarks. The incident played directly into the narrative of Romney as a candidate who favored the interests of the wealthy, a perception that was supported by polling research (Rutenberg and Parker 2012).

Mitt Romney came out swinging in the first debate and remained on his game throughout. Whether it was too little preparation, lack of enthusiasm, or as former Democratic presidential nominee Al Gore suggested, the altitude in Denver, Barack Obama's performance in the debate was lackluster. Americans prefer candidates who exhibit strength and leadership; Obama appeared tired and reticent. Romney managed to get in 541 more words than Obama in four fewer minutes (Zuckerman 2012). The debate set off an intense media frenzy fueled by social media that enabled immediate, unfiltered, and widespread commentary. News stories contrasted the candidates' performance and fact-checked their statements. Both camps attempted to corral the media agenda and quickly distributed post-debate ads with messages they reinforced on the stump. Obama took the gloves off while campaigning in Colorado and questioned Romney's authenticity and trustworthiness, a message he reinforced in a television spot. The Republican National Committee released an ad called "Smirk" that spotlighted Obama's uncomfortable and off-putting body language as Romney talked about the failure of Obama's policies. The ad was reminiscent of George H. W. Bush checking his watch during a debate with Democratic candidate Bill Clinton in 1992, a move that drew an unfavorable reaction from voters. The Romney campaign was able to reset after his solid performance in the first presidential debate. The media's horse-race coverage played up changes in the polls in favor of Romney, and he was treated more favorably in news stories.

The vice presidential debate between Joe Biden and Paul Ryan enlivened media coverage, even if vice presidential debates rarely influence the course of campaigns. Ryan was articulate and competently reinforced the Republican campaign's key talking points about taxes and the economy. However, Biden's off-the-cuff responses and snarky side comments—calling Ryan's statements "malarkey" and "a bunch of stuff"—made for better copy. Biden was unfazed by the split-screen television presentation that showed his facial expression ranging from amused to annoyed. He received high marks from the public and the press for his performance. Of the four candidates, Biden received by far the most favorable media coverage throughout the campaign (Project for Excellence in Journalism 2012c). His performance in the debates set the media pendulum swinging slowly back in favor of the Democratic camp.

Romney and Obama went on the attack during the second presidential debate, which featured a town hall format. They confronted each other using verbal and physical tactics, including shouting and moving around the stage. Candidates typically have more congenial exchanges in a town hall debate because they are attempting to appeal to the citizen questioners, but that rule of thumb did not pertain. The debate put the spotlight on undecided voters, who asked the questions on issues ranging from education and the economy to foreign affairs. Analysts gave the edge to Obama because he performed better than expected in the debate and seemed to come out on top of a heated exchange over the attacks in Benghazi, Libya, that resulted in the deaths of four Americans. The third presidential debate focused on foreign policy issues. The press gave the edge to Obama because he showed a command of foreign policy while keeping Romney on the defensive. Polls following the third debate indicated that Romney had maintained momentum from the first debate and that the candidates appeared to be in a dead heat.

As the candidates headed into the final lap of the campaign, Hurricane Sandy hit the East Coast of the country, leaving a path of devastation. Romney and Obama sought to emphasize their leadership abilities as well as their humanity. They temporarily suspended campaigning, with Obama overseeing the government response to the storm and Romney raising funds and collecting supplies for victims. Journalists expressed concerns that Sandy would disrupt polling operations and that they would not have much to report on about the campaign. Instead, they turned to speculation about how the storm might influence the outcome of the election. Stories focused on how President Obama was receiving unlikely support from Republicans, such as New Jersey governor Chris Christie, for his handling of the storm crisis (McGregor 2012), and the horse race began to shift in his favor.

The Social Media Campaign

Social media outlets have come a long way since their debut in the 2008 campaign. When Barack Obama announced his candidacy in 2007, the iPhone did not exist, Facebook had been online for three years, and Twitter was a fledgling platform whose users were considered cutting-edge (Ouimet 2012). In 2012, voters had a much wider choice of social media options, as users turned to Pinterest, Reddit, Google+, Instagram, Tumblr, and Foursquare in addition to Facebook and Twitter, which had become the social medium de jour in the 2010 midterm elections. Social media options were standard on most news and election-related websites. Social networking is the fastest-growing digital media activity (Mlot 2012). At the time of the 2012 election, the number of social media users had topped 1.43 billion worldwide (Nielsen 2012). Two-thirds of Internet users were on social networks (Brenner 2012). Daily, 2.5 billion pieces of content were shared on Facebook, and Twitter hosted 230 million tweets. Americans spent over 121 billion minutes per month on social media sites, or 23 percent of their time online (Nielsen 2012).

With the tremendous growth in social media options as well as the size of the potential audience, candidate committees, political parties, and media organizations made extensive use of social media in the 2012 election. Social media platforms were an integral and strategic campaign tool for candidates and political parties. The news media's social media presence was prominent and slick. Journalists, such as CNN's Wolf Blitzer, were active on Twitter and regularly reported on the election's social media buzz. The campaign was one of the most heavily covered events in social media history. Social media became a barometer for measuring shifts in campaign momentum and a mechanism for tracking the public's interest in campaign events and their views on issues (Strong 2012). Social media activity surged in response to campaign events, such as Clint Eastwood's speech with the empty chair at the Republican National Convention and the presidential debates, as users sought to share the experience with their networks. A photo of Barack and Michelle Obama embracing after he was declared the winner of the election that was posted on Twitter broke records, with over 700,000 "retweets" and 3.5 million Facebook "likes" (Foulger 2012).

In 2008, the use of social media in campaigns was pathbreaking. Social media platforms not only offered new mechanisms for distributing information; they also facilitated active participation through their capacities for networking, collaboration, and community building. They offered new ways of accomplishing traditional campaign tasks, such as fundraising, volunteer recruitment, publicity, event organizing, and advertising. Citizens, especially young voters, were integral to the social media revolution. Social media sparked spontaneous grassroots electoral engagement. Voters innovated with social media and became involved in the campaign in novel ways without consulting campaign organizations, parties, and political organizations. Voters created videos in support of their candidate, covered campaign events live, posted information online, and encouraged their peers to take part in the election (Owen 2009). They established online organizations with people who shared their views or group identities that performed functions traditionally relegated to political parties, such as issue agenda-setting, voter registration, and get-out-the-vote drives (Owen 2012). In 2008, the Obama campaign embraced voters' independent social media ventures on its behalf and harnessed their enthusiasm without entirely co-opting their efforts (Plouffe 2009). According to Richard Slaby, the Obama campaign's technology officer in 2008, his team members were "opportunistic consumers of technology" who were willing to use trial and error to gain an advantage in an election they felt they could not win using traditional techniques.

In 2012, the Obama and Romney campaigns invested significant resources to mount extensive social media operations. The candidates' social media teams managed their presence across a range of social media platforms and pushed out a tremendous amount of information. However, there was a significant difference in the approach to social media taken by the campaigns in this election compared to the previous presidential contest. Slaby argues that the campaigns were "strategic integrators of technology" that carefully devised social media tactics for organizing (Cruz 2012). The user-led social media innovation that had been the hallmark of the 2008 election was largely lacking in 2012 because voters were less enthusiastic about the candidates, and the novelty of social media had worn off. As a result, the candidates' use of social media was aimed less at encouraging active voter engagement and more at getting their message out, fundraising aggressively, and attracting mainstream media attention. In essence, social media applications were treated like an extension of broadcast technology rather than as platforms for engaging in dialogue with voters (Higgins 2012). Although candidates were quick to hop on the latest social media bandwagon, they did little to explore innovative uses of these media that might invest voters more solidly in the campaign. The campaigns and political parties posted thousands of messages, videos, and ads to the candidates' social media pages, YouTube channels, and video hosting platforms. Both campaigns repurposed material posted by supporters on social media as part of their strategy—a photo taken by a supporter at an election rally might be reposted with a campaign-supplied caption that tied into the candidate's messaging.

The campaigns used social media to achieve specific goals. Social media channels are conducive to conveying material more candidly, and both sides used social media to make their candidates more personally relatable to voters. The candidates' favorite films and music playlists were publicized along with pictures of them socializing informally with family and friends. The candidates' wives featured prominently in this effort. Michelle Obama scored high marks on social media after her speech at the Democratic National Convention, where she sought to convey the personal side of her husband. The White House posted on Twitter a photo of Barack Obama and his daughters, Sasha and Malia, curled up on the couch watching the speech, which reinforced the message (Serjeant 2012). The candidates also used social media to appeal to young voters. The campaigns kept digital scrapbooks of the campaign on Tumblr and Pinterest and made frequent references to popular culture, such as the television program *Parks and Recreation* (Wortham 2012a).

The candidates' social media reflected their distinctly different styles and personalities. Obama's social media sought to appeal to young voters by being hip and edgy. His sites featured parodies, animation, and posts by younger celebrities. His social media accounts were updated frequently, which met the expectations of tech-savvy voters and kept them returning to the platforms. Romney's digital postings, like the candidate, were more restrained and buttoned-down. His team posted fewer moving images, with his platforms supporting more still photos of the campaign trail or posters with slogans. Rarely did the candidates use social media themselves or provide much opportunity for conversation with voters (Project for Excellence in

Table 2.1 Number of Social Media Followers for Barack Obama and Mitt Romney

	Obama	*Romney*
Facebook likes	31,101,000+	10,200,000+
Twitter followers	20,420,000+	1,225,000+
YouTube followers	233,000+	21,000+
Pinterest	42,000+	12,000+
Instagram	1,400,000	38,000
Spotify subscribers	14,654+	402+

Source: Compiled from Wortham (2012b).

Journalism 2012b). Barack and Michelle Obama occasionally authored their own tweets, which they designated with their initials, bo and mo.

The social media war between the Obama and Romney camps was covered extensively by the press. The Obama social media team had a significant head start on the Romney campaign, which had to work hard to catch up throughout the campaign. The Project for Excellence in Journalism found that early in the campaign, Obama averaged 29 tweets a day to Romney's one. Obama had twice as many posts on his campaign website than Romney and more than twice as many YouTube videos (Project for Excellence in Journalism 2012a). As the campaign came to a close, however, the Romney organization had closed this gap considerably (Cruz 2012). Obama's social media presence was far more robust than Romney's based purely on the number of followers. As Table 2.1 shows, Obama outpaced Romney in terms of followers on all forms of social media. Obama had over 20 million more Facebook likes than Romney and 19 million more Twitter followers. Although these metrics provide a rough picture of the relative size of the candidates' social media networks, they do not tell the entire story. Romney's social media users tended to interact more with the platforms, posting more and retweeting items, than Obama's users (Darwell 2012).

Social media networks offer campaigns the opportunity for real-time engagement. Keeping current 24/7 has replaced the deadlines associated with traditional media (Cruz 2012). The candidates' social media teams were quick to post reactions to key campaign events in a manner that appealed to the young, niche audiences for particular types of social media. Remixed video clips with commentary or captions were launched on microblogging sites, such as Twitter and Tumblr, to attract attention. Mitt Romney's remark during the first presidential debate that he was going to stop subsidizing PBS even though he liked Big Bird ignited the campaign social media universe. A Twitter account with handle @FiredBigBird was created while the debate was in progress and immediately attracted thousands of followers (Eversley 2012). The Obama campaign reacted quickly to the comment that attacked an icon of the younger generation by posting an image of Big Bird with a caption about Romney wanting to fire him, an image that went viral (Wortham 2012b).

Old-School New Media

Old-school digital platforms have been adapted to the new era of campaigning and maintain a strong foothold in the process. The Romney and Obama candidate websites were central hubs for the campaigns' digital media presence. The Republican and Democratic parties also maintained websites that complemented the candidates' online media. Since 2008, campaign websites have become full-service, multimedia platforms that integrate the candidates' social media. Voters can find extensive information about the candidates and election logistics on the websites. The sites allow voters to access and share videos, view ads, post blogs, provide commentary, donate, take part in volunteer activities, and purchase campaign logo wear. The 2012 presidential candidates used their websites to exercise further control over their messaging. Users of the candidates' social media were driven to their websites to view videos and read documents (Project for Excellence in Journalism 2012a). Typically, websites are accessed by between 20 percent and 30 percent of the electorate. Mobile applications, or apps, for visiting the candidates' websites were a new development in 2012. Approximately 20 percent of smartphone users visited Romney's or Obama's website using an app at least weekly during the campaign (Statista 2012).

E-mail, another old-style new medium, proved to be a useful tool for candidates. The Obama campaign employed a staff of twenty to craft and distribute e-mails. Both campaigns employed e-mail outreach and fundraising strategies that bordered on overkill, as voters on their lists received multiple message per day from the candidates and their surrogates asking for money. The candidates, the candidates' wives, prominent politicians, and celebrities used emotion, fear, and humor to appeal for support and dollars. Voters had the opportunity to win dinner with Mitt Romney or Barack Obama for a small donation of $3 or $5. People receiving Obama e-mails were tempted to open them with subject lines that read, "Hey," "Wow," and "Some scary numbers." Fundraising through e-mail and social networking sites proved to be lucrative, as micro-donations averaging $40 or less contributed online added up. The Obama campaign raised $690 million online, with most of it generated through e-mails (Green 2012; Flock 2012). Thirty-four percent of Obama's total receipts for the campaign came from these small donations, compared to 18 percent for Romney (Goldman 2012). Obama had an e-mail advantage over Romney because he had begun developing his subscriber list five years earlier. Thirteen million people were on Obama's e-mail list; 68 percent of his messages made it to subscribers' e-mail inboxes, and 27 percent were opened. Romney had one-fifth as many subscribers as Obama; only 50 percent of his messages made it to users' inboxes, and 22 percent were opened (Prakash 2012).

Microtargeting

Some analysts argue that the most important development involving social media during the 2012 presidential campaign was not the visible ruckus on social media sites, but instead microtargeting efforts that were being orchestrated behind the scenes (Sifry 2011). Microtargeting is the process of mining personal data and devising directed messages that appeal to particular voters. In 2008, the Obama campaign employed microtargeting methods, such as the use of focused text messages and e-mails to reach specific constituencies, including young people, strong partisans, and issue publics. This strategy used commercially available data on demographics, zip codes, shopping preferences, and television-viewing habits to develop voter profiles. Microtargeting was raised to the next level in 2012. The campaigns used information gleaned from social media analytics to expose voters' digital habits, political preferences, and consumer behavior to target their campaign messages. They sifted through "big data" archives, seeking to find actionable insights that would direct their ad placements (Cruz 2012). Microtargeting takes advantage of the trail of information that users leave when they use digital media. This information is matched to publicly available digitized voter rolls that let analysts know how often a voter has cast a ballot since the 2000 election. Algorithms are used to match individuals to personalized messages for fundraising and voter contact (Fouhy 2012). Facebook, Google, YouTube, and Twitter also used demographic information that they collect on users to target online campaign ads. Visitors to a candidate's website might later have seen display ads for that candidate popping up on their Facebook pages. A Google search for information about a candidate might have prompted a short promotional video about that candidate the next time the user visited a social media site (Fouhy 2012).

The Obama campaign's use of analytical techniques to manage voters in the most recent election was unmatched. The campaign hired a team of dozens of data scientists who secretly created a massive integrated voter data file and developed models that were used to refine the ground game. The models helped to increase the effectiveness of voter outreach techniques ranging from personal approaches, such as door knocks, to direct mail and e-mail messages. The strategy was used in battleground states and helped Obama gain an advantage (Scherer 2012).

Microtargeting using big data raises questions about voters' privacy and civil liberties, especially given that most people are not aware that their information is being collected and used in this way by political campaigns. As a CNN reporter noted, with the sophisticated microtargeting techniques available today, campaigns may know you better than you know yourself (Brennan 2012). Proponents argue that this type of targeting is beneficial because it matches voters to the issues they care about, helping them to sort through the glut of campaign information. However, an Annenberg School of Communication study found that 86 percent of Americans do not want political ads targeted at them in this way (Turow et al. 2012).

Third-Party and Nonpartisan Voter Engagement Platforms

In the period prior to the general election, virtual third-party movements and nonpartisan social media–based platforms for electoral engagement were launched and represented a novel approach to campaign involvement. These online organizations tapped into some citizens' frustration with the American party duopoly. They used the interactive features of the Internet to form online political communities to facilitate discussion and take political action (Owen 2012). Americans Elect (http://www.americanselect.org/), the most visible and well financed of these organizations, attempted to put forward a bipartisan presidential ticket through an online nomination process. In the end, the effort was not successful. Still, Americans Elect generated a great deal of discussion about how elections might be contested differently, the impact of partisan bickering, and the quality of presidential nominees. The organization also managed to get laws passed in over thirty states that would allow candidates nominated through online processes to get on the ballot, setting the stage for future online presidential candidate recruitment efforts (Cillizza and Blake 2012). Other online organizations set more modest goals of hosting discussion platforms and connecting people with like-minded views. Some of these groups, such as Votifi (http://votifi.com/) and Votocracy (http://www.votocracy.com/), have survived beyond the presidential election.

Advertising Overkill

Advertising contributed mightily to the media overkill and campaign negativity in 2012. In addition to traditional thirty-second televised ads, spots were placed online and distributed through websites, video sharing sites, social media, and e-mail messages. They could be readily accessed through computers, tablets, and cell phones. The amount of money spent producing and placing ads reached a historic high at over $1 billion. The Obama campaign spent $333 million on television ads compared to $147 million for Romney. During the final ten-day push, the campaigns spent over $40 million on ads in battleground states trying to win over the few remaining undecided voters (*Washington Post* 2012). The vast majority of televised campaign ads were negative. Eighty-five percent of Obama's TV ads and 91 percent of Romney's spots were negative. The candidates' committees allocated significant resources to online ads. The Obama campaign committed over $52 million to online ads, and Romney spent about half that amount, $26.2 million. The amount spent by the campaigns on online advertising represented a 251 percent increase over 2008 (Rosen 2012).

The advertising overload was abetted by federal court decisions. In *Citizens United v. the Federal Election Commission,* the Supreme Court outlawed restrictions on independent expenditures by corporations and trade unions. The District of Columbia Circuit Court's *Speechnow.org v. Federal Election Commission* decision authorized the establishment of independent expenditure–only political action committees, or "Super PACs." This decision has made it possible for independent groups to run ads for or against candidates as long as they do not coordinate with the candidates' campaign organizations, a standard that is difficult to enforce. Super PACS, groups whose sole purpose is to make independent expenditures in campaigns, and tax-exempt advocacy organizations that engage in voter mobilization and issue-awareness activities ran more ads in the presidential contest than the Republican and Democratic parties (Center for Responsive Politics 2012). Advertising by outside groups is almost entirely negative, and a majority of spots include deception (Brader 2006; Jamieson 2012). Outside groups spent over $522 million on advertising and were especially active in the Republican nominating campaign. The Super PAC Restore Our Future spent more than $40 million on behalf of Mitt Romney in the nominating campaign. It ran ads alleging that Rick Santorum had voted to allow violent felons to vote and that Newt Gingrich had partnered with Democrat Nancy Pelosi in support of a United Nations program "supporting China's brutal 'one child' policy" (PolitiFact 2012). Super PACs and advocacy groups such as American Crossroads and Americans for Prosperity ran more than 270,000 ads on behalf of Romney during the 2012 campaign (Baum 2012b). Newt Gingrich and Rick Santorum benefited from Super PAC ads that allowed them to stay in the running for longer than expected (Confessore 2012). Outside groups were active down the stretch in the general election, running ads in battleground states in an effort to influence the election outcome (Blumenthal 2012).

A study by the Wesleyan Media Project found that the candidates, political parties, and independent groups aired more than one million campaign ads between June 1 and Election Day, which was 39 percent more than in 2008 and 41 percent more than in 2004. The Romney and Obama campaigns each developed over 100 separate television ads compared to the fewer than 30 spots that the Reagan campaign made in 1984 (Geer 2012). The Obama campaign aired 503,255 ads, far outpacing Romney's organization, which aired 190,784 ads. Voters in battleground states experienced the full force of the ad wars, whereas other media markets were ignored (Baum 2012a).

In addition to political ads, voters were able to access other types of video content online, ranging from cell phone camera videos from the campaign trail to professional recordings of full speeches. According to data from the Project for Excellence in Journalism, a majority of voters—55 percent—watched political videos online, and 52 percent circulated videos to people in their networks. Voters were more likely to watch video news reports (48 percent); prerecorded videos of candidates' speeches, press conferences, or debates; informational videos about political issues (39 percent); and humorous or parody videos (37 percent) than political ads online. Twenty-eight percent watched the candidates live. Only one percent of voters created their own online videos about politics or the election, which was down from 2008 (Smith and Duggan 2012).

The onslaught of campaign ads and video content did not appear to assist voters much in making their decisions about candidates. It is unclear whether voters gained much information from campaign ads, and they may have been turned off by the constant barrage of highly negative messages. Pew Research Center data reveal that a majority of voters (54 percent) felt that campaign commercials did not help them at all in making campaign decisions, and 18 percent found that ads were not too helpful. Fifteen percent of the electorate believed that ads were somewhat helpful, and only 9 percent found spots to be very helpful.

The Tone and Content of Campaign Messages

Election media messages in 2012 were especially nasty. As Table 2.2 indicates, mainstream media stories about the candidates were decidedly more negative than positive. In the 2008 campaign, Barack Obama enjoyed more positive (35 percent) than negative (29 percent) press coverage. After four years in office, the percentage of negative coverage Obama received remained stable at 30 percent, but only 19 percent of stories about him were positive. Mitt Romney did not fare as well as Obama in the mainstream media. Thirty-eight percent of his coverage was negative, and 15 percent was favorable. Democratic vice presidential candidate Joe Biden was treated better by the press than his opponent, Republican Paul Ryan. Biden's coverage was 16 percent negative compared to 28 percent negative for Ryan. Ryan was far less visible in the mainstream media than his counterpart in 2008, Sarah Palin; he received one-third as much coverage as Palin (Project for Excellence in Journalism 2012c).

The heightened volume of social media content in the 2012 campaign contributed to the nasty tone of coverage. Since social media now are scoured routinely by journalists seeking material, the highly negative tone of social media content made its way into mainstream press stories. As depicted in Table 2.2, Twitter, Facebook, and blog posts were decidedly less favorable in their treatment of the presidential candidates than mainstream media.

Table 2.2 Tone of Mainstream Media Coverage and Digital Media Content August 27–October 21, 2012

		Mainstream media	Twitter	Facebook	Blogs
Positive	Obama	19%	25%	24%	19%
	Romney	15%	16%	23%	18%
Negative	Obama	30%	45%	53%	44%
	Romney	38%	58%	62%	46%
Mixed	Obama	51%	31%	22%	37%
	Romney	47%	25%	15%	36%

Source: Project for Excellence in Journalism, *Winning the Media Campaign 2012*.

Twitter and Facebook users were much harsher in their treatment of Romney than Obama, especially the Twitterverse. Fifty-eight percent of tweets about Romney were negative versus 45 percent for Obama. A higher percentage of tweets about Obama (25 percent) were positive than were tweets about Romney (16 percent). This trend may be due to the fact that the Obama campaign was more aggressive than the Romney team about posting messages to social media (Wortham 2012b). Bloggers were more evenhanded in their treatment of the two presidential contenders, although a much higher percentage of their posts about both candidates were negative rather than positive. Social media content is far more polarized than mainstream media stories. The percentage of "mixed" content is substantially lower for Twitter, Facebook, and blogs than for the mainstream press, where nearly half of all stories are neutral in tone.

A number of factors account for the tone of mainstream and social media content. Positive and negative stories in the mainstream press often are associated with horse-race coverage. Negative horse-race coverage focuses on candidates' failure to appeal to voters and gain traction in the polls, on who's behind in fundraising, and on who lost a debate. Horse-race coverage was especially prominent during the Republican nominating campaign. Poll-driven stories were used to track shifts in the momentum behind the large field of candidates and to keep public interest alive during a drawn-out campaign. According to the Center for Media and Public Affairs, television reports covered the horse race six times as much as they reported on issues (Center for Media and Public Affairs 2012). A report by the Project for Excellence in Journalism revealed that 64 percent of stories in print, on television, online, and on radio dealt with poll results, campaign strategies, and fundraising tallies. Twelve percent of stories covered personal issues related to the candidates, 9 percent reported on domestic issues, 6 percent on the candidates' public record, 1 percent on foreign issues, and 6 percent on other topics (Project for Excellence in Journalism 2012d). However, horse-race journalism did not dominate coverage throughout the general election. Overall, poll-related stories accounted for 22 percent of all stories, which was far less than the 53 percent in 2008. Poll stories increased in prominence around the debates, rising to more than 40 percent of coverage (Project for Excellence in Journalism 2012c).

Horse-race coverage accounts for much of the gap in the amount of negative press received by the presidential candidates, given that Romney was trailing in the polls for much of the campaign. When horse-race coverage is removed from the calculation, both Obama and Romney received an equal amount of negative coverage: 32 percent (Project for Excellence in Journalism 2012c). The campaign horse race has now carried over prominently to social media. Campaigns post polling information with strategic spin on social media, hoping that it will be picked up by the mainstream press and circulated by voters in their social networks. Major mainstream media organizations, such as the *Washington Post* and CNN, have established digital platforms that present reams of polling data and invited discussion. Statistician Nate Silver's blog, *FiveThirtyEight,* which is licensed by the *New York Times,* became a focal point for much discussion about the 2012 campaign horse race. Silver correctly predicted the outcome of the presidential election in all fifty states. Although many technical reports on the horse race remain inside baseball pitched at political junkies (Kludt 2012), poll-driven information makes its way to the wider public largely through televised reports, complete with visually stunning graphics.

The media's obsession with candidate gaffes—real and overstated—also contributed to the negative coverage in 2012. A statement made by Barack Obama at a rally in Roanoke, Virginia, came back to haunt him throughout the campaign: "If you've got a business, you didn't build that; somebody else made that happen." The comment sparked negative press reports and campaign ads as well as a pro-Romney catchphrase, "We built it," that appeared on T-shirts and billboards. Obama's remark at a news conference that the "private sector is doing fine" also generated substantial negative coverage that highlighted the country's economic woes during his tenure in office. Mitt Romney's refusal to release his tax records and his comment that 47 percent of Americans expect government support generated volumes of unfavorable press. He also was criticized in the media for his quick indictment of President Obama in the immediate aftermath of the death of an American diplomat and three others during an attack in Benghazi, Libya (Dickerson and Kirk 2012). But although the press has a field day with candidate gaffes, evidence suggests that many people are unaware of gaffes, and few voters change their minds about whom to support as a result (Sides 2012).

Another aspect of the gaffe-obsessed media was the excessive fact-checking of campaign messages. Since the 1980s, traditional notions of journalistic fact-checking and sourcing, where reporters carefully verify information before publishing, have fallen by the wayside as entertainment media have played a more prominent role in the political process (Davis and Owen 1998). Reputable academic fact-checking efforts, notably the Annenberg Public Policy Center's FactCheck.org, stepped in to fill the gap. In 2012, journalists adopted this new style of fact-checking, and fact-checking stories emerged as their own category of news. The statements, ads, and social media postings of candidates and their surrogates were subjected to incessant inspection by academics, media organizations, and the general public. Candidates' comments in speeches, position papers, and tweets were combed for inconsistencies and erroneous claims. Fact-checks most often are performed on brief summary statements or sound bites that encapsulate complex issue stances and that may be taken out of context. Candidates rarely are given the opportunity to clarify their comments before the fact-check goes public. The quality of third-party sources used to verify facts varies greatly (Crovitz 2012). Some fact-checkers are associated with partisan and ideological groups and have their own political agendas; fact and opinion can become blurred. Campaign operatives, who long have engaged in fact-checking the opposition, now can publicize their findings extensively through social media. It was quite common in the 2012 campaign to find fact-checks of the same material verified against different sources with conflicting results (Hermes 2012).

Journalists view fact-checking as an extension of their watchdog role. They claim that their goal is to better inform voters about the candidates' stands on issues. In reality, fact-check reporting is a type of gotcha journalism that contributes to the negativity of campaign coverage. Reporters in the 2012 campaign often were concerned more with exposing falsehoods than with finding truth. The overarching fact-checking story line was that the candidates were continually deceiving the public even as journalists continually corrected their errors (Hermes 2012). Fact-checking was especially rampant during the presidential debates. Mainstream media organizations and the public, via crowdsourcing on social media, fact-checked the candidates' statements in real time. Post-debate news stories focused heavily on whether or not the candidates were deceptive in their statements. Following the third presidential debate, the *Washington Post* admitted on its blog *The Fact Checker* that fact-checking is challenging. "Foreign policy is generally a difficult area to fact check—differences can be more of opinions than numbers—but that did not stop President Obama and former governor Mitt Romney from making questionable claims" (Kessler 2012). This statement was followed by a laundry list of fact-checked candidate comments. At times, the media fact-checking overreached badly. A comment made by First Lady Michelle Obama in her speech at the Democratic National Convention suggesting that her husband "was always ready to listen to good ideas" was fact-checked by conservative Fox News and shown to be misleading (Carr 2012).

The Election News Audience

Television remained firmly the medium of choice for voters in the 2012 election, followed by the Internet, which has overtaken print media. According to the Pew Research Center, 76 percent of the electorate relied on television as their main source of information during the nominating campaign, which was up from 68 percent in 2008 (see Table 2.3). Television was the main news source for 67 percent of voters during the general election, which was almost the same percentage as four years earlier. Cable news (42 percent) is the most popular television source, followed distantly by network evening news (19 percent) and local news (11 percent). The percentage of people relying on the Internet as a campaign news source has grown steadily since 1996, when 3 percent of voters used online media. In 2012 the Internet was a main campaign news source for 47 percent of voters, up from 36 percent in 2008. Fewer people (36 percent) considered the Internet a main source in the primaries. It is interesting to note that this pattern is reversed for television, which lost viewers during the general election. It may be the case that television was a more accessible source of information for some voters than online media during the primaries, when there was less interest in the campaign than during the general election and thus less motivation to seek out online sources.

Print newspapers have experienced a precipitous decline in popularity as an election news source since 1996, when they were read by 60 percent of the electorate. The percentage of people who consider newspapers to be a main election news source dropped to an all-time low of 23 percent in the primaries and 27 percent in the 2012 general election. The percentage of readers was down almost 10 percentage points from 2008. A very small percentage of the population—3 percent in the last two presidential election cycles—considers print magazines to be their primary news source. The radio audience has increased since 1988, as talk radio has established a dedicated audience in the new media era. Seventeen percent of voters relied on radio, both talk and news formats, as a main source in the 2012 primaries, and 20 percent did so in the general election, which is consistent with radio's popularity in 2008.

Table 2.3 Main Source of Election News in the Presidential Primaries and General Election

	Television	Newspapers	Radio	Magazines	Internet
Primaries	74%	23%	17%	3%	36%
General election	67%	27%	20%	3%	47%

Sources: For primaries, Pew Research Center for the People and the Press, Political Communication and Methods Study, January 2012; for general election, Pew Research Center for the People and the Press, November 2012 Post Election Survey.

Note: Survey respondents could choose more than one source.

The Social Media Audience

There is good reason for candidates to engage in a vigorous social media strategy. Social media users tend to be more politically engaged than other citizens. Eighty-eight percent of adult social media users are registered voters. Sixty-six percent of voters use Facebook, and 15 percent use Twitter. Social media users are five times more likely than other citizens to attend a campaign rally and are twice as likely to vote (Ouimet 2012). However, although there is potential to reach a sizable portion of the electorate through social media, the number of voters who use social media for campaign-related purposes remains relatively small. According to the Pew Research Center, 12 percent of voters used Facebook for campaign purposes, 4 percent used Twitter, and 3 percent used YouTube. Twitter use increased slightly in 2012, but fewer voters accessed YouTube.

Although older Americans increasingly are using social media, the audience for politics continues to skew heavily in favor of younger people. Ninety-two percent of 18- to 29-year-olds who are online use social media, compared to 73 percent of 30- to 49-year-olds, 57 percent of 50- to 64-year-olds, and 38 percent of those age 65 and older. The patterns are similar for Twitter use; 32 percent of the youngest age group are on Twitter compared to 15 percent of 30- to 49-year-olds, 9 percent of 50- to 64-year-olds, and 4 percent of those 65 and older (Pew Internet and American Life Project 2012b).

Social media users also differ in terms of their political ideology. A higher percentage of liberals (79 percent) use social media, followed by moderates (70 percent) and conservatives (63 percent). The same trend pertains for Twitter use, although the percentages are lower. Liberals (37 percent) also were more likely to use their cell phones to get information about the 2012 election campaign than were moderates (28 percent) and conservatives (25 percent) (Pew Internet and American Life Project 2012b).

Conclusion

The 2012 presidential campaign provides a glimpse of what the future may hold for elections in the frenzied media age. Citizens have access to an overwhelming amount of election-related content through countless platforms. But are voters getting the information they need to make informed choices in elections? Quality information—quite a bit of it—is available to voters, but it can be difficult to locate amid the avalanche of media messages. Voters are not always willing to invest the time and effort needed—nor do many have the specialized skills—to sort through the media din to find the kernel of information that they are seeking. With fewer trained journalists providing firsthand coverage of the campaign trail, it is more difficult for voters to assess the quality and significance of much of the campaign news, even that produced by sources with long-standing reputations. Data-driven stories focusing on campaign dynamics do little to enlighten voters who seek to learn about candidates' views on foreign policy. The media proclaimed that this was the most fact-checked election of all time, which it was, but the somewhat questionable methodologies employed in verifying statements and the sensational style of fact-check reporting may undercut their utility for voters' decision making (Carr 2012). Voters were highly dissatisfied with campaign media and were especially discouraged by the high level of negativity (Pew Research Center 2012). It may well be the case that less is more in campaigns and that making available materials that cut through the clutter and clearly articulate the candidates' position will be appreciated by voters.

Another question raised by the 2012 campaign is this: do elections in the current era facilitate meaningful citizen involvement and encourage voter turnout? On the one hand, social media platforms have made possible new avenues for engagement that allow citizens to bypass boundaries that previously prevented them from being more than spectators or workers in campaigns. Social media can shatter hierarchies and level the playing field for voters who want to take part in campaigns without the intervention of institutional intermediaries. As the 2008 campaign illustrates, these possibilities can be realized when citizens take the initiative and when elites are receptive to their efforts.

However, it is necessary to temper enthusiasm about the potential for new media to engage citizens based on voters' experience in 2012. Campaign committees, parties, and news organizations can dominate message production and promotion and marginalize citizen engagement. Further, the emphasis on social media may exacerbate gaps in political participation among those who are least connected in society. Fifteen percent of the U.S. population does not use the Internet, precluding these citizens from engaging online. People with lower levels of education and income and older people are the least likely to have online access (Pew Internet and American Life Project 2012a). This represents a sizable segment of the population that has limited access to other political resources as well. This issue of accessible, useful information for political decision making pertains beyond the electoral arena.

REFERENCES

Baker, Peter, and Ashley Parker. 2012. "Before Debate, Tough Crowds at the Practice." *New York Times,* September 28. http://www.nytimes.com/2012/09/29/us/politics/cramming-and-pruning-for-first-presidential-debate.html?pagewanted=all (accessed November 1, 2012).

Barbaro, Michael, and Michael D. Shear. 2012. "Before Eastwood's Talk with a Chair, Clearance from the Top." *New York Times,* August 31. http://www.nytimes.com/2012/09/01/us/politics/romney-aides-scratch-their-heads-over-eastwoods-speech.html?_r=0 (accessed November 21, 2012).

Baum, Laura. 2012a. "2012 Shatters 2004 and 2008 Records for Total Ads Aired." Wesleyan Media Project: Political Advertising Analysis. http://mediaproject.wesleyan.edu/2012/10/24/2012-shatters-2004-and-2008-records-for-total-ads-aired/.

Baum, Laura. 2012b. "Presidential Ad War Tops 1M Airings." Wesleyan Media Project: Political Advertising Analysis. http://mediaproject.wesleyan.edu/2012/11/02/presidential-ad-war-tops-1m-airings/.

Blumenthal, Mark. 2011. "Republican Polls' Roller Coaster Powered by News Coverage." *Huffington Post,* October 21. http://www.huffingtonpost.com/2011/10/21/republican-presidential-polls-powered-by-news-coverage_n_1025219.html (accessed December 1, 2012).

Blumenthal, Paul. 2012. "Citizens United Ruling in Full Force as October Influence Spending Skyrockets." *Huffington Post,* October 16. http://www.huffingtonpost.com/2012/10/16/citizens-united-ruling-effects-october-spending_n_1971323.html (accessed November 22, 2012).

Brader, Ted. 2006. *Campaigning for Hearts and Minds.* Chicago: University of Chicago Press.

Brennan, Allison. 2012. "Microtargeting: How Campaigns Know You Better Than You Know Yourself." CNN, November 5. http://www.cnn.com/2012/11/05/politics/voters-microtargeting/index.html (accessed November 20, 2012).

Brenner, Joanna. 2012. "Pew Internet: Social Networking." Pew Internet and American Life Project. http://pewinternet.org/Commentary/2012/March/Pew-Internet-Social-Networking-full-detail.aspx (accessed November 20, 2012).

Carr, David. 2012. "A Last Face Check: It Didn't Work." *New York Times,* November 6. http://mediadecoder.blogs.nytimes.com/2012/11/06/a-last-fact-check-it-didnt-work/ (accessed December 1, 2012).

Center for Media and Public Affairs. 2012. "Study: TV News Bashes Romney, Boosts Horse Race." Press release. http://www.cmpa.com/media_room_press_1_18_12.html (accessed February 5, 2013).

Center for Responsive Politics. 2012. "Outside Spending." OpenSecrets.org. http://www.opensecrets.org/outsidespending/ (accessed November 12, 2012).

Cillizza, Chris, and Aaron Blake. 2012. "Americans Elect and the Death of the Third Party Movement." *Washington Post,* May 18. http://www.washingtonpost.com/blogs/the-fix/post/americans-elect-and-the-death-of-the-third-party-movement/2012/05/17/gIQAIzNKXU_blog.html (accessed November 12, 2012).

Colbert, Annie. 2012. "Eastwooding! Clint's 'Invisible Obama' Routine Inspires Meme." *Mashable,* August 30. http://mashable.com/2012/08/30/clint-eastwood-chair-meme/ (accessed November 21, 2012).

Confessore, Nicholas. 2012. "Result Won't Limit Campaign Money Any More Than Ruling Did." *New York Times,* November 11. http://www.nytimes.com/2012/11/12/us/politics/a-vote-for-unlimited-campaign-financing.html?pagewanted=all (accessed November 24, 2012).

Crovitz, L. Gordon. 2012. "Double-Checking the Journalist 'Fact Checkers.'" *The Wall Street Journal,* September 9. http://online.wsj.com/article/SB10000872396390443686004577639743922340620.html (accessed February 5, 2012).

Cruz, Laurence. 2012. "The Social Media Election?" *The Network,* September 3. http://newsroom.cisco.com/feature/1006785/2012-The-Social-Media-Election- (accessed November 20, 2012).

Darwell, Brittany. 2012. "Obama and Romney Facebook Stores and Donation Apps Tied for Users." *Inside Facebook,* November 6. http://www.insidefacebook.

com/2012/11/06/obama-and-romney-facebook-stores-and-donation-apps-tied-for-users-but-obama-2012-app-beats-commit-to-mitt/ (accessed November 20, 2012).

Davis, Richard, and Diana Owen. 1998. *New Media and American Politics.* New York: Oxford University Press.

Dickerson, John, and Chris Kirk. 2012. "The 2012 Campaign Decoder." *Slate,* October 29. http://www.slate.com/articles/news_and_politics/politics/2012/10/the_campaign_decoder_sorting_the_presidential_campaign_s_gaffes_antics_and_false_controversies_from_the_stuff_that_actually_matters_.html (accessed November 20, 2012).

Ellis, Justin. 2012. "Election Night Traffic, Trends, and Strategies from the *New York Times,* CNN, BuzzFeed, and More." *Nieman Journalism Lab,* November 9. http://www.niemanlab.org/2012/11/election-night-traffic-trends-and-strategies-from-the-new-york-times-cnn-buzzfeed-and-more/ (accessed November 24, 2012).

Erikson, Robert S., and Christopher Wlezien. 2012. *The Timeline of Presidential Elections.* Chicago: University of Chicago Press.

Eversley, Melanie. 2012. "Romney's 'Big Bird' Comment Stirs Social Media." *USA Today,* October 4. http://www.usatoday.com/story/onpolitics/2012/10/03/big-birg-romney-debate-pbs/1612171/ (accessed November 20, 2012).

Fitzgerald, Britney. 2012. "Eastwooding: Clint Eastwood's 'Chair' Speech at Republican National Convention Inspires New Meme." *Huffington Post,* August 31. http://www.huffingtonpost.com/2012/08/31/eastwooding-clint-eastwood-chair_n_1846414.html (accessed November 24, 2012).

Flock, Elizabeth. 2012. "The Wacky Obama Campaign E-mails That Didn't Work." *Business Week,* December 5. http://www.businessweek.com/articles/2012-11-29/the-science-behind-those-obama-campaign-e-mails (December 5, 2012).

Fouhy, Beth. 2012. "2012 Election: Campaigns Mine Online Data to Target Voters." *Huffington Post,* May 28. http://www.huffingtonpost.com/2012/05/28/2012-election-internet-data_n_1550720.html (accessed November 20, 2012).

Foulger, Matt. 2012. "Social Media's Role in the 2012 U.S. Election: Obama Breaks Twitter Records." *TootSource,* November 7. http://blog.hootsuite.com/election-tracker-results/ (accessed November 20, 2012).

Geer, John. 2012. "The News Media and the Rise of Negativity in Presidential Campaigns." *PS: Political Science & Politics* 45 (3): 422–27.

Goldman, Julianna. 2012. "Obama Winning Social Media, If #Hashtagwars Really Matter." *Bloomberg,* October 22. http://www.bloomberg.com/news/2012-10-22/obama-winning-social-media-if-hashtagwars-really-matter.html (accessed November 20, 2012).

Green, Joshua. 2012. "The Science behind Those Obama Campaign E-Mails." *Bloomberg Business,* November 29. http://www.businessweek.com/articles/2012-11-29/the-science-behind-those-obama-campaign-e-mails (accessed November 30, 2012).

Hermes, Jeffrey P. 2012. "The Thankless Task of the Political Fact-Checker." *Citizen Media Law Project,* November 27. http://www.citmedialaw.org/blog/2012/thankless-task-political-fact-checker (accessed December 1, 2012).

Higgins, Caroline. 2012. "The 2012 Presidential Campaign and Social Media: A New Age?" *Flip the Media,* August 31. http://flipthemedia.com/2012/08/the-2012-presidential-campaign-and-social-media-a-new-age/ (accessed November 20, 2012).

Itzkoff, Dave. 2012. "D'Oh! Eastwood's Convention Speech Spawns Fake 'Simpson' Meme." *The Caucus* (blog), *New York Times,* http://thecaucus.blogs.nytimes. com/2012/08/31/doh-eastwoods-convention-speech-spawns-fake-simpsons-meme/ (accessed November 20, 2012).

Jamieson, Kathleen Hall. 2012. "Third-Party Dollars Spent on Deceptive Ads: Update." Annenberg Public Policy Center, October 19. http://www.flackcheck.org/press/ third-party-dollars-spent-on-deceptive-ads-update-through-10192012/ (accessed November 29, 2012).

Jamieson, Kathleen Hall, and David S. Birdsell. 1988. *Presidential Debates: The Challenge of Creating an Informed Electorate.* New York: Oxford University Press.

Kessler, Glenn. 2012. "Fact Checking the Third Presidential Debate." *Washington Post,* October 23. http://www.washingtonpost.com/blogs/fact-checker/post/ fact-checking-the-third-presidential-debate/2012/10/23/91dbdc4a-1c61-11e2-ba31-3083ca97c314_blog.html (accessed December 1, 2012).

Kludt, Tom. 2012. "Voters Still Trust Gallup Polls More Than Nate Silver." *Business Insider,* December 5. http://www.businessinsider.com/voters-trust-gallup-more-than-nate-silver-2012–12 (accessed December 5, 2012).

Kois, Dan. 2012. "'I've Barely Prepared for This Debate. Gonna Wing It!'—Mitt Romney." *Slate,* October 1. http://www.slate.com/articles/news_and_politics/ low_concept/2012/10/barack_obama_and_mitt_romney_debate_who_can_set_ expectations_lowest_for_the_first_presidential_debate_.html (accessed November 1, 2012).

Lehrer, Jim. 2011. *Tension City.* New York: Random House.

Lewandowski, Andrew D. 2012. "The Rise of the Visual Political Meme." *Electronic Media and Politics,* April 2. http://www.emandp.com/post/single/the_rise_of_ the_visual_political_meme (accessed November 22, 2012).

McGregor, Jena. 2012. "In Superstorm Sandy, Gov. Chris Christie Praises Obama's Crisis Leadership." *Washington Post,* October 30. http://www. washingtonpost.com/national/on-leadership/in-superstorm-sandy-new-jersey-governor-chris-christie-praises-president-obamas-crisis-leadership/2012/10/30/ 89769e32-22b5-11e2-ac85-e669876c6a24_story.html (accessed November 24, 2012).

Mlot, Stephanie. 2012. "Social Media Use Exploded in 2012, Led by Pinterest." *PC Magazine,* December 3. http://www.pcmag.com/article2/0,2817,2412785,00. asp (accessed December 3, 2012).

Nielsen. 2012. *State of the Media: The Social Media Report 2012.* New York: Nielsen.

Ouimet, Maeghan. 2012. "Who's Winning the 2012 Social Media Election." *Inc.,* September 8. http://www.inc.com/maeghan-ouimet/social-meda-campaigns-election-2012-obama-romney.html (accessed November 20, 2012).

Owen, Diana. 2009. "The Campaign and the Media." In *The American Elections of 2008,* ed. Janet M. Box-Steffensmeier and Steven E. Schier. New York: Routledge.

Owen, Diana. 2012. "Political Parties and the Media: The Parties Respond to Technological Innovation." In *The Parties Respond,* ed. Mark Brewer and L. Sandy Maisel. Boulder, CO: Westview Press.

Pew Internet and American Life Project. 2012a. "Internet Adoption, 1995–2012." http://www.pewinternet.org/Static-Pages/Trend-Data-(Adults)/Internet-Adoption.aspx (accessed November 20, 2012).

Pew Internet and American Life Project. 2012b. "Digital Politics." November 29. http://pewinternet.org/Infographics/2012/Digital-Politics.aspx (accessed December 3, 2012).

Pew Research Center for the People and the Press. 2012. "Low Marks for the 2012 Election." November 15. http://www.people-press.org/2012/11/15/low-marks-for-the-2012-election/ (accessed November 24, 2012).

Plouffe, David. 2009. *The Audacity to Win*. New York: Viking.

PolitiFact. 2012. "Super PAC Says New Gingrich and Nancy Pelosi Teamed Up to Support China's 'One Child' Policy." January 12, http://www.politifact.com/florida/statements/2012/jan/12/restore-our-future/newt-gingrich-nancy-pelosi-china-one-child-policy/ (accessed February 5, 2013).

Prakash, Neha. 2012. "Which Presidential Candidate Is Ruling the Email Election?" *Mashable,* October 18. http://mashable.com/2012/10/18/election-emailing/ (accessed November 12, 2012).

Project for Excellence in Journalism. 2012a. "How the Presidential Candidates Use the Web and Social Media." August 15. http://www.journalism.org/node/30477 (accessed November 20, 2012).

Project for Excellence in Journalism. 2012b. "Internet Gains Most as Campaign News Source but Cable TV Still Leads." October 25. http://www.journalism.org/commentary_backgrounder/social_media_doubles_remains_limited (accessed November 20, 2012).

Project for Excellence in Journalism. 2012c. *Winning the Media Campaign 2012* (report). November 2. http://www.journalism.org/node/31438 (accessed November 25, 2012).

Project for Excellence in Journalism. 2012d. *How the Media Covered the 2012 Primary Campaign* (report). April 23. http://www.journalism.org/analysis_report/romney_report?src=prc-headline (accessed November 24, 2012).

Reeve, Elspeth. 2012. "Obama and Romney's Ritual Pre-Debate Lovefest." *The Atlantic,* September 27. http://www.theatlanticwire.com/politics/2012/09/obama-and-romneys-ritual-pre-debate-lovefest/57336/ (accessed November 12, 2012).

Rosen, Kenneth. 2012. "Who Spent More on Online Ads This Election?" *Mashable,* November 5. http://mashable.com/2012/11/05/online-ads-election/ (accessed November 12, 2012).

Rutenberg, Jim, and Ashley Parker. 2012. "Romney Says Remarks on Voters Help Clarify Position." *New York Times,* September 18. http://www.nytimes.com/2012/09/19/us/politics/in-leaked-video-romney-says-middle-east-peace-process-likely-to-remain-unsolved-problem.html?pagewanted=all (accessed November 20, 2012).

Scherer, Michael. 2012. "How Obama's Data Crunchers Helped Him Win." *Time,* November 8. http://www.cnn.com/2012/11/07/tech/web/obama-campaign-tech-team/index.html (accessed November 20, 2012).

Schroeder, Alan. 2008. *Presidential Debates: Fifty Years of High-Risk TV.* New York: Columbia University Press.

Serjeant, Jill. 2012. "Michelle Obama Wows Social Media, TV Audience Soars." Reuters, September 5. http://news.yahoo.com/michelle-obama-wows-social-media-tv-audience-steady-183557328.html (accessed November 20, 2012).

Sides, John. 2012. "Mitt Romney and that 47%." *The Monkey Cage,* September 17. http://themonkeycage.org/blog/2012/09/17/mitt-romney-and-that-47/ (accessed November 12, 2012).

Sifry, Micah L. 2011. "Election 2012: It's Not Facebook. It's the Data, Stupid." *TechPresident,* April 20. http://techpresident.com/blog-entry/election-2012-its-not-facebook-its-data-stupid (accessed November 20, 2012).

Smith, Scott. 2012. "Does Print Have a Place in Data-Driven News?" *Lean Back 2.0,* November 13. http://www.economistgroup.com/leanback/new-business-models/does-print-have-a-place-in-data-driven-news/ (accessed November 24, 2012).

Smith, Aaron, and Maeve Duggan. 2012. "Online Political Videos and Campaign 2012." Report, Pew Internet & American Life Project, November 2, http://pewinternet.org/Reports/2012/Election-2012-Video.aspx (accessed February 5, 2012).

Statista. 2012. "2012 Election: Percentage of Smartphone Users Who Visited Candidates' Mobile Website." http://www.statista.com/statistics/245378/percentage-of-us-smartphone-users-who-visited-presidential-candidates-mobile-website/ (accessed November 20, 2012).

Strong, Frank. 2012. "How Much Will Social Media Really Affect the U.S. Election?" PBS, September 6. http://www.pbs.org/mediashift/2012/09/how-much-will-social-media-really-affect-the-us-election250.html (accessed November 20, 2012).

Turow, Joseph, Michael X. Delli Carpini, Nora Draper, and Rowan Howard-Williams. 2012. "Americans Roundly Reject Tailored Political Advertising." Annenberg School for Communication, University of Pennsylvania, http://www.asc.upenn.edu/news/Turow_Tailored_Political_Advertising.pdf (accessed February 5, 2013).

Washington Post. 2012. "Campaign 2012: Mad Money: TV Ads in the 2012 Presidential Campaign." *Washington Post Politics.* http://www.washingtonpost.com/wp-srv/special/politics/track-presidential-campaign-ads-2012/whos-buying-ads/ (accessed November 12, 2012).

Wortham, Jenna. 2012a. "Campaigns Use Social Media to Lure Younger Voters." *New York Times,* October 7. http://www.nytimes.com/2012/10/08/technology/campaigns-use-social-media-to-lure-younger-voters.html?_r=0 (accessed November 24, 2012).

Wortham, Jenna. 2012b. "The Presidential Campaign on Social Media." *New York Times,* October 8. http://www.nytimes.com/interactive/2012/10/08/technology/campaign-social-media.html (accessed November 20, 2012).

Zuckerman, Esther. 2012. "Romney Spoke Four Minutes Less, but Got in 541 More Words." *The Atlantic Wire,* October 4. http://www.theatlanticwire.com/politics/2012/10/romney-spoke-four-minutes-less-got-541-more-words/57608/ (accessed November 25, 2012).

3   Fighting Off Challengers

The 2012 Nomination of Mitt Romney

Barbara Norrander

Looking at the end results of the 2012 Republican presidential nomination, one might conclude that Mitt Romney sailed to an easy victory. After all, he won 32 out of 40 presidential primaries, and he was being called the presumptive nominee of the Republican Party by April. Even in the year before the election, Romney was considered by many to be the front-runner, having amassed the most money for his own campaign. In addition, Romney for several years had quietly built support among Republican activists with early visits to their states and had established ties with state and local Republican candidates with contributions from his Free and Strong America PAC. Yet in late 2011, Romney could not maintain a lead in the public opinion polls, and in 2012, he faced a series of challenges to his front-runner status as other candidates won early primaries or caucuses. Former president Bill Clinton on *The Daily Show* colorfully described Romney's path to the Republican nomination as akin to a game of "Whac-A-Mole."[1] Each week seemed to bring a new challenger to Romney's claim to be the front-runner for the 2012 Republican Party's presidential nomination.

The diverse composition of the Republican Party contributed to Romney's problems. Although most Republicans consider themselves to be conservatives, they mean different things by this term. Christian conservatives are concerned foremost with social issues, such as abortion and same-sex marriage. Main-street Republicans favor pro-business policies, such as lower taxes and fewer regulations, and might want to downplay social issues to attract more independent voters. Libertarian-leaning Republicans stress minimum government in all spheres, joining with other Republicans in support of smaller government on most domestic policies, but setting themselves apart by opposing military intervention abroad and government interference with personal freedoms at home. Tea Party activists, galvanized by their opposition to Obama's Affordable Care Act (i.e., Obamacare) and the growing federal deficit, reject compromises to what they view as core conservative principles. Finally, neoconservative Republicans focus on foreign policy and stress intervention by the United States to expand democratic rule and protect our national interests. These multifaceted components of the Republican Party fit within the notion of political parties as networks of policy-demanding groups and activists (Bawn et al. 2012). Sometimes these groups coordinate behind a single candidate, signaling this agreement with numerous elite endorsements (Marty Cohen et al. 2008). Yet in other years, such as with the Republicans in 2012, these diverse factions provided a base of support for several challengers.

To illustrate how Romney secured the nomination and how his competitors, one by one, fell by the wayside, this chapter begins with the strengths and weaknesses of the 2012 candidate field. Next, we turn to the new set of Republican Party rules for 2012, which led some to fear in the middle of the nomination battle that no candidate would secure the nomination before the national convention. We then focus on the unfolding of the Republican nomination race, first during the pre-election invisible primary stage and next in the early months of actual primary and caucus results. Despite numerous obstacles, Romney would secure the Republican nomination by mid-April as most other challengers bowed out. The chapter concludes with a brief recap of how other parties chose their 2012 presidential nominees, including the easy renomination of Barack Obama by the Democrats.

The 2012 Republican Candidates

When a major political party has neither a sitting president nor a vice president seeking the nomination, the field of candidates grows large. Thus, in 2008, eight candidates vied for the Democratic nomination, and seven faced off in the Republican race. The 2012 Republican contest was no exception either. Listed in Table 3.1 are 12 candidates who made formal announcements to run, though not all of these candidates were of equal stature and likely to win the nomination. The winning candidate is often the one who leads in the national polls in the year before the election or who has raised the most money (Mayer 1996; Dowdle, Adkins, and Steger 2009). Results from early caucuses and primaries, however, can upset even the best-laid plans of a front-runner. Still, an apt description of the presidential nominating process is that of an attrition game (Norrander 2006). One by one, each candidate withdraws from the contest. Some quit before the first votes are cast, most typically because they have failed to raise sufficient campaign funds to be competitive. Several more candidates withdraw after the first few primaries, having received few votes. At this point, the field of candidates narrows to three or four main contenders, but these candidates too eventually lag behind in primary victories and the resulting convention delegates. In many recent election years, the nomination contest was over by mid-March, with only one serious contender still in the race (Norrander 2000). This contender is then considered to be the party's presumptive nominee,

Table 3.1 The 2012 Republican Candidates

Candidate	Last political office	Home state	Primary victories	Withdrawal date
Tim Pawlenty	Governor	Minnesota	0	Aug. 14, 2011
Thaddeus McCotter	U.S. House	Michigan	0	Sept. 22, 2011
Herman Cain	None	Georgia	0	Dec. 3, 2011
Gary Johnson	Governor	New Mexico	0	Dec. 28, 2011
Michele Bachmann	U.S. House	Minnesota	0	Jan. 4, 2012
Jon Huntsman	Governor	Utah	0	Jan. 16, 2012
Rick Perry	Governor	Texas	0	Jan. 19, 2012
Buddy Roemer	Governor	Louisiana	0	Feb. 23, 2012
Rick Santorum	Senator	Pennsylvania	6	Apr. 10, 2012
Newt Gingrich	U.S. House	Georgia	2	May 2, 2012
Ron Paul	U.S. House	Texas	0	May 14, 2012
Mitt Romney	Governor	Massachusetts	32	

though the official nomination is not bestowed until the national convention at the end of the summer.

If there was a Republican front-runner in 2011, it was former Massachusetts governor Mitt Romney, who had run for the presidential nomination in 2008 as well. As a former governor, Romney had a typical background for presidential nominees. Governorship has been the office held by the largest number of presidential nominees in recent years, though typically more senators than governors seek the nomination (Burden 2002). Romney also laid claim to a successful career in business and to civic positions—for example, as the head of the 2002 Winter Olympics in Utah. In addition, Romney had been more or less campaigning for the nomination since losing in 2008. During this time he had developed many contacts with Republican activists and donors throughout the nation. Such contacts, along with the endorsements Romney received from the party's elites, are vital resources for winning the nomination (Marty Cohen et al. 2008). However, Romney had fewer elite endorsements than leading contenders in prior years (Silver 2012c), perhaps another sign of a weak front-runner status. Romney also had difficulty in maintaining a lead in the national polls. Only in fundraising totals did Romney dominate the field of candidates.

Five other governors ran for the 2012 Republican nomination. Texas governor Rick Perry initially appeared to be the strongest contender among this group, but missteps during the early campaign doomed his chances. Former Minnesota governor Tim Pawlenty had even less luck, being the first candidate to withdraw from the contest in the middle of 2011. Gary Johnson, Jon

Huntsman, and Buddy Roemer all had their own weak points. New Mexico's former governor, Gary Johnson, made little headway in the Republican race, competing for the same libertarian voters as Ron Paul. Johnson dropped out early but eventually became the Libertarian Party's presidential nominee instead. Jon Huntsman, once the governor of Utah, failed to convince Republican voters that his moderate issue positions would make him more electable in the fall campaign. Finally, former Louisiana governor Buddy Roemer had not held elective office since 1992 and was not considered a major candidate in 2012.

Remarkably, only one senator contested the 2012 Republican presidential nomination, and Rick Santorum was initially viewed as a weak choice since he had lost his last bid for reelection as Pennsylvania's senator by 18 percentage points. Still, Santorum would become the favored candidate of the important religious voting bloc within the Republican Party. Members of the U.S. House of Representatives are candidates less frequently, since they need to run for reelection in the same election cycle. Further, House members have previously won only in their smaller, more homogeneous congressional districts versus the more competitive statewide senatorial and gubernatorial contests. Yet the 2012 Republican contestants included four current or former members of the U.S. House. Minnesota representative Michele Bachmann was a leader of the Tea Party caucus in the House and did well in some pre–election year events, but she struggled in the final run-up to the Iowa caucuses. Former Georgia congressman Newt Gingrich had been out of political office for more than a decade, but in 1994 he had led the Republican Party to win control of the House for the first time in 40 years with his "Contract with America." Gingrich was praised for his grand ideas, but former colleagues faulted his ability to follow through on initiatives. His intervening career as a Washington consultant and his third marriage also were dents to Gingrich's reputation and fodder for attack ads against him. Texas congressman Ron Paul was making his third bid for the presidency, having failed to win the Republican nomination in 2008 and having run as the Libertarian Party candidate in 1988. Paul's staunch libertarian positions won him ardent admirers, many of them young adults, but his candidacy lacked a wider berth of support. Michigan congressman Thaddeus McCotter was a marginal candidate for president, and failing to file the proper paperwork for his reelection bid to the U.S. House, he withdrew from that contest as well.

It is rare for a presidential candidate not to have held elective office. The last major party nominee without a previous public office was Dwight Eisenhower in 1952. Eisenhower, however, was a famous World War II general. Wendell Willkie, the Republican nominee in 1940, was the last businessman nominated for the presidency who had not held a previous public office. Without a prior bid for elective office, candidates are unfamiliar with campaign strategies and technologies and may underestimate the intrusive glare of the media coverage. Businessman Herman Cain hoped to break this pattern in 2012. Cain was the former CEO of Godfather's Pizza and more recently a radio talk show host. He also would be the only African American to run for the Republican nomination. In 2011, Cain gained traction with his 9-9-9 tax plan. The proposal called for a 9 percent national sales tax, a 9 percent business tax, and a flat 9 percent tax on personal income. Cain briefly led in some national polls in October 2011, but his fortunes began to fall with indications that he lacked knowledge of international issues. Allegations of sexual harassment during Cain's time leading the National Restaurant Association and of a long-term extramarital affair led Cain to suspend his bid for the nomination on December 3.

Sometimes election contests are decided not so much by who runs as by who does not. Several candidates who could have been serious challengers to Mitt Romney decided not to pursue the presidency in 2012. Among those who were mentioned but who declined to run were Indiana governor Mitch Daniels, New Jersey governor Chris Christie, Mississippi governor Haley Barbour, congressman Paul Ryan, and former Arkansas governor and 2008 presidential nomination-seeker Mike Huckabee. Sarah Palin, the 2008 Republican vice presidential nominee and former Alaska governor, kept the media guessing about her intentions throughout much of 2011. In May, she staged a family vacation and, it seemed, a campaign bus tour that concluded in New Hampshire on the same day that Romney was making his formal announcement of candidacy. She appeared in Iowa on the day of the Ames straw poll, though she was not a participant. Her frequent tweets, Facebook updates, and role as a commentator on Fox News kept her in the public eye. Her position as a Tea Party favorite and her successful endorsement of candidates in 2010 lent credence to a potential bid. Yet on October 5, 2011, she announced she would not seek the nomination.

The New 2012 Rules

In 2012, for the first time in modern nomination history, the Republican Party instituted national rules on how states could distribute their delegates among candidates winning votes in their presidential primaries. Voters in presidential primaries cast ballots for one of the national candidates, but in reality, they are setting the stage for the selection of national convention delegates who are committed to support their preferred candidates. This two-component primary vote and delegate-selection process is analogous to the popular vote and electoral college vote in presidential elections. The Democratic Party has had uniform rules since the mid-1990s. The Democratic rules require that all states allocate delegates by proportional representation rules. If a candidate wins a primary with 40 percent of the vote, that candidate is awarded 40 percent of the delegates. The remaining 60 percent of the delegates are distributed among the other candidates based on their vote totals. The Democratic Party requires a candidate to receive a minimum of 15 percent of the vote to receive any delegates, and two-thirds of the delegates are allocated based on voting results at the congressional district level and one-third are allocated based on statewide vote totals.

Before 2012, the Republican Party allowed states to select their own method for distributing delegates among the candidates receiving votes. One option for distributing delegates is winner-take-all: whichever candidate wins the most votes in a primary receives all of the state's delegates. This method is similar to that used by 48 states for the allocation of their electoral college votes (Maine and Nebraska allocate part of their electoral college votes on the basis of the vote within each congressional district). The simplest formula for winner-take-all is to allocate all delegates to the winner of the statewide vote, whether or not the winner received a majority of the vote. Some modifications for winner-take-all include requiring a candidate to earn a certain level of support, such as a majority of the statewide vote, in order to win all of the state's delegates. Alternatively, some states allocate part of their delegates on a winner-take-all basis in each congressional district and award the other delegates to the statewide winner. Another option available for the selection of Republican delegates has been for voters to directly elect them. This is typically done with a two-part ballot—voters demonstrate their support for the national candidates with a preference vote and cast a second series of votes for individuals running to be national convention delegates. The direct delegate-election format was the most typical form for presidential primaries held in the earliest part of the twentieth century, but few states have chosen this option in recent decades. Finally, before 2012, states could also select proportional representation rules for their Republican as well as their Democratic primaries. Many Republican caucus states had no formal rules for the selection of national convention delegates, and these delegates were often selected not at the original caucuses but at later midlevel or state-level conventions.

For 2012, the national Republican Party instituted a rule that states could not use the statewide winner-take-all method of delegate allocation if they chose to hold their presidential primaries before April 1. National party leaders hoped this new rule would convince states to hold later primaries, so that not all primaries would be clustered at the front of the election calendar. For several decades, the two political parties at the national level have tried to control the nomination calendars with a carrot and stick approach (Norrander 2013). In the past, one or the other party tried to persuade states to hold later primaries by offering them more convention delegates if they did so. On the other hand, the national parties penalized states that went too early by reducing their delegate totals. The 2012 Republican plan added a new carrot. States presumably like to use statewide winner-take-all delegate allocation rules to be more attractive to a candidate who thinks he or she can win the state and capture a large batch of delegates.

Most of the parties' previous carrots and sticks had minor influence on the actions of the states. Some states want more clout in the presidential nomination process. Such states often feel that an early primary will gain them more attention from the candidates and, subsequently, the media. Thus, these clout-seeking states select an early date for their primaries, contributing to the front-loading of the primary calendar. Other states select primary dates based on local political needs. In 2012, a number of states moved the dates of their primaries backward on the election calendar to save money. A late presidential primary can be held on the same date as the state's primaries for statewide and local offices. Thus, California in 2008 moved its primary forward to February 5, Super Tuesday, to gain clout, but in 2012, it moved its presidential primary back to its historical date of the first Tuesday in June, to coincide with its statewide primary. Holding all of its primaries on one day saved California nearly $100 million over holding two separate primaries.

In 2012, the less front-loaded primary calendar had more to do with state politics, especially thinly stretched government budgets, than the carrot of winner-take-all rules. In addition, even in 2008, most Republican primaries were not the simple statewide winner-take-all format. Twelve of the 37 Republican primaries in 2008 were simple winner-take-all, four used statewide winner-take-all if the first-place candidate won a majority of the vote, and ten states combined statewide and congressional district winner-take-all rules. The remaining 2008 Republican primaries used proportional representation (nine states) or direct election of delegates (two states) (Norrander 2010). In 2012, seven of 40 Republican primaries were simple winner-take-all, nine used statewide winner-take-all if the first-place candidate won a majority of the vote (often combined with winner-take-all at the district level), and four used winner-take-all separately at the state and district levels. Fifteen states used proportional representation (three combined with winner-take-all at the district level), three states used direct election of delegates, and the last two states held primaries that were not connected to delegate selection.[2] Thus, in both 2008 and 2012, Republican presidential primaries were considerably more diverse than a simple winner-take-all format.

The Republican Party punished five states for holding 2012 presidential primaries too early. These states lost half of their delegate totals. Before the start of the campaign, both the Democratic and Republican parties agreed to a common start for the nomination calendar. Iowa, New Hampshire, South Carolina, and Nevada could hold their caucuses or primaries starting on February 1. All other states could set their nominating events beginning with the first Tuesday in March. Yet just as was the case in 2008, some states fought back against this predetermined calendar. Florida and Michigan violated the calendar rules in 2012, as they had in 2008, and Arizona joined in on the rebellion in 2012. As these states moved to the front of the election calendar, three of the four preestablished early states moved their primary or caucus dates even earlier, just as they had in 2008. The result in 2012 was that the Iowa caucuses once again moved into the first week of January, New Hampshire positioned its primary for January 10, and South Carolina selected January 21. Nevada maintained its caucuses on February 4. This maneuvering by the states led the Republican Party to cut the delegate allocations of New Hampshire, South Carolina, Florida, Arizona, and Michigan. The too-early caucus states (Iowa, Colorado, Maine, and Minnesota) and Missouri's nonbinding primary were not punished because no convention delegates were selected in these contests.

The Invisible Primary 2011–2012

The actual voting for the presidential nominee begins in the early months of the election year, but candidates' activities in the year (or two) before the election can be as important to their fates as the actual primary outcomes. The pre–election year period is traditionally referred to as the "invisible primary," as candidates quietly lay the groundwork for their campaigns. During the invisible primary stage, candidates crisscross the country to raise campaign funds and court party activists. Thus, in the summer of 2010, Minnesota governor Tim Pawlenty made several trips to Iowa, meeting with small groups of voters and working the crowds at the Iowa State Fair. He was not alone; 11 other potential candidates made early trips to Iowa (Zeleny 2010). Romney campaigned in 25 states during the summer of 2010, and he made alliances with more than 200 state and local Republican candidates by giving them contributions from his political action committee (Balz 2010). Palin, Pawlenty, and Gingrich too organized PACs that allowed them to build support by making contributions to a wide variety of Republican candidates (Peoples 2010). During this pre-election period, the presidential candidates also organize their campaign staffs, test out their stump speeches, and plan their strategies. Sometimes, upheavals during this initial organizing stage make the national news, such as when most of Gingrich's staff quit in the summer of 2011 over differences in strategies. More typically, candidates seek out positive media attention by participating in debates and straw polls. The pre–election year events have become more visible.

On August 13, 2011, the Iowa Republican Party once again held a straw poll. This straw poll is not a scientific measure of candidate preferences among Iowa Republicans. Rather, the straw poll counts the preferences of party activists who are enthusiastic enough about their candidate to gather in Ames, Iowa, for a daylong event of political activity. Nevertheless, this straw poll has figured prominently in pre–election year skirmishes in recent years. It is seen as a harbinger of the candidates' abilities to organize in Iowa, where the caucus format depends as much on getting supporters to the precinct meetings as it does on the overall popularity of the candidate.

To influence the outcome of the Iowa straw poll, candidates hire buses to bring their supporters to Ames, they set up campaign booths providing free food and entertainment, and some candidates even pay the $30 cost of casting a ballot. Thus, the event is a fundraiser for the Iowa Republican Party; it charges candidates for setting up their booths and charges individuals to cast ballots. Minnesota congresswoman and Tea Party favorite Michele Bachmann won the 2011 Iowa straw poll with 4,823 votes, 29 percent of the total. Ron Paul was a close second, at 4,671. Former Minnesota governor Tim Pawlenty came in a distant third, with 14 percent of the vote.[3] However, since Pawlenty had committed considerable resources to the bid, and candidates are expected to do well in states next door to their home states, Pawlenty withdrew from the Republican race after the Iowa straw vote. The eventual winner of the Iowa caucuses, Rick Santorum, finished fourth in the straw poll, with 10 percent of the vote. Mitt Romney skipped the straw polls in 2011 (Cillizza 2011).

The Iowa straw poll was not the only one scheduled. Numerous straw polls were taken at Republican or conservative political events in 2011. Ron Paul won a large number of these because of the willingness of his supporters to attend these events (Knickerbocker 2011). Yet straw polls have little relationship to the outcome of the subsequent primaries and caucuses, and they reflect only the preferences of the small number of people who attend the conference or meeting. Most straw polls receive little national media attention, and no candidate withdrew because of poor performance except for Pawlenty.

The most publicized events during 2011 were the candidate debates. Twenty debates were held between some or all of the Republican contenders between May 2011 and February 2012. Debates were sponsored by major media outlets, interest groups, or components of the Republican Party. Providing little other information on the abilities and qualities of the candidates, these debates influenced candidates' standings in the national polls. Candidates' fates could rise or tumble based on their debate performance. Rick Perry occasionally stumbled over his own words. The most infamous event occurred at the November 9, 2011, debate in Rochester, Michigan, where he was unable to name all three government departments he said he favored abolishing. His 53 seconds of a stumbling response ended with "Sorry. Oops." Perry's stammering was a hit on the Internet and was mocked on TV's *Saturday Night Live*. Meanwhile, Perry's policies received mixed reactions during the debates. His support for more moderate immigration policies drew hostile reactions, but his tough stance on capital punishment mirrored most conservatives' beliefs. Newt Gingrich was often powerful in his speech, and he craftily attacked the other candidates and sometimes the moderators, but he advocated some unusual positions, such as mining colonies on the moon. Mitt Romney, as the presumed front-runner, was frequently attacked from all sides. Although Romney was not a natural debater, his performance improved over time. Ron Paul stood out from the crowd with his more libertarian positions, and Jon Huntsman did so with his more moderate stances. Twenty debates between up to eight candidates at a time, however, often left a muddled picture of which candidate was ahead.

Two more concrete measures of candidates' strengths are available in the invisible primary stage. The first is standing in the national polls, and the second is fundraising totals. Romney was the clear front-runner in the latter category, but the 2011 and early 2012 public opinion polls revealed a series of changes in the front-runner. This instability in the pre–election year polls is unusual on the Republican side, where in many election years an early front-runner emerges. Yet both 2008 and 2012 showed a different pattern of no single candidate dominating the early public opinion polls of Republican-leaning voters (Saad 2011).

Figure 3.1 traces preferences of Republicans for their presidential nominee between May 2011 and April 2012 according to Gallup Poll surveys.[4] Gallup conducted daily tracking polls in 2012, averaging the results over five days. In 2011, polls were done on a monthly basis until December, when daily tracking polls commenced. This variance in timing explains the less dense data on the left side (2011) of Figure 3.1 versus the right side (2012). The bold solid line is

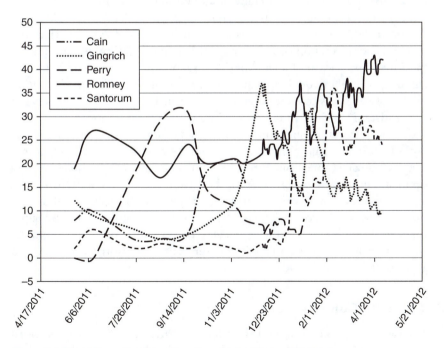

Figure 3.1 Republican Candidate Standings in the National Polls
Source: Gallup polls.

Romney's standing in the poll. Although he led part of the time in 2011, Rick Perry surged ahead in August and September, and Herman Cain tied Romney in the November survey. At the beginning of December, Gingrich pulled ahead of Romney, but Romney retook the lead at the end of December. The polls remained volatile in the beginning months of 2012 as well. Gingrich once again led in the polls in the middle of January. Gingrich's support faded after that, but Rick Santorum took over first place in the polls in early February, before Romney permanently regained the lead in late February.

The 2011 campaign finance picture revealed a sizable lead for Romney. By the end of 2011, Romney had raised $56.5 million. Ron Paul had half as much, at $25.9 million. Rick Perry raised $19.8 million; Herman Cain brought in $16.8 million; and Newt Gingrich garnered $12.6 million. Raising less than $10 million were Michele Bachmann ($9.2 million), Jon Huntsman ($5.8 million), and Rick Santorum ($2.2 million). Barack Obama, who as the sitting president was unopposed for his renomination, far outraised all the Republican contenders, drawing in $125 million.[5]

The candidates' own fundraising was only half the money story in 2011–2012. In the aftermath of the Supreme Court's ruling in *Citizens United v. Federal Election Commission* (2010) and other court rulings, a variety of groups formed to support the Republican candidates. A typical format was the Super PAC. These Super PACs could raise unlimited amounts of money from individuals and economic interests, including corporations and unions. Some of the Super PACs received large donations from a single individual, with casino owner Sheldon Adelson contributing $20.5 million to Winning Our Future, the Super PAC backing Newt Gingrich.[6] Super PACs could spend unlimited amounts of money for or against particular candidates. The one limitation on Super PACs was that they could not coordinate their efforts with that of a candidate. However, a number of the managers and donors to the Super PACs had previous connections with the candidates. For example, $2.2 million of the $3.2 million raised by the Our Destiny PAC, which supported Jon Huntsman, came from his father, Jon Huntsman Sr.[7] Mitt Romney's campaign ultimately benefited from the advertising by Restore Our Future, an organization led by top Romney campaign aides from his 2008 bid for the presidency, Charles R. Spies and Carl Forti.[8] The money spent by Super PACs could exceed that of the candidates. For example, in the run-up to the South Carolina primary, Super PACs were outspending the candidates on advertising by two-to-one (Eggen 2012).

The Early Contests

The Iowa caucuses once again led off the intraparty battle for the presidential nomination. Caucuses are conducted by the political parties, and the format is less structured than a primary conducted by the state government. The 2012

Iowa caucuses brought the sometimes informal structure of the caucus voting procedures to the public's attention, when an 8-vote victory for Mitt Romney on caucus night was reversed to a 34-vote margin in favor of Rick Santorum two weeks later after the Iowa Republican Party certified its final vote count. However, even then, the outcome of the Iowa caucuses was in doubt, since results from 8 of 1,774 precincts were lost. In the end, as Table 3.2 shows, it is best to view the Iowa caucus vote totals as a tie between Romney and Santorum. How these caucus votes translated into delegates was even more tenuous. On caucus night, various media sources made estimates, ranging from a five-way split of delegates by CNN (7 each for Romney, Santorum, and Paul and 2 each for Gingrich and Perry) to a two-way split by the Associated Press (12 for Santorum and 13 for Romney).

Yet in the end, none of these disputed caucus votes or estimated delegates won had any legal significance. The caucus-night preference poll is nonbinding, meaning the actual selection of Iowa's Republican convention delegates does not necessarily follow the outcome of the initial caucus-round vote totals. Rather, Iowa's Republican national convention delegates are selected in a series of subsequent conventions. Delegates selected from the local caucuses attend a county convention, which in turn selects delegates to attend a congressional district convention. Each of Iowa's six congressional district conventions selects three delegates to the Republican national convention. Iowa's remaining 23 delegates are selected at the state's Republican convention, which in 2012 was held on June 16. By that time, Santorum was out of the race, and Ron Paul supporters were more persistent in attending the subsequent conventions. Thus, the final delegate total for Iowa was 22 delegates for Paul and 6 for Romney.[9]

At the time of the Iowa caucuses, the Romney campaign was not focused on Santorum as the main challenger. Instead, they were worried about Newt Gingrich, who led in the December national polls. As a consequence, Gingrich faced a barrage of negative advertising in Iowa, with 45 percent of all Iowa advertisements attacking him (Wolf 2011). These advertisements came from the opposing candidates but also—and more often in 2012—from Super PACs. For example, Restore Our Future, the Super PAC supporting Romney, created advertisements painting Gingrich as someone with "a ton of baggage," given that he had been charged for violating ethics rules in the U.S. House and for receiving millions in consulting fees from Freddie Mac, the floundering home mortgage security company (Shear 2011). Under this barrage of attacks, Gingrich finished fourth in the Iowa caucuses. With the attack ads focused on Gingrich, Santorum was able to build support among Iowa's conservative Christian voters, much like Mike Huckabee had done in Iowa in 2008. Ron Paul held his own in the Iowa caucuses, finishing third, because of his support among the libertarian wing of the Republican Party. Michele Bachmann had a disappointing sixth-place finish, after having won

Table 3.2 2012 Republican Primaries and Caucus Results

Primary	Date	Romney	Santorum	Gingrich	Paul	Total vote
New Hampshire	Jan. 10	39	9	9	23	248,211
South Carolina	Jan. 21	28	17	40	13	603,770
Florida	Jan. 31	46	13	32	7	1,676,176
Missouri	Feb. 7	25	55		12	252,185
Arizona	Feb. 28	47	27	16	9	511,239
Michigan	Feb. 28	41	38	7	12	996,499
Georgia	March 6	26	20	47	7	901,470
Massachusetts	March 6	72	12	4	10	316,383
Ohio	March 6	38	37	15	9	1,213,879
Oklahoma	March 6	28	34	27	10	286,523
Tennessee	March 6	28	37	24	9	554,573
Vermont	March 6	39	24	8	25	60,850
Virginia	March 6	60			40	265,570
Alabama	March 13	29	35	29	5	621,731
Mississippi	March 13	31	33	31	4	293,787
Puerto Rico	March 18	83	8	2	1	128,834
Illinois	March 20	47	35	8	9	933,454
Louisiana	March 24	27	49	16	6	186,410
Maryland	April 3	49	29	11	10	248,468
Washington, DC	April 3	70		11	12	5,104
Wisconsin	April 3	44	37	6	11	787,847
Connecticut	April 24	67	7	10	13	59,578
Delaware	April 24	56	6	27	11	28,592
New York	April 24	62	10	13	15	190,515
Pennsylvania	April 24	58	18	10	13	808,115
Rhode Island	April 24	63	6	6	24	14,564
Indiana	May 8	65	13	6	15	635,589
North Carolina	May 8	66	10	8	11	973,206
West Virginia	May 8	70	12	6	11	112,416
Nebraska	May 15	71	14	5	10	185,402
Oregon	May 15	71	9	5	13	287,955
Arkansas	May 22	68	13	5	13	152,360
Kentucky	May 22	67	9	6	13	176,160
Texas	May 29	69	8	5	12	1,449,477
California	June 4	80	5	4	10	1,924,970
Montana	June 4	68	9	4	14	140,457
New Jersey	June 4	81	5	3	10	231,465
New Mexico	June 4	73	11	6	10	90,113
South Dakota	June 4	66	11	4	13	51,145
Utah	June 26	93	1	0	5	242,272

Sources: Primary vote totals from states' secretary of state or election board websites. Caucus totals from *The Green Papers website*. No candidate preference vote totals are available for the following caucuses: American Samoa (March 13), Missouri (March 17), and Louisiana (April 28). Iowa caucus total vote from official recount. Blanks indicate that a candidate was not on the ballot.

the summer 2011 Iowa straw poll and after spending 81 days campaigning in the state. However, during the latter half of 2011, Bachmann had stumbled with numerous misstatements, and other candidates challenged her for the support of conservative Christian voters. The day after the Iowa caucuses, Bachmann suspended her presidential campaign.

New Hampshire traditionally holds the first primary contest. The primary electorate is larger and more diverse than caucus attendees. The composition of the New Hampshire Republican Party also is different than that found in Iowa. Most notably, in the northeastern states the Republican Party contains few fundamentalist Christian voters. Since Rick Santorum's base was among these religious voters, he faced an uphill battle to do as well in New Hampshire as he had done in Iowa. Meanwhile, Romney had the advantage of having served as a governor in a nearby northeastern state, and he had been diligently campaigning and contributing to New Hampshire Republican candidates over the past four years (Confessore 2012). Jon Huntsman, who had skipped the Iowa caucuses, focused all of his early campaigning on New Hampshire, hoping the state's voters would support his more moderate issue positions. Instead, Romney decisively won in New Hampshire, followed by Ron Paul in second place. Within a few days, both Huntsman and Rick Perry withdrew from the race. The Republican field was now down to four main contenders: Romney, Santorum, Gingrich, and Paul.

South Carolina's primary often plays a pivotal role in the early rounds of the Republican contest. In 2000, a victory in South Carolina's primary helped George W. Bush rebound from a loss to John McCain in the New Hampshire primary. But South Carolina losses have doomed the prospects of other candidates, such as in 2008 when Fred Thompson put all of his efforts into the state, only to place third. The question in 2012 was whether Newt Gingrich would be able to recover from earlier losses to compete well in South Carolina. Gingrich had served as a congressman from Georgia, so a southern state was part of his natural base. The southern Republican electorates also have a larger number of religiously conservative voters, and Gingrich courted the support of these voters. But he would have to vie with Santorum for this section of the Republican electorate. Gingrich did win in South Carolina. His victory was helped by the Super PAC Winning Our Future, which aired advertisements critical of Romney's tenure at Bain Capital. Further, Gingrich performed well in the two debates prior to South Carolina's primary. Finally, Gingrich benefited from Rick Perry's withdrawal and endorsement of him. Gingrich's victory in South Carolina meant that the first three Republican contests in 2012 had produced three different winners.

Next up was Florida. Gingrich had momentum from his South Carolina victory. However, momentum can be fleeting and countered by the strategies of opposing candidates. In Florida, the financial advantages of Romney's own campaign and his supporting Super PAC would once again take their toll on

Gingrich's image. Romney and the Super PAC supporting him spent $13.3 million on Florida advertising, whereas Gingrich and his supporting groups mustered "only" $2.5 million (Dodge and Lerer 2012). Anti-Gingrich ads once again reminded viewers of his ethics violations in the House. Romney also put in an impressive debate performance, and Gingrich was hammered for his pre-debate promise to establish a permanent moon colony by 2020. Romney won in Florida, reviving his claim to front-runner status, and he followed this up with a victory in the Nevada caucuses.

The next series of early events included caucuses and Missouri's nonbinding primary (Missouri's delegates would be selected at later caucuses and conventions). Other than Iowa, and to a lesser extent Nevada, caucus states typically receive less attention from the candidates and the media. However, Barack Obama's string of caucus victories in 2008 had shown that attention to these caucus states could assist in the eventually important delegate counts and in gaining some media attention for caucus victories. Rick Santorum hoped a strategy of paying attention to this round of caucus states would pay off. He did win the Colorado and Minnesota caucuses and Missouri's nonbinding primary on February 7. Momentum seemed to shift to Santorum.

After a two-week break in the schedule, the next stages were Arizona's and Michigan's primaries on February 28. The Arizona primary received scant attention once public opinion polling showed a strong lead for Romney, who was aided by key endorsements from top Republican officials and a significant Mormon contingency among Republican voters. Thus, all eyes turned to Michigan. Romney should have been an easy front-runner in Michigan, a state he had won in the 2008 nomination battle against John McCain and where his father had been governor. Yet Santorum could claim momentum from his earlier victories. In addition, Santorum had the conservative and Christian wings of the party to himself, with Gingrich skipping these primaries to focus on the upcoming Super Tuesday events. The pro-Santorum Super PAC—the Red White and Blue Fund—committed $600,000 toward advertisements. Santorum also courted crossover votes from Democrats who could participate in Michigan's open primary.

Still, Romney narrowly beat out Santorum, 41 percent to 38 percent, in the Michigan primary. According to the exit polls, 60 percent of the voters identified themselves as Republicans, and Romney won this group with 48 percent of their support; only 9 percent were Democrats, but these voters supported Santorum by 53 percent; and the two candidates evenly split the vote of independent identifiers.[10] More tellingly, Santorum continued to draw his support from voters who called themselves very conservative and from strong supporters of the Tea Party movement, born-again Christians, and those who opposed abortion in all cases.

The split of early primary and caucus victories between Romney, Santorum, and Gingrich led some Republican leaders and media commentators to ponder the possibility of a brokered convention. A brokered convention is one in which no candidate has the needed number of delegates to win on the first roll call of states, and multiple rounds of voting are required to name a presidential nominee. Such a multi-ballot convention had not occurred since 1948, when Thomas Dewey won the Republican nomination on the third ballot. It was believed that conditions within the 2012 Republican race could produce the first such brokered convention in 50 years. With three candidates continuing in the race, each winning and losing in different states, no one could amass the 50 percent of convention delegates needed to win the nomination by the close of the primary and caucus season in June. Some critics also pointed to the new restrictions on statewide winner-take-all delegate distribution during the early primaries as a mechanism for a long, drawn-out Republican contest (Hamby 2012). Others blamed either Gingrich or Santorum for not bowing out or Romney for not being more effective in winning decisively across a number of states. In addition, Ron Paul was expected to remain in the race, siphoning off the support of the libertarian wing of the party. Republican critics feared that a prolonged intraparty battle would disadvantage the eventual nominee, while benefiting President Obama, who faced no primary challenger.

However, Romney regained his footing with the Super Tuesday primaries and won most of the subsequent primaries. Further, the early Republican delegate distribution rules were not strictly proportional; many states were using the allowable method of winner-take-all at the congressional district level. And once again, the other leading contenders would withdraw, though not as early as in some years. The Republican nomination would be decided well before the August convention.

Super Tuesday and Beyond: Romney Becomes the Presumptive Nominee

Super Tuesday 2012 was not as massive as Super Tuesday 2008. In 2008, half of the states held their primaries or caucuses on the same day. In 2012, seven primaries (Georgia, Massachusetts, Ohio, Oklahoma, Tennessee, Virginia, and Vermont) and four caucuses (Alaska, Idaho, North Dakota, and Wyoming) were held on March 6. Super Tuesday 2012 also would not bring the Republican nomination to a close, as it had for all intents and purposes for John McCain's nomination in 2008. Nevertheless, Romney won seven states on Super Tuesday. He won in Massachusetts, where he had been expected to win as the former governor. In Virginia, Romney and Ron Paul were the only two candidates on the ballot; the other candidates had failed to meet complex requirements for a large number of signatures dispersed across 11 congressional districts. Romney won 60 percent of the vote in Virginia. Romney's Ohio victory was the most important of the day, and he edged out Santorum by less than a percentage point; early organizational deficiency continued to plague Santorum's ability to win convention delegates, his campaign having failed to file full delegate slates across all of Ohio's congressional districts. Santorum did win two primary states, Oklahoma and Tennessee, and the North Dakota caucuses. Gingrich won only his home state of Georgia. Thus, Romney did well on Super Tuesday, but not well enough to bring the nomination race to a close. He continued to have problems gaining the support of the more conservative elements of the Republican Party, such as Tea Party supporters and evangelical Christians.

With the more numerous contests on Super Tuesday, the number of delegates won by each candidate begins to matter in the race for nomination. The early contests are all about momentum and attrition. Candidates want to win, or do well, in the early contests to gain media attention and additional campaign resources. Candidates who do poorly leave the race. Not much attention is given to delegate counts because few are chosen in these early states. Some of the states are small in population, such as Iowa and New Hampshire, and other states have had their delegate totals diminished for violating party rules on calendar dates, such as Florida. On Super Tuesday, in contrast, 419 delegates were available in 2012, and 1,144 delegates were needed to clinch the Republican nomination. As Figure 3.2 shows, with his

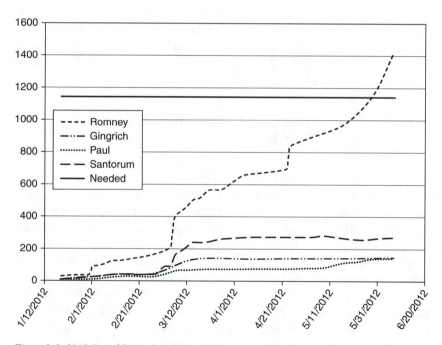

Figure 3.2 2012 Republican Candidate Delegate Vote Totals
Source: Delegate totals as published on CNN web pages.

Super Tuesday victories, Romney's delegate total climbed from 207 to 404, and he led Santorum by 239 delegates and Gingrich by 298. Neither of these latter two candidates would be able to catch up to Romney's ever-growing delegate lead with subsequent primary victories.

After Super Tuesday, the question became whether Santorum and Gingrich would continue to split the non-Romney vote. In some ways, Romney would be at an advantage if two candidates divided the opposing vote. As long as the opposition did not consolidate behind a single challenger, Romney could continue to gain in the delegate count, even if he periodically lost to one challenger or the other. Gingrich and Santorum also were competing for the same groups of voters within the Republican Party, the more conservative voters and the more religious voters. A three-way race made it more difficult for one of the challengers to catch up to Romney in the delegate count. On the other hand, the two challengers could each win enough delegates to make it difficult for Romney to capture the support of the 50 percent of all delegates needed to secure the nomination.

The three-candidate contest, however, would not endure. Gingrich won none of the remaining contests. In the immediate post–Super Tuesday period, Santorum fared better, winning primaries in Alabama, Mississippi, and Louisiana as well as the Kansas caucuses. Santorum was winning in states with large numbers of religiously conservative Republican voters. Meanwhile, Romney won in six caucus events and gained another crucial victory in the Illinois primary. Romney had struggled against Santorum for voter support in the Midwest and South, but once again, Santorum appeared unprepared for all elements of a national campaign. He misallocated time to the Puerto Rico caucuses, a contest he was unlikely to win, especially after he advocated a requirement for an official English statute for the island before consideration of statehood. In Illinois, Santorum's chances—and the delegate totals—were greater, but his campaign did not file full delegate slates. Santorum's missteps, Romney's seven-to-one advantage in advertising (Hunt 2012), and large urban areas in Illinois (more favorable to Romney) overshadowing less populous rural portions (more favorable to Santorum) combined to give Romney a 12 percentage point victory over Santorum. A next-day comment by Romney advisor Eric Fehrnstrom, however, put a bit of a damper on Romney's win. Fehrnstrom told CNN that Romney would be able to move his positions back to the middle when he won the nomination and used a phrase that provided some new ammunition for Santorum and Gingrich. Fehrnstrom avowed that with the fall campaign, "everything changes. It's almost like an Etch A Sketch. You can kind of shake it up and we start all over again" (Davis and Tiron 2012).

Nevertheless, Romney's decisive win in Illinois led more Republican leaders to endorse him and to calls for the other candidates to drop out. Most notably, Jeb Bush, the former governor of Florida, publically endorsed

Romney after the Illinois victory. Romney was not winning every contest, but he had victories in the Northeast (New Hampshire, Massachusetts), the South (Florida, Virginia), the West (Arizona, Nevada), and finally, the Midwest (Michigan, Ohio, Illinois). Even though Santorum won the March 24 Louisiana primary, Romney was steadily adding to his delegate totals. By the close of March, Romney was halfway to the ultimate goal of 1,144 delegates. Romney controlled 568 delegate votes and led Santorum by 307 delegates and Gingrich by 431. Romney's delegate leads over Santorum and Gingrich were in the range, calculated as a percentage of the delegates needed for the nomination, at which most candidates in prior years had decided to leave the contest (Norrander 2000).

The Wisconsin primary scheduled for April 3 would turn out to be the last battle between Romney and Santorum. As the Wisconsin primary approached, the Santorum campaign had little to spend on advertising (about $800,000) compared to the Romney campaign and the pro-Romney Super PAC (combined total around $3.1 million) (O'Connor and Yadron 2012). Romney also was endorsed by the largest-circulation newspaper in the state, the *Milwaukee Journal Sentinel,* and by Wisconsin congressman Paul Ryan. Equally important, Wisconsin voters were distracted by state political battles over an upcoming recall election against Republican governor Scott Walker, whose successful legislation to limit collective bargaining for state employees had led to massive protests but had galvanized the GOP base. Republican activists were preparing for the recall battle and were unavailable for mobilizing efforts by Santorum. Romney defeated Santorum in the Wisconsin primary, 44 to 37 percent.

The two other primaries on April 3, Maryland and Washington, DC, were easy victories for Romney and helped to push his delegate total to 654. Still, Santorum vowed to continue in the race and especially to hold out until his home-state primary in Pennsylvania on April 24. But Santorum switched his position and withdrew from the race on April 10. He had suffered a string of crucial primary losses, and his campaign simply did not have the money to compete with Romney on a nationwide basis. In addition, Republican leaders were moving to endorse Romney and urging his opponents to withdraw. Gingrich remained in the race for nearly another month, but by the end of April, his campaign was $4 million in debt, and he withdrew from the race. That left Ron Paul, who ended his active campaigning for the nomination on May 14, while indicating his supporters would continue to pursue delegate slots.

As the 2012 primary season progressed, Romney became increasingly viewed as the inevitable nominee. Media coverage had changed after Romney's February 28 primary victory in Michigan. Coverage of Romney became more positive, and reporting on his opponents became more critical and less frequent. More media attention was given to delegate totals and how the math supported Romney as the inevitable nominee (Rosenstiel et al.

2012). Romney also stabilized his position as the front-runner in the national polls after the Michigan victory (Silver 2012b). After Romney's victories in Wisconsin, Maryland, and Washington, DC, on April 3, more journalists and bloggers viewed Romney as the inevitable nominee (e.g., Micah Cohen 2012). Nate Silver's projections gave Romney a 96 percent chance of winning the needed delegates after these three victories (Silver 2012a). More concrete evidence on Romney's inevitability emerged when Santorum withdrew on April 10, leaving only Gingrich and Paul in the race. Gingrich had won only two primaries, and Paul, none.

Thus, Romney remained the only credible candidate by the second week in April. The Republican National Committee declared Romney as the party's presumptive nominee on April 24. On May 29, Romney secured the required support of one-half of the convention delegates after winning the Texas primary. Romney became the official nominee during the Republican National Convention held in Tampa, Florida, from August 27 to August 30. The convention also confirmed Romney's choice for vice president, Wisconsin congressman Paul Ryan.

Other Parties' Nominating Contests

Barack Obama received no challenge for the Democratic presidential nomination. In recent decades, a sitting president has rarely been challenged for his party's nomination. George W. Bush, Bill Clinton, and Ronald Reagan were renominated without opposition. George H. W. Bush was opposed by political commentator Pat Buchanan, who served as a vehicle for protest votes against Bush's breaking of his no-new-tax promise. Only President Jimmy Carter in 1980 and President Gerald Ford in 1976 faced more serious challengers (i.e., Ted Kennedy and Ronald Reagan). Thus, it was not unusual that in 2012 Obama quietly swept through the Democratic primaries and caucus.

A few minor candidates won scattered votes across the primaries, but they generally failed to file delegate slates and won no delegates. The most notable of these minor-candidate protest votes occurred in the West Virginia primary, where a fringe candidate won 41 percent of the vote because of voters' concerns over potential Environmental Protection Agency rulings that would adversely affect the state's coal industry. Unofficially, Obama controlled the necessary one-half of the delegate total at the close of the Wisconsin, Maryland, and Washington, DC, primaries on April 3. Obama and Vice President Joe Biden were officially renominated at the Democratic National Convention held in Charlotte, North Carolina, from September 3 to September 6. As the unchallenged Democratic nominee throughout 2012, Obama had the advantage of preparing for the fall campaign since January 1, if not earlier.

Various third parties nominated presidential candidates. For example, the Libertarian Party selected Gary Johnson as its presidential candidate during its convention held in May. The Green Party chose Dr. Jill Stein as its nominee at its July convention. A new nominating procedure was tested in 2012 but ultimately failed to draw enough support. A nonpartisan group called Americans Elect decided to hold a national presidential primary using the Internet to name a third-party candidate. The proposal called for a series of online ballots to narrow down alternatives to six candidates by April, with a winner to be named by June. Simultaneously, the organization would gather the necessary voters' signatures to place the Americans Elect nominee on all 50 state ballots. To pay for this undertaking, the group aimed to raise $35 million to finance the operations, and contributions came from small donors and about 50 wealthy individuals (Altman 2011). Despite some national publicity, the effort failed to catch on. Americans Elect suspended its efforts in May 2012 when no candidate had attained the required number of votes.

Conclusion

The 2012 Republican nomination ended in the same manner as the 2008 Republican contest and many recent nominations. One by one, candidates withdrew, leaving one candidate to be the presumptive nominee midway through the primary and caucus calendar. Early primary and caucus states played an important role in winnowing some candidates, while providing an aura of momentum for others. Somewhat unusual in 2012 was the early back-and-forth between Romney and several other candidates for the claim of front-runner status and the momentum advantage. Yet as the primary season progressed, and delegate totals became more important after Super Tuesday, Romney's delegate numbers consistently climbed. In addition, Romney possessed some of the traditional advantages of winning candidates. His own campaign fundraising totals greatly exceeded those of the other candidates, and Romney's prior experience as a presidential nomination seeker gave him the skills to compete effectively across the nation. His competitors often had ardent supporters among one wing of the Republican Party, but they failed to expand their base, had less of their own financial resources, and made strategic mistakes. Super PACs could bring in additional advertising support for these other candidates, but the pro-Romney Super PACs could hammer back with attack ads. Equally as important, Republican primary voters were anxious to nominate a candidate who could beat Obama in the fall election, and throughout the primary season, more often than not, Romney was viewed as possessing this trait (DePinto and Dutton 2012).

But did the nomination process hurt Romney's chances to win the presidential election? Since the beginning of the primary-dominated presidential nomination era in the 1970s, a tension has existed between the openness of the process, which allows millions of Americans to take part in the nomination process, and the potential to acerbate divisions within the party. On the one hand, the primary process allows American voters to feel that they are part of the nomination process, even if their preferred candidate does not win. In 2012, 19 million Republicans voted in a primary or participated in a caucus. A smaller number became activists who helped staff local headquarters, spreading the candidate's message to their friends and neighbors and participating in get-out-the-vote drives. Modern technology allowed more people to participate in the campaign through social media connections as well. In addition, millions of Americans gave small contributions to the candidates, though recent Supreme Court rulings allow the super-wealthy to funnel millions of dollars to Super PACs.

On the other hand, all of this openness during the intraparty nomination battles brings up concerns as well. Are primary contests too divisive, creating passionate supporters for candidates who eventually lose the nomination? The party's nominee may need to woo back such voters in time to reunite the party for the fall campaign. Other concerns focus on how the primary campaign may harm the candidate who ultimately wins the nomination. Does the successful candidate have to move too far to the extremes to win the nomination? Do opposing candidates open up criticisms of the nominee during the primary campaign that can be reused against the party's nominee in the fall? In the aftermath of the 2012 general election, some conservative Republicans felt that Romney lost the election because he had not successfully carried their message to the general election voter, whereas other Republicans pondered whether Romney had moved too far to the right during the primaries to court the support of the conservative wing of the party.

The more decisive part of the 2012 presidential nominations might have occurred on the Democratic side. Because Obama faced no opposition to his renomination, he was able to focus on the general election well before Romney unofficially secured his nomination. Indeed, no sitting president without an intraparty challenge to his renomination (e.g., Reagan, Clinton, and George W. Bush) has lost the general election since the start of the primary-dominated presidential nomination era in the 1970s.

NOTES

1. *The Daily Show with Jon Stewart,* "Bill Clinton Pt. 1," September 20, 2012. http://www.thedailyshow.com/watch/thu-september-20-2012/bill-clinton-pt-1 (accessed November 12, 2012).
2. Delegate selection rules came mainly from *The Green Papers,* http://www.thegreenpapers.com/P12/ (accessed November 9, 2012).
3. Iowa straw vote totals are from *The Green Papers,* http://www.thegreenpapers.com/P12/IA-R (accessed September 7, 2012).

4. The data were downloaded from the Gallup website, from the tracking polls at the end of December 2011 and the final tracking polls ending on April 9, 2012. http://www.gallup.com/.

5. Federal Election Commission, "Presidential Pre-Nomination Campaign Receipts through December 31, 2011," http://www.fec.gov/press/summaries/2012/ElectionCycle/file/presidential_summaries/Pres1ye2011.pdf (accessed September 10, 2012).

6. "Winning Our Future," OpenSecrets.org, http://www.opensecrets.org/outside spending/detail.php?cmte=C00507525&cycle=2012 (accessed September 9, 2012).

7. "Our Destiny PAC," OpenSecrets.org, http://www.opensecrets.org/outside spending/detail.php?cmte=C00501098&cycle=2012 (accessed September 9, 2012).

8. "Restore Our Future," OpenSecrets.org, http://www.opensecrets.org/outside spending/detail.php?cmte=C00490045&cycle=2012 (accessed September 9, 2012).

9. The CNN delegate totals from the January 4, 2012, posting; the Associated Press delegate totals as posted on the *New York Times* website on January 19, 2012; and the final delegate count from *The Green Papers,* accessed on November 9, 2012.

10. Michigan primary exit poll as posted on the CNN website, http://www.cnn.com/election/2012/primaries/epolls/mi (accessed November 12, 2012).

REFERENCES

Altman, Alex. 2011. "Can Well-Heeled Insiders Create a Populist Third-Party Sensation?" *Time,* December 21. http://swampland.time.com/2011/12/21/americans-elect-can-a-well-heeled-group of-insiders-create-a-populist-third-party-sensation/ (accessed September 9, 2012).

Balz, Dan. 2010. "Romney Gets Ready for 2012." *Washington Post,* October 30. http://www.washingtonpost.com/wpdyn/content/article/2010/10/30/AR2010103002819.html?pid=topnews (accessed October 30, 2010).

Bawn, Kathleen, Martin Cohen, David Karol, Seth Masket, Hans Noel, and John Zaller. 2012. "A Theory of Political Parties: Groups, Policy Demands and Nominations in American Politics." *Perspectives on Politics* 10 (3): 571–597.

Burden, Barry. 2002. "United State Senators as Presidential Candidates." *Political Science Quarterly* 117: 81–102.

Cillizza, Chris. 2011. "Why Ron Paul Keeps Winning Straw Polls." *Washington Post,* June 20. http://www.washingtonpost.com/blogs/the-fix/post/why-ron-paul-keeps-winning-straw-polls/2011/06/20/AGu2qvcH_blog.html (accessed September 7, 2012).

Cohen, Marty, David Karol, Hans Noel, and John Zaller. 2008. *The Party Decides: Presidential Nominations Before and After Reform.* Chicago: University of Chicago Press.

Cohen, Micah. 2012. "Political Geography: Wisconsin." *FiveThirtyEight* (blog), *New York Times,* April 3. http://fivethirtyeight.blogs.nytimes.com/2012/04/03/political-geography-wisconsin/ (accessed November 12, 2012).

Confessore, Nicholas. 2012. "For Romney, Close Ties to Officials Bear Fruit." *New York Times,* January 9. http://www.nytimes.com/2012/01/10/us/politics/innh allies-in-high-places-help-power-the-romney-machine.html (accessed October 19, 2012).

Davis, Julie Hirshfield, and Roxana Tiron. 2012. "Romney Gets Endorsement While Facing Etch A Sketch Issue." *Bloomberg,* March 21. http://www.bloomberg.com/news/2012-03-21/romney-beats-santorum-in-illinois-as-long-race-remains-ahead.html (accessed October 8, 2012).

DePinto, Jennifer, and Sarah Dutton. 2012. "How Mitt Romney Became the Presumptive Nominee." CBS News, April 12. http://www.cbsnews.com/8301503544_162-57412775-503544/how-mitt-romney-became-the-presumptive nominee/ (accessed November 12, 2012).

Dodge, Catherine, and Lisa Lerer. 2012. "Romney Wins Florida Primary, Frontrunner Again." *Bloomberg,* January 31. http://www.bloomberg.com/news/2012-02-01/romney-wins-florida-primary-re-establishing-him-as-republican-frontrunner.html (accessed October 19, 2012).

Dowdle, Andrew J., Randall E. Adkins, and Wayne P. Steger. 2009. "The Viability Primary: Modeling Candidate Support before the Primaries." *Political Research Quarterly* 62: 77–91.

Eggen, Dan. 2012. "Super PACs Dominate Republican Primary Spending." *Washington Post,* January 16. http://www.washingtonpost.com/politics/superpacs-dominate-republican-primary-spending/2012/01/11/gIQAdcoq3P_story.html (accessed September 9, 2012).

Hamby, Peter. 2012. "Republicans Feud over Drawn-Out Nominating Calendar." CNN, March 4. http://www.cnn.com/2012/03/04/politics/gopnominating-calendar/index.html (accessed August 29, 2012).

Hunt, Kasie. 2012. "Endorsements, Dollars Shift to Romney. Can He Close the Deal?" *The Christian Science Monitor,* March 21. http://www.csmonitor.com/USA/Latest-News-Wires/2012/0321/Endorsements-dollars-shift-to-Romney.-Can-he-close-the-deal (accessed October 8, 2012).

Knickerbocker, Brad. 2011. "Ron Paul Wins Yet Another Straw Poll. So Why Are the Media Ignoring Him?" *Christian Science Monitor,* November 6. http://www.csmonitor.com/USA/Elections/President/2011/1106/Ron-Paul-wins-yet-another-straw-poll.-So-why-are-the-media-ignoring-him (accessed November 18, 2012).

Mayer, William G. 1996. "Forecasting Presidential Nominations." In *In the Pursuit of the White House,* ed. William G. Mayer. Chatham, NJ: Chatham House.

Norrander, Barbara. 2000. "The End Game in Post-Reform Presidential Nominations." *Journal of Politics* 62: 999–1013.

Norrander, Barbara. 2006. "The Attrition Game: Initial Resources, Initial Contests and the Exit of Candidates during the US Presidential Primary Season." *British Journal of Political Science* 36: 487–507.

Norrander, Barbara. 2010. *The Imperfect Primary: Oddities, Biases and Strengths in U.S. Presidential Nomination Politics.* New York: Routledge.

Norrander, Barbara. 2013. "Parties and the Presidential Nominating Contests: The Battles to Control the Nominating Calendar." In *The Parties Respond,* 5th ed., ed. Mark D. Brewer and L. Sandy Maisel, 161–180. Boulder, CO: Westview Press.

O'Connor, Patrick, and Danny Yadron. 2012. "Santorum's Other Wisconsin Fight." *Wall Street Journal,* March 30. http://online.wsj.com/article/SB10001424052702304177104577312163593351148.html (accessed October 8, 2012).

Peoples, Steve. "2012 Hopefuls Gave Big to 2010 Candidates." *Roll Call,* December 5. http://www.rollcall.com/news/-201171-1.html (accessed December 6, 2010).

Rosenstiel, Tom, Amy Mitchell, Mark Jurkowitz, and Tricia Sartor. 2012. "How the Media Covered the 2012 Primary Campaign." Pew Research Center's Project for Excellence in Journalism, April 23, http://www.journalism.org/sites/journalism.org/files/2012PrimaryCampaignReport.pdf (accessed November 12, 2012).

Saad, Lydia. 2011. "Lack of GOP Front-Runner for 2012 Is Atypical." Gallup Poll, March 7. http://www.gallup.com/poll/146489/Lack-GOP-Front-Runner-2012-Atypical.aspx (accessed March 9, 2011).

Shear, Michael D. 2011. "PAC Backing Romney Shows Anti-Gingrich Ad." *New York Times,* December 14. http://thecaucus.blogs.nytimes.com/2011/12/14/super-pac-backing-romney-up-with-anti-gingrich-ad/ (accessed October 19, 2012).

Silver, Nate. 2012a. "Romney 96 Percent Likely to Clinch Delegate Majority?" *FiveThirtyEight* (blog), *New York Times,* April 3. http://fivethirtyeight.blogs.nytimes.com/2012/04/03/live-coverage-of-the-wisconsin-maryland-and-d-c-primaries/ (accessed November 12, 2012).

Silver, Nate. 2012b. "Romney's Michigan Win Stands as Climatic Moment in Campaign." *FiveThirtyEight* (blog), *New York Times,* April 4. http://fivethirtyeight.blogs.nytimes.com/2012/04/04/romneys-michigan-win-stands-as-climactic-moment-in-campaign/ (accessed November 12, 2012).

Silver, Nate. 2012c. "Some Signs G.O.P. Establishment's Backing of Romney Is Tenuous." *FiveThirtyEight* (blog), *New York Times,* January 23. http://fivethirtyeight.blogs.nytimes.com/2012/01/23/some-signs-g-o-p-establishments-backing-of-romney-is-tenuous/ (accessed September 9, 2012).

Wolf, Z. Byron. 2011. "Nearly Half of Iowa Ads Were Negative, Anti Gingrich." ABC News, December 30. http://abcnews.go.com/blogs/politics/2011/12/nearly-half-of-iowa-ads-were-negative-anti-gingrich/ (accessed November 12, 2012).

Zeleny, Jeff. 2010. "In Iowa Tour (Yes, Already), A Republican Tests His Voice." *New York Times,* August 2, A9, A11.

4　The General Election Campaign

Steven E. Schier and Janet M. Box-Steffensmeier

Once Mitt Romney had secured the Republican presidential nomination, many imposing questions surrounded the fall general election contest. Would the difficult economy cause the voters to turn against President Barack Obama? Could Mitt Romney appear as a credible alternative to the presidential incumbent? Would either presidential campaign accrue a decisive financial advantage in the fall contest? Might the rise of Super PACs and unprecedented campaign spending tilt the race in one direction or another? How would media coverage, candidate debates, and campaign events affect the 2012 election outcome?

This chapter relates the 2012 fall campaign's answers to these questions. Underlying such uncertainties, however, were conditions that pointed to a close and competitive election. Political scientists produced an array of statistical models, based on historical conditions and the results of prior presidential elections, for predicting 2012's presidential election outcome. Among 13 models released in September 2012, 8 predicted an Obama victory and 5 a Romney win. Across the 13 models, however, the average predicted Obama percentage was 50.2 percent, and the average Romney percentage was 49.8 percent of the two-party vote.[1] In the models, the most common variables employed to estimate the election result were economic conditions and the job approval of the incumbent president. Economic variables in many models pointed against Obama's reelection, but the president's job approval in surveys, averaging close to 50 percent during 2012, indicated that reelection was quite possible.

As the fall campaign began, a mix of positive and negative polling evidence could be found for both presidential candidates. On the eve of the parties' national conventions in August, average approval of President Obama's job performance stood at 47.9 percent, but Gallup found August approval of his economic stewardship lagged at only 36 percent.[2] Yet 54 percent of the public blamed his predecessor, Republican president George W. Bush, and his party for the bad economic conditions, whereas only 38 percent laid the blame on Obama and the Democrats (CNN 2012a). On average, the public thought the nation was on the "wrong track" in late August by a margin

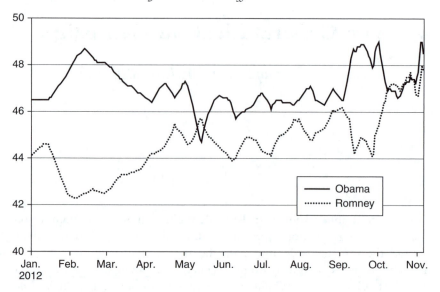

Figure 4.1 National Presidential Election Poll Trend: Obama and Romney
Source: Huffington Post National Dashboard of Polls.

of 61.3 percent to 32 percent.[3] The president, however, was personally more popular in August than his rival Romney, with an August Gallup "favorable" rating of 53 percent compared to Romney's 48 percent (Jones 2012b). Obama's foreign policy leadership also had on average a narrow margin of approval—49.6 percent to 43.8 percent disapproving—among those polled in August 2012 (Huffington Post 2012a).

It was far from clear whether former governor Romney could take advantage of Obama's poll weaknesses. By late summer, Romney was one of the least personally popular major party nominees in the history of polling. Of 38 polls released from July 23 to September 5, 25 polls registered a net-negative rating for Romney, meaning more respondents had a negative view of him than had a positive view of him (Romano 2012). Through most of 2012, however, Republicans in national polls had indicated more enthusiasm about voting than had Democrats. Obama's campaign had to narrow that gap. All this portended a close horse race in 2012, and that is what transpired, as evident in Figure 4.1.

Initial Campaign Strategies

Obama's general election strategy involved lots of campaign spending, and the financial playing field had altered greatly from that of 2008. First, for the first time since the creation of publicly financed general election campaigns in 1976, both major party nominees declined public funds and instead decided to raise funds privately. Though individual contributions to presidential campaigns were legally limited to $5,000 during the election year ($2,500 for the nomination contest and $2,500 for the general election), overall spending was for the first time unlimited for both nominees' campaigns. Second, the Supreme Court in its 2010 *Citizens United v. Federal Election Commission* ruling held that corporations, unions, and nonprofit groups have the same political speech rights as individuals under the First Amendment. The Court found no "compelling government interest" for prohibiting corporations and unions from using their general treasury funds to make election-related independent expenditures. For the first time since 1990, corporations and labor unions could now spend unlimited amounts of money on "express advocacy"—advertisements that explicitly announced the sponsor's support or opposition to a candidate. They are not required to disclose the sources of their contributions to the public. Third, the District of Columbia Circuit Court's *Speechnow.org v. Federal Election Commission* decision authorized the establishment of independent expenditure–only political action committees, or "Super PACs." These PACs could receive unlimited contributions from individuals, corporations, and unions. They could use this money for express advocacy, as long as they disclosed the sources of their contributions and did not coordinate their activities with candidates. Together, these three developments ensured that if candidates and contributors complied with the restrictions on how different types of campaign organizations could raise and spend money, there were effectively no financial limits in place in the 2012 election.

President Obama and his campaign initially discouraged the creation of Democratic Super PACs. The president had previously labeled such undisclosed spending as "a threat to our democracy" (CBS News 2012). But he and members of his campaign changed their minds in the wake of bustling GOP Super PAC activity in 2012. Prominent GOP Super PACs included American Crossroads, founded by Karl Rove, former campaign strategist and White House deputy chief of staff for George W. Bush; Restore Our Future, founded before the primary season to boost Romney's candidacy; and the Club for Growth Action PAC, sponsored by the anti-tax group of the same name. Other nonprofit organizations such as Americans for Prosperity, formed by the Koch Brothers, and Rove's Crossroads GPS also engaged in election-related spending. In August 2012 alone, Restore Our Future and Americans for Prosperity spent $31 billion in anti-Obama ads (Levinthal 2012). In response, Obama and his campaign encouraged the creation of Democratic Super PACS to counter the potential GOP Super PAC spending advantage. The main pro-Obama Super PAC was Priorities USA, which raised $10 million in August 2012 (Confessore 2012). Though fundraising for Obama's Super PACs initially trailed behind that of the GOP groups, cash flowed to it in larger sums as the autumn campaign progressed.

The Obama strategy at the end of the primary season was to reinforce Romney's low personal popularity ratings so that he would be "damaged goods" in the fall. The summer of 2012 featured large TV advertising sums spent nationally and in a small number of 12 "battleground states" whose electoral votes were in play and would determine the election outcome. The 12 composing the battleground were Virginia, North Carolina, Nevada, Colorado, Ohio, Florida, New Hampshire, Iowa, Michigan, New Mexico, Pennsylvania, and Wisconsin. The ads, paid for by the Obama campaign and newly created friendly Super PACs, were responsible for a major portion of the high "burn rate" of spending by Obama and his allies. From May to August, the Obama campaign alone spent over $100 million on ads attacking Romney in the 12 battleground states (*Washington Post* 2012). Among the charges hurled at Romney were that he had "something to hide" because he refused to release tax returns beyond those of the last two years; that during his time as head of the Bain Capital investment firm, he had shipped jobs overseas; and that he was a rich man "out of touch" with average Americans. An Obama Super PAC even accused him of causing the cancer death of a worker who had lost his job when Bain shuttered his factory (Lee 2012). In fact, the onset of the cancer had occurred years after the man lost his job and after the family declined health insurance offered by a new employer.

The Romney campaign, for its part, attempted to focus on the troubled economy and fundraising during the summer months. The campaign faced a money squeeze because federal campaign finance laws prevented candidates from spending funds raised for the general election until after the national conventions, and Romney had largely exhausted his funds raised for securing the nomination. The Obama campaign faced no such problem because, since he had run unopposed in the primaries, the president had not exhausted his primary funds as Romney had during the competitive GOP nomination contest. Romney's campaign borrowed $20 million dollars against future contributions to buoy the summer campaign (Eggen and Rucker 2012). Obama's summer barrage of negative ads largely went unanswered on the airwaves by the Romney campaign. Meanwhile, GOP Super PACs spent millions in negative ads to counter Obama. By mid-September, Republicans had spent $314 million on ads, with Romney's campaign accounting for just 27 percent ($86 million) of that total. Democrats had spent $277 million on ads, with Obama accounting for 80 percent ($222 million) of that total (Cillizza and Blake 2012). Super PACs, however, had to pay higher per-ad rates than the candidate campaigns, allowing the Obama campaign to run far more ads during the summer than Romney and his friendly Super PACs.

Romney surprised many observers on August 12 with his choice of Republican U.S. representative Paul Ryan as his running mate. Ryan, then in his eighth term and serving as chair of the House Budget Committee, had emerged as a fiscal policy leader in the GOP ranks. He had developed a controversial long-term fiscal plan, known as the "Roadmap for America's Future," which called for large cuts in federal spending and reconfiguration of popular government programs such as Medicare, which provides federal health insurance for the elderly, and Social Security, which provides federal retirement benefits. Ryan was a hero among many conservative Republican activists and pundits, and they warmly greeted his selection. He was largely unknown to the broader public, however, and initial polls showed that the reaction to his selection broke along partisan lines, with Democrats cool to him and Republicans supportive of him. The impact of Ryan on the presidential race was far from clear at the time of his selection.

The Party Conventions

By the time of the conventions, the race remained close, with most polls showing a small Obama lead. On the day before the GOP convention, the *Huffington Post* Election Dashboard average of polls, created by political scientist Charles Franklin of the University of Wisconsin–Madison, found the race at 46.7 percent for Obama and 45.5 percent for Romney, a 1.2 percent lead for the president (Huffington Post 2012b). Romney's campaign viewed the Republican convention as an opportunity to introduce its candidate to many in the public who had not yet "tuned in" to the presidential race. However, Republicans encountered problems in making the most of their convention opportunity.

The first day of the Republican convention was canceled because of a tropical storm threatening the Tampa area. Then as the storm hit the Gulf Coast later in the week, it stole headlines from the GOP event and raised memories of the political disaster that had befallen GOP president George W. Bush when Hurricane Katrina hit in 2005. The three main speakers at the convention—Ann Romney, Paul Ryan, and Mitt Romney—gave sound speeches, but ratings for their prime-time orations were historically low. Other speakers at the convention, notably New Jersey governor Chris Christie and Florida senator Marco Rubio, spent little time during their remarks touting the virtues of Mitt Romney. Any convention "bounce" in the polls may have shrunk because of the onset of the Democratic convention shortly after the GOP conclave concluded. The bounce Romney did receive from the convention proved minimal, estimated by *New York Times* election analyst Nate Silver at only 2.5 percent, the third smallest since 1968 (Silver 2012).

The two GOP nominees emphasized in their convention speeches the nation's economic distress and their desire to alleviate it. Paul Ryan portrayed America's fiscal problems as dire: "Before the math and the momentum overwhelm us all, we are going to solve this nation's economic problems. And I'm going to level with you: We don't have that much time. But if we are serious, and smart, and we lead, we can do this." In his acceptance speech, Mitt

Romney contrasted his focus on American's economic problems with the president's rhetoric: "President Obama promised to begin to slow the rise of the oceans and heal the planet. My promise . . . is to help you and your family."

Democrats conducted a more successful convention. The event featured four important speeches by First Lady Michelle Obama, former president Bill Clinton, Vice President Joe Biden, and President Barack Obama that gained large audiences and that the viewers received, on balance, favorably. Viewership was higher than for the GOP convention (Hartman 2012). President Clinton argued on Obama's behalf: "President Obama started with a much weaker economy than I did. Listen to me, now. No president—no president, not me, not any of my predecessors, no one—could have fully repaired all the damage that he found in just four years." The president, for his part, cast the GOP as backward-looking: "They want your vote, but they don't want you to know their plan. And that's because all they have to offer is the same prescriptions they've had for the last 30 years. Have a surplus? Try a tax cut. Deficit too high—try another." In polls, Democratic enthusiasm rose after the convention, and Obama's competitive standing in the race improved. One week after the Democratic convention, polling averages put Obama at 48.5 percent and Romney at 44.8 percent, giving Obama a 3.7 percent lead, up from a 46.4 to 46.2 Romney edge on September 3 when the Democratic convention began (Huffington Post 2012b).

The Tempests of September

In September, in the wake of the conventions, both candidates encountered difficulties. On September 11, U.S. Ambassador to Libya J. Christopher Stevens and three other personnel were assassinated at the U.S. Consulate in Benghazi, Libya. The ensuing week witnessed anti-American protests in at least 18 countries with large Muslim populations, which recurred sporadically in various countries later in the month. At first, the administration for eight days claimed the killing was the result of a spontaneous protest triggered by the distribution of an anti-Muslim Internet video made in America. American intelligence sources eventually revealed that terrorists, perhaps allied with al-Qaeda, had planned and performed an attack on the Benghazi consulate. Subsequent press reports disclosed that Benghazi had been the site of multiple terrorist attacks on diplomats in recent months and that security at the consulate was inadequate. Eventually, in late September, the administration admitted that the assassination was a terrorist incident. Media scrutiny of the administration's explanation of the assassination and handling of embassy security grew and a GOP-majority House oversight committee promised hearings in October.

Mitt Romney immediately criticized the administration's response to the anti-American protests in the Middle East. As a large protest erupted outside of the American Embassy in Cairo, the embassy issued a statement that contained this sentence: "The Embassy of the United States in Cairo condemns the continuing efforts by misguided individuals to hurt the religious feelings of Muslims—as we condemn efforts to offend believers of all religions." Within hours of the issuance of that statement, Mitt Romney responded with strongly worded criticism via a statement and press conference: "I think it's a terrible course for America to stand in apology for our values. That instead, when our grounds are being attacked and being breached, that the first response of the United States must be outrage at the breach of the sovereignty of our nation. An apology for America's values is never the right course." The campaign press corps challenged Romney about the appropriateness of his criticism in the midst of a trying international situation. The Obama campaign accused Romney of shooting first and asking questions later. The incident placed Romney on the political defensive as the campaign media labeled Romney's hasty remarks a campaign gaffe, despite the protests of Republicans and conservatives.

Romney's difficulties multiplied with disclosure on September 17 of a videotape of his remarks before a private fundraiser earlier in 2012. Romney appears on tape making the following statement:

> There are 47 percent of the people who will vote for the president no matter what. All right, there are 47 percent who are with him, who are dependent upon government, who believe that they are victims, who believe the government has a responsibility to care for them, who believe that they are entitled to health care, to food, to housing, to you-name-it—that that's an entitlement. And the government should give it to them. And they will vote for this president no matter what. . . . These are people who pay no income tax. . . . My job is not to worry about those people. I'll never convince them they should take personal responsibility and care for their lives. (ABCnews 2012)

The comments produced a firestorm of criticism from the Obama campaign and a declaration of a second monumental "gaffe" for Romney by the campaign media. Romney initially termed the remarks "inelegant" and explained that his comments targeted Obama's project of making America into a "government centered society." He eventually admitted in an October 4 television interview that his initial comments about the 47 percent were "wrong."

The critical media coverage of Romney in September generated many public criticisms of his campaign by fellow GOPers. Former Reagan speechwriter Peggy Noonan suggested that the campaign was floundering and needed an "intervention" (Noonan 2012). The coverage also prompted several leading conservatives to attack campaign media as biased in their reporting on Romney and in their campaign polling. A letter signed by two dozen conservative media figures labeled the mainstream media "out of control with a deliberate and unmistakable leftist agenda" (CBS DC 2012). Conservatives also decried several polling organizations for producing samples with too many Democrats that showed Obama moving into a lead over Romney as September progressed.

The public, for its part, found some problems with campaign coverage. A September Gallup poll found that 60 percent of American adults had not very much or no confidence in the mass media, an all-time high. Democrats claimed a great deal or fair amount of trust in the media at 58 percent, but only 31 percent of political independents and 26 percent of Republicans had comparable faith in the media (Morales 2012). A Fox News poll in late September found that 64 percent of likely voters thought the media focused on "silly issues of little importance to the country" (Blanton 2012). A Pew Research Center survey also released in late September, however, found that equal pluralities—46 percent—of the public thought media coverage of both Obama and Romney was "fair." Twice as many thought the media was too easy on Obama as thought the media was too hard on him (28 to 15 percent), and opinion on similar coverage of Romney split evenly (21 to 20 percent) (Pew Research Center 2012a).

By the end of September, Obama held a small lead in national polls and in the swing states of Ohio, Florida, Virginia, Nevada, and Colorado. Though benefiting from Romney's misfortunes, the president was still averaging less than 50 percent in the national polls and running behind the September poll averages of successfully reelected incumbents Ronald Reagan, Bill Clinton, and George W. Bush. Romney, despite his rough September, was within striking distance of the president. The October debates held the potential to reshape the presidential race.

The Season of Debates

Presidential debates at times have altered the competitive standing of presidential candidates. The most recent instances resembling 2012 occurred in 1984, 1992, 1996, and 2004, when incumbent presidents sought reelection. In 1984, the two debates made no difference in the polling margins between incumbent Ronald Reagan and challenger Walter Mondale. Bill Clinton as a challenger in 1992 lost six points in his poll standing with incumbent George H. W. Bush during their three debates but still went on to win the election. When Clinton ran for reelection in 1996, he gained five points during his two debates with challenger Robert Dole and won that race comfortably. George W. Bush in 2004 lost a full eight points during his three debates with John Kerry, with Bush's margin shrinking to just three points after the debate—the eventual margin of his reelection victory (American Enterprise

Institute 2012). All this suggested that in a highly competitive presidential race, the debates could prove decisive.

On October 3, the day of the first presidential candidate debate, President Obama averaged a 3.1 percent lead over former governor Romney in the national polls, 48.6 percent to 45.5 percent, and led in most of the major battleground states as well (Huffington Post 2012b). By October 24, after the conclusion of three presidential debates and one vice presidential debate, the candidates were tied: Obama with 47.6 percent and Romney with 47.4 percent (Huffington Post 2012b). Romney clearly gained on Obama during the debate season. Why?

The signal moment boosting Romney was his performance in the first debate in Denver, which drew the largest television audience of any debate: 67.2 million people (Byers 2012). With each candidate at the podium and a loose debate structure, there was considerable latitude in how each could approach the confrontation. President Obama, who on the eve of the debate complained that debate preparation was a "drag," appeared passive and unenergetic during the event. Romney, in contrast, assertively and confidently challenged the president. The debate's topic—domestic policy—further favored Romney, as he frequently repeated an array of troubling economic statistics in the form of an indictment of Obama's record.

The result was a resounding Romney debate victory by the largest margins ever recorded in post-debate polls reaching back to 1984. In several surveys, more than 70 percent of respondents named Romney the victor, and in no survey did those naming Obama the victor reach 30 percent. In a CNN poll of debate watchers, more than 6 in 10 thought the president had done worse than expected, but 82 percent thought Romney had performed better than expected. Majorities in the poll picked Romney over Obama as better able to address the economy, health care, the federal budget deficit, and taxes. By 58 to 37 percent, Romney "seemed a stronger leader" to poll respondents (CNN 2012b).

Shortly after Romney's victory in the first debate came the debate between the two vice presidential candidates on October 11. Vice President Biden, in a pre-debate tweet, promised more "fight" than the president had delivered in the first debate. Biden delivered a feisty performance, replete with aggressive assertions, verbal gesticulations, and animated facial expressions. Paul Ryan, for his part, did not respond in kind, adopting a more restrained demeanor and only occasionally needling his opponent. An audience of 51.4 million watched the debate, in which the candidates sat next to each other at a table (Byers 2012). Polls of debate viewers yielded a mixed result from the contest, with some labeling Biden the victor and others deeming Ryan the top performer. Each candidate scored equally well regarding viewers' perceptions of their traits. A Pew Research Center poll, however, found that among the electorally important group of political independents, 50 percent thought Ryan had won, but only 39 percent preferred Biden (Pew Research Center 2012b). Fifty-three percent of debate watchers found Ryan "more likeable" compared to 41 percent for Biden, and 70 percent thought Biden "spent more time attacking his opponent" compared to only 17 percent who attributed that activity to Ryan (CNN 2012c).

The relative success of Romney and Ryan during the first two debates led to a tightening in the polls. By October 16, the day of the second presidential debate, Romney had regained the lead in the polling average, with 47.5 percent to the president's 46.8 percent. This produced complaints from Obama's pollster, Joel Benenson, that recent surveys were undersampling Democratic voters (Gabriel 2012). The shoe was now on the other foot.

The president knew he had to improve his performance in the final two debates, and he did. The second presidential debate involved a town hall format, with questions on both foreign and domestic issues posed to the candidates by an audience of undecided voters. It drew a television audience of 65.6 million people, almost as many as the first debate (Byers 2012). From the outset, the president was more demonstrative and energetic in presenting his positions and challenging his opponent. Romney for his part committed no major gaffes and again emphasized America's economic problems in his responses. Polls of debate viewers gave a narrow victory to the president. The CNN survey, for example, found that Obama won the debate 46 percent to 39 percent. Seventy-three percent thought Obama had performed better than they had expected, but only 37 percent though Romney had performed better than expected. Majorities of poll respondents, however, thought Romney was "better able to handle" the economy, health care, taxes, and the budget deficit. Only in foreign policy, by 49 to 47 percent, did respondents find Obama better able to handle the task (CNN 2012b). A national survey found that of the likely voters who were second debate viewers and who had changed their candidate support, 57 percent switched to Romney compared to 32 percent to Obama (Monmouth University 2012).

Obama had improved his performance, but the second debate did not reverse the advantageous public perceptions or momentum Romney had gained in the first debate. That made the third debate an important, last opportunity for Obama to even the overall debate score. It focused on foreign policy, a topic that might favor the president, given his greater experience with it. Foreign issues, however, ranked low among voter concerns in 2012, with none named as a "most important issue" by more than 4 percent of respondents in a mid-October survey, compared with 37 percent naming the economy, 26 percent naming unemployment, and 12 percent naming the federal budget deficit (Saad 2012).

The debate featured the two candidates seated at a table. It drew the smallest presidential debate audience, 59.2 million viewers (Byers 2012). Obama seized the opportunity to challenge Romney for his supposedly erratic positions and inexperience, claiming that on some issues he was "all over the map." Romney in reply presented a calm demeanor, but he did castigate Obama for leaving the Middle East in "shambles" and engaging in a Mideast "apology" tour when he first took office. Post-debate polls gave Obama the victory by varying margins. The CNN poll found that Obama won 48 percent to 40 percent, but his 8 percent advantage was within the survey's margin of error. Romney, however, could claim some gains as well. According to the same poll, 25 percent of respondents indicated that the debate had made them more likely to vote for Romney, compared to 24 percent for Obama. Sixty percent thought Romney better able to handle the job of commander in chief, compared to 63 percent for Obama (CNN 2012d).

Obama gained an edge in certain respects during the third debate, but his performance in the final two presidential debates did not reverse Romney's gains in the polling horse race. By the end of the debate season, the race had moved from a three-point Obama edge to a tie at 47 percent each. Ron Fournier, *National Journal's* editor in chief, in his summary of the third debate, explained the broader consequences: "Mitt Romney wins. That's not to say he won Monday night's debate or the presidential campaign, but it's safe to say he won an important chapter: the debate season" (Fournier 2012).

Though poet W. H. Auden termed April "the cruelest month," October has often played that role for presidential incumbents seeking reelection. In Gallup surveys for incumbents seeking reelection in 1956, 1972, 1980, 1984, 1996, and 2004, polls on average tightened between six and seven points between incumbents and challengers (Cost 2012). Only in 1956 did an incumbent, Dwight Eisenhower, expand his lead in October. In the waning days of October, the president's three-point lead at the month's outset had vanished, and he was in a tied race with his support at 47 percent, below the vital 50 percent mark needed for reelection. The debates had hindered Obama's reelection efforts, and congressional hearings into the assassination of the Libyan ambassador proceeded during the month, giving no comfort to the White House. The election's outcome was anyone's guess. It would depend on three forces: the quality of each campaign's get-out-the-vote "ground game" in key battleground states, the messaging efforts by candidates and campaigns ads, and any unforeseeable campaign events that might tip the outcome either way.

The Endgame

Two days after the final debate, Obama and Romney were tied in the polls, with the president averaging 47.3 percent support to Romney's 46.9 percent (Huffington Post 2012b). Events during the last week of the campaign, however, advantaged the president. The arrival of the severe Hurricane Sandy along the Atlantic coast on Monday, October 29, took President Obama away from the campaign trail and enmeshed him in crisis management. His steady addressing of the situation, coupled with an on-air hug from GOP New Jersey governor Chris Christie during Obama's visit to the state, made the president appear competent, bipartisan, and above politics. The four-day disaster also removed Mitt Romney and his campaign message from the headlines. Two leading Republicans, Mississippi governor Hayley Barbour and strategist Karl Rove, later noted that the hurricane helped Obama at a crucial time in the campaign (Leahy and Sullivan 2012; Davenport 2012).

The "ground game" of each of the candidates would shape the election's result. Obama's campaign had several advantages in this regard. Lacking primary opposition, the reelection effort had spent over a year establishing a network of hundreds of field offices throughout key swing states. The offices made contacts throughout the Latino, African American, and young voter communities that constituted the president's electoral base. Obama's campaign also employed innovative persuasion techniques, drawing on social science research regarding effective means of interpersonal contact. The Obama effort also heavily utilized social media over many months to precisely and effectively reach voters open to their message (Issenberg 2012).

The Romney "ground game" gained shape much later, with authority for its operation dispersed among the national party, the state parties, and the Romney campaign itself. Contact with voters came later, and such contact was less likely to be interpersonal or to employ social media as precisely as the Obama effort. The national GOP unveiled a computer-driven voter turnout effort, named ORCA, which generated many technical problems and ultimately crashed on Election Day (Haberman and Burns 2012). Obama's ground game advantage proved to be a considerable one as Election Day proceeded.

As the campaign wound to a close, the Obama effort continued to run more ads than did the Romney/GOP effort. Obama's campaign had bought ad time earlier and in better programming markets. Romney's late purchases were more costly, and the campaign and its kindred organizations produced fragmented messages throughout the fall. The fragmentation resulted from the fact that the national party, the Super PACs, and the Romney campaign all were spending on the candidate's behalf but could not by law coordinate all of their activities. This produced a profusion of pro-Romney messages that lacked overall coherence. In contrast, the Obama campaign centrally produced the large majority of ads for its candidate, allowing the campaign more tactical control over campaign ad messaging.

In the campaign's closing days, the two presidential campaigns had different expectations about the election. Obama's strategists argued that the 2012 electorate would closely resemble that of 2008, with high turnout of younger voters, African Americans, and Latinos and a proportion of white voters below the 74 percent that composed the 2008 electorate. This would produce an overall electorate with approximately 7 percent more Democrats than Republicans, the partisan balance of the 2008 electorate.

The Romney campaign, for its part, assumed that the electorate would include about the same proportion of whites as in 2008 and would feature lower turnout of younger voters, Latinos, and African Americans. By its calculation, the number of Democrats would be only slightly higher—a few percentage points at most—than the number of Republicans in the electorate. The Romney campaign and GOP operatives argued in the campaign's closing days that many public opinion polls were oversampling Democrats and falsely indicating Obama leads in the swing states.

As Election Day approached, Obama's lead in the national polls increased slightly, resting at 48.2 percent for Obama and 46.7 percent for Romney by November 4 (Huffington Post 2012b). Late deciders seemed to be moving in Obama's direction. Most swing-state polls registered either dead heats or narrow Obama leads; Romney on average led in few of them. The late evidence tended to favor the Obama campaign's expectations about the electorate.

The Election Result

Exit polls on Election Day vindicated the Obama campaign's expectations. Table 4.1 indicates that Democrats had a six-point advantage over Republicans in the electorate—38 to 32 percent—very close to the 39–32 Democratic advantage in 2008 (CNN 2012e). Obama won a somewhat narrow victory in the popular vote, 51.0 percent to Romney's 47.2 percent. The president won all of the swing states with the exception of North Carolina and, in all the swing states but Ohio, by margins larger than his national advantage over Romney. This produced a convincing 332 to 206 win for the president in the Electoral College. As Figure 4.2 reveals, the geography of the Electoral College vote closely resembled that of 2008, with only Indiana and North Carolina switching to the Republican candidate.

Table 4.2 indicates that 2012 marked the second presidential election in a row in which Democrats gained a majority of the popular vote. Since 1992, Democrats have won the presidential popular vote over the GOP in every election except that of 2004. Election turnout in 2012 was lower than that of 2008. In 2012, 58.7 percent of eligible citizens voted, compared to 62.2 percent in 2008, 60.7 percent in 2004, and 55.3 percent in 2000 (United States Election Project 2013).

On election night, before a large and enthusiastic crowd in Chicago, President Obama invoked a theme of national unity, a reprise of his breakthrough speech at the 2004 Democratic National Convention:

> I believe we can seize this future together because we are not as divided as our politics suggests. We're not as cynical as the pundits believe. We are greater than the sum of our individual ambitions and we remain more than a collection of red states and blue states. We are, and forever will be, the United States of America.

An ironic result of the election was that despite the president's rhetoric, the statewide results evidenced more polarization than any election since 1948.

Table 4.1 Group Support in the 2008 and 2012 Presidential Elections

2012 voters (%)	2008 voters (%)	Characteristic	For Romney (%)	For Obama 2012 (%)	For McCain (%)	For Obama 2008 (%)
		Party				
38	39	Democrat	7	92	10	89
32	32	Republican	93	6	90	9
29	29	Independent	45	50	44	52
		Ideology				
25	22	Liberal	11	86	10	89
41	44	Moderate	41	56	39	60
35	34	Conservative	82	17	78	20
		Ethnic group				
72	74	White	59	39	55	43
13	13	Black	6	93	4	95
10	9	Hispanic	27	71	31	67
3	2	Asian	26	73	35	62
		Sex/ethnicity				
34	36	White men	62	35	57	41
38	39	White women	56	42	53	46
5	5	Black men	11	87	5	95
8	7	Black women	3	96	3	96
		Sex/marital status				
29	33	Married men	60	38	53	45
31	32	Married women	53	46	50	47
18	14	Unmarried men	40	56	38	59
23	21	Unmarried women	31	67	29	71
		Age				
19	18	18–29 years old	37	60	32	66
27	29	30–44 years old	45	54	46	52
38	37	45–64 years old	51	47	49	50
16	16	65 years and older	56	44	53	45
		Education				
3	4	Not a high school grad	35	64	35	63
21	20	High school graduate	48	51	46	52
29	31	Some college education	48	49	47	51
29	28	College graduate	51	47	48	50
18	17	Postgraduate education	42	55	40	58

(Continued)

Table 4.1 Continued

2012 voters (%)	2008 voters (%)	Characteristic	For Romney (%)	For Obama 2012 (%)	For McCain (%)	For Obama 2008 (%)
		Religion				
53	54	Protestant	57	42	54	45
39	42	White Protestant	69	30	65	34
15	15	Attend church weekly	70	29	67	32
26	26	White evangelical	78	21	74	24
25	27	Catholic	48	50	45	54
11	12	Attend church weekly	57	42	50	49
2	2	Jewish	30	69	21	78
		Family Income				
21	19	Under $50K	38	60	38	60
59	62	$50–100,000	52	46	49	49
28	—	$100,000+	54	44	49	49
18	21	*Union household*	40	58	42	57
		Population of area				
11	11	Large city	29	69	28	70
21	19	Small city	21	58	39	59
47	49	Suburbs	50	48	48	50
8	7	Small town	56	42	53	45
14	14	Rural	61	37	53	45
		Most important issue				
59	63	Economy	51	47	44	53
18	9	Health care	24	75	26	73
15	—	Budget deficit	66	32	—	—
5	—	Foreign policy	33	59	—	—
—	7	Energy policy	—	—	46	50
—	10	Iraq	—	—	39	59
—	9	Terrorism	—	—	86	13

Source: National exit polls conducted by Edison Research for the National Election Pool.

Inclusion of "—" indicates that the question was not asked in that year.

Counting the number of states where the winner's share of the statewide vote was at least 10 points higher or lower than the candidate's nationwide vote, 2012 produced 19 states with such polarized results, compared to 18 in 2008, 15 in 2004, and 16 in 2000. Only one election from 1948 to 1996 featured more than 11 such polarized states (the tumultuous year of 1968, with 15).

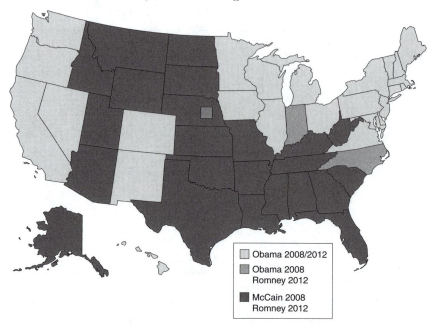

Figure 4.2 Electoral Vote Map for the Two Major Parties, 2008 and 2012

Polarization now seems an enduring feature of our politics. National unity may prove to be an elusive goal for Obama during his second term.

In 2012, Table 4.1 reveals, big divisions also appeared in the voting behavior of groups within the electorate, as they had four years before. As in 2008, Obama's win hinged on the support of four demographic groups: African Americans, Latinos, young voters, and highly educated voters. Obama scored a resounding 93 percent vote from African Americans, whose ranks had grown from 11 percent of the electorate in 2004 to 13 percent in 2008 and 2012. Latino turnout, rising from 9 percent to 10 percent of the electorate in four years, yielded strong support for Obama. Latino support for the Democratic candidate grew to 71 percent, up from 67 percent in 2008 and 53 percent in 2004. Since the Latino proportion of the population is projected to grow in coming years, this is very good news for Democrats. Young voters 18–29 also made up a sizable 19 percent of the electorate, up from a previous high of 18 percent in 2008. Though Obama's margin among them dropped from 66–32 in 2008 to 60–37 in 2012, they remained a major source of his electoral advantage. Obama also managed to carry those with postgraduate degrees by 55 to 42 percent, a bit smaller than his 58 to 40 percent margin four years earlier.

Obama's reduced margin of victory compared to 2008 came from lesser support among the highly educated and young, noted previously, as well as declining backing elsewhere in the electorate. Though Obama carried the suburbs narrowly in 2008 by 50–48, he lost that region by the same margin in

Table 4.2 Presidential Popular Vote and Electoral College Results by State, 2008 and 2012

State	Electoral Vote 2012		Electoral Vote 2008		Popular Vote 2012		Popular Vote 2008		Popular Vote 2012 (%)		Popular Vote 2008 (%)	
	Romney	Obama	McCain	Obama	Romney	Obama	McCain	Obama	Romney	Obama	McCain	Obama
Alabama	9		9		1,255,925	795,696	1,264,879	811,764	61	38	61	39
Alaska	3		3		164,676	122,640	192,631	122,485	55	41	60	38
Arizona	11		10		1,233,654	1,025,232	1,132,560	948,648	53	44	54	45
Arkansas	6		6		647,744	394,409	632,672	418,049	61	37	59	39
California		55		55	4,839,958	7,854,285	4,554,643	7,441,458	37	60	37	61
Colorado		9		9	1,185,050	1,322,998	1,020,135	1,216,793	46	51	45	54
Connecticut		7		7	634,899	905,109	620,210	979,316	41	58	38	61
Delaware		3		3	165,484	242,584	152,356	255,394	40	59	37	62
DC		3		3	21,381	267,070	14,821	210,403	7	91	7	93
Florida		29		27	4,163,447	4,237,756	3,939,380	4,143,957	49	50	49	51
Georgia	16		15		2,078,688	1,773,827	2,048,244	1,843,452	53	45	52	47
Hawaii		4		4	121,015	306,658	120,309	324,918	28	71	27	72
Idaho	4		4		420,911	212,699	400,989	235,219	64	32	61	36
Illinois		20		21	2,135,216	3,019,512	1,981,158	3,319,237	41	58	37	62
Indiana	11			11	1,420,543	1,152,887	1,341,667	1,367,503	54	44	49	50
Iowa		6		7	730,617	822,544	677,508	818,240	46	52	45	54
Kansas	6		6		692,634	440,726	685,541	499,979	60	38	57	41

(Continued)

Table 4.2 Continued

State	Electoral Vote 2012		Electoral Vote 2008		Popular Vote 2012		Popular Vote 2008		Popular Vote 2012 (%)		Popular Vote 2008 (%)	
	Romney	Obama	McCain	Obama	Romney	Obama	McCain	Obama	Romney	Obama	McCain	Obama
Kentucky	8		8		1,087,190	679,364	1,050,599	751,515	61	38	58	41
Louisiana	8		9		1,152,262	809,141	1,147,603	780,981	58	41	59	40
Maine		4		4	292,276	401,306	296,195	421,484	40	55	41	58
Maryland		10		10	971,869	1,677,844	956,663	1,612,692	36	62	37	62
Massachusetts		11		12	1,188,314	1,921,290	1,104,284	1,891,083	37	61	36	62
Michigan		16		17	2,115,256	2,564,569	2,044,405	2,867,680	45	54	41	57
Minnesota		10		10	1,320,225	1,546,167	1,275,409	1,573,354	45	53	44	54
Mississippi	6		6		710,746	562,949	687,266	520,864	55	44	57	43
Missouri	10		11		1,482,440	1,223,796	1,445,812	1,442,180	54	44	50	49
Montana	3		3		267,928	201,839	241,816	229,725	55	42	50	47
Nebraska	5		4	1	475,064	302,081	448,801	329,132	60	38	57	42
Nevada		6		5	463,567	531,373	411,988	531,884	46	52	43	55
New Hampshire		4		4	329,918	369,561	316,937	384,591	46	52	45	54
New Jersey		14		15	1,478,088	2,122,786	1,545,495	2,085,051	41	58	42	57
New Mexico		5		5	335,788	415,335	343,820	464,458	43	53	42	57
New York		29		31	2,485,432	4,471,871	2,576,360	4,363,386	35	63	37	62
North Carolina	15			15	2,270,395	2,178,391	2,109,698	2,123,390	50	48	49	50
North Dakota	3		3		188,320	124,966	168,523	141,113	58	39	53	45

Ohio		18		20	2,661,422	2,827,663	2,501,855	2,708,685	48	51	47	51
Oklahoma	7		7		891,325	443,547	959,745	502,294	67	33	66	34
Oregon		7		7	754,175	970,488	699,673	978,605	42	54	41	57
Pennsylvania		20		21	2,680,434	2,990,274	2,586,496	3,192,316	47	52	44	55
Rhode Island		4		4	157,204	279,677	165,389	296,547	35	63	35	63
South Carolina	9		8		1,071,645	865,941	1,034,500	862,042	55	44	54	45
South Dakota	3		3		210,610	145,039	203,019	170,886	58	40	53	45
Tennessee	11		11		1,462,330	960,709	1,487,564	1,093,213	59	39	57	42
Texas	38		34		4,569,843	3,308,124	4,467,748	3,521,164	57	41	55	44
Utah	6		5		740,600	251,813	555,497	301,771	73	25	63	34
Vermont		3		3	92,698	199,239	98,791	219,105	31	67	31	68
Virginia*		13		13	1,822,522	1,971,820	1,726,053	1,958,370	47	51	47	53
Washington		12		11	1,290,670	1,755,396	1,098,072	1,548,654	41	56	41	58
West Virginia	5		5		417,655	238,269	394,278	301,438	62	36	56	43
Wisconsin		10		10	1,407,966	1,620,985	1,258,181	1,670,474	46	53	43	56
Wyoming	3		3		170,962	69,286	160,639	80,496	69	28	65	33
Total	206	332	173	365	60,928,981	65,899,625	58,348,877	66,877,438	47	51	46	53

Sources: CNN, New York Times, National Association of Secretaries of State.

2012. Mitt Romney carried white voters by 59 to 39 percent, a big increase over John McCain's 55–43 edge in 2008. Romney's win among white voters was the largest of any candidate since Ronald Reagan's landslide victory in 1984. The changing demographics of the electorate, however, meant that such an edge could not deliver victory. Whites made up 72 percent of the 2012 electorate, in line with the Obama campaign's expectations, compared to 74 percent in 2008. Obama also lost independents to Romney by 50–45, compared to a 52–44 win for the president in 2008.

Romney also won older and rural voters by comfortable margins. However, the rural population is not growing as a proportion of the American population, and older voters will not help build future Republican electoral majorities. Romney also suffered from public perceptions regarding whom to blame for current economic conditions, which 77 percent of voters labeled "not so good" or "poor." Fifty-three percent of voters blamed George W. Bush for those conditions, and only 38 percent blamed Obama. Romney's at-times self-induced "callous rich guy" image also hurt him at the polls. Eighteen percent of voters named "cares about people" as the most important candidate quality, and Obama carried these voters easily, earning a whopping 81 percent of their votes, versus Romney's 18 percent. Romney also failed to "close the sale" on his claims of superior economic stewardship. Forty-nine percent of voters labeled him "better able to handle the economy," but 48 percent so labeled Obama (CNN 2012d).

One puzzle of the election involves the case of the missing white voters. Election analyst Sean Trende identified a decline of the white electorate by as many as seven million voters, which was possibly crucial to Obama's victory by a bit more than three million votes. Trende's explanation of their absence is plausible:

> My sense is these voters were unhappy with Obama. But his negative ad campaign relentlessly emphasizing Romney's wealth and tenure at Bain Capital may have turned them off to the Republican nominee as well. The Romney campaign exacerbated this through the challenger's failure to articulate a clear, positive agenda to address these voters' fears, and self-inflicted wounds like the '47 percent' gaffe. Given a choice between two unpalatable options, these voters simply stayed home. (Trende 2012)

Voters did not have to look far for a reason to stay home. The campaign featured huge levels of negative messaging. Eighty-five percent of the Obama campaign's ads and ninety-one percent of the Romney campaign's ads were negative, an all-time high in presidential campaigns since analysis of ad content began (Andrews, Keating, and Yourish 2012). Super PACs on both sides also contributed a plethora of negative ads.

Lower turnout occurred despite record spending by both sides in the presidential campaign. In summing the amount spent by each presidential campaign and supportive groups and Super PACs, the pro–Obama forces expended approximately 1 billion dollars and the Romney camp about 1.2 billion dollars (Vogel 2012). What gave Obama the edge, however, was how his forces spent their cash. More of the funds spent were concentrated within the Obama campaign itself, giving the campaign better tactical control over their allocation. The absence of a primary opponent gave the Obama campaign an 18-month head start in the ground game of voter mobilization, which they used to their advantage. Obama's campaign advantages helped to limit the damage to his campaign from his poor first debate performance and frequent campaign gaffes by Vice President Biden.

The 2012 victory was less impressive than Obama's 2008 triumph on several counts. It marked the first time since 1832 that a president gained reelection with a smaller share of the popular vote than he had received in his first election. Obama lost the support of important swing groups—in the suburbs and with independents—but avoided defeat by turning out unprecedented numbers of his base supporters among Latinos, African Americans, and young voters. His win in 2012 most closely resembled George W. Bush's narrow reelection margin in 2004. Bush received 50.7 percent of the vote, Obama 51.0 percent.

The Broader Consequences

One term seldom encountered in post-election analyses was "realignment." Election scholars coined the term "realignment" to connote an unusual election or series of elections that reconfigures electoral politics for the long term. Such elections feature sharp changes in issues, party leaders, and the regional and demographic bases of the two parties, creating a new competitive situation in national elections and often a dominant majority party. A classic realignment occurred in 1932, when Franklin Delano Roosevelt's landslide victory brought new groups—African Americans and blue-collar workers—into an enlarged Democratic coalition and reshaped electoral competition around a variety of new social welfare issues. The Democratic "New Deal Coalition" dominated American politics until the 1960s, when it was replaced by a "no majority party" alignment that persists to this day (Schier and Eberly 2012).

Little, if any, evidence suggests that 2012 was a realigning election. Political scientist John Sides terms it a "status quo" election that returned divided government—a Democratic president and Senate and a Republican House—to power. Even modest GOP gains among Latinos, Sides notes, could return the Republican Party to victory in future presidential elections. He identifies two additional arguments against the label of realignment:

> The growth of pro-Democratic constituencies is happening far too slowly to insulate the party from the natural swings that occur because of

economic fundamentals. If there is a recession in 2016, the Republicans will be likely to take back the White House. . . . the "Obama coalition" may prove to be exactly that: a coalition specific to Obama. When he is no longer at the top of the ticket, will groups like Latinos and African-Americans turn out in such numbers, and with such strong support for the Democratic candidate? (Sides 2012)

Research on the continuity of electoral alignments since the 1960s reveals that 2012 was not a radical departure from previous elections, as previous realigning elections have been (Schier and Eberly 2013).

How then shall we explain the 2012 election outcome? It is helpful to consider both short- and long-term explanations. The short-term explanations concern matters specific to the election that may not reoccur in the future. Hurricane Sandy is an obvious example. Obama won a majority of late-deciding voters, and fully 15 percent of the electorate indicated the hurricane was the most important factor in their vote decision. They opted for Obama by 73 to 26 percent (Temp 2012). Another short-term effect was the Obama campaign operation. Its advantages of an early start and innovative voter contact techniques may not appear in future campaigns. Obama campaign director David Plouffe said in a post election interview, "We just can't transfer this. All of the door-knocking on Election Day, the contributions and the phone calls made are because they believed in Barack Obama" (Crabtree 2012). Both parties, for example, replicated in the next two elections the campaign innovations that had contributed to George W. Bush's reelection in 2004. It is up to the GOP, however, to learn the 2012 Obama campaign techniques—and soon.

Another short-term explanation involves more favorable public attitudes about the nation's course, the president's conduct of his job, and identification with the president's party. Gallup surveys noted that although several public opinion indicators remained negative in November 2012, they had improved markedly over the previous 12 months. During that time, Obama's job approval rose from 43 to 50 percent, Democratic Party identification grew from 43 to 50 percent, Gallup's economic confidence index improved 34 points, and satisfaction with the nation's course rose from 12 to 33 percent (Jones 2012a). Recent changes in public opinion provided just enough impetus to make Obama's victory possible.

We must also add GOP mistakes and problems to the list of short-term factors affecting the election result. Control of campaign funds and messaging was dispersed widely among the Romney campaign, the national party, and Super PACS, unlike Obama's more centralized effort. Romney forces failed to respond adequately to the deluge of swing-state negative advertising by the Obama campaign during the summer of 2012. September publicity surrounding Romney's "47 percent" statement made his electoral climb that much steeper. A controversial Romney campaign ad in the crucial swing state of Ohio, charging that Chrysler and General Motors were shipping jobs overseas, received much criticism from car companies and the media in the campaign's final days (Moore 2012). The GOP's ORCA get-out-the-vote effort did not function well on Election Day.

The central GOP error was Republicans' flawed assumptions about the likely 2012 electorate. The campaign's inaccurate polling helped confirm these assumptions. This produced flawed planning about where to spend money and what states the candidates and their surrogates should visit. Their overestimation of success prevented a strategic change that might have allowed Romney to gain the presidency.

The main long-term influence on the 2012 election results, and an important influence on future elections, is the gradually changing demographic composition of the country and its electorate. The growing number of heavily Democratic Latinos and the strong Democratic advantage among young voters portends a Democratic advantage in future elections, all other things being equal.

But will all else be equal? Presidential second terms are usually difficult, and midterm elections during a second term very often result in gains for the nonpresidential party. Will the economy recover, or will it remain a problem for ruling Democrats in future elections? Can America's growing national debt and huge, looming federal budget deficits be satisfactorily resolved in Obama's second term? Problems overseas may also afflict the president and his party. Europe remains in the economic doldrums, Iran continues progress toward creating nuclear weapons, the Middle East continues to be in turmoil, and the threat of revived global terrorism remains.

In the wake of the 2012 election, however, the Republican Party faces the bigger political task. It must find a way to appeal to younger voters and the growing ranks of Latinos. The party also must upgrade its polling analysis and master new methods of voter persuasion and turnout pioneered by the 2012 Obama campaign.

The 2012 presidential election, by reaffirming the Washington status quo in the face of large national and international problems, has left America's political future uncertain. The Duke of Wellington referred to his victory in the Battle of Waterloo as "the nearest run thing that you ever saw in your life," one that easily could have resulted in defeat. So was the case for the 2012 election for President Obama. America's future contains similar possibilities for good or ill.

NOTES

1. The prediction models appear in *PS: Political Science and Politics* 45, no. 4 (October 2012): 610–674.

2. The Obama job approval percentage comes from the average job approval for August 26, 2012, at realclearpolitics.com (accessed October 8, 2012). Gallup's Obama economic job approval measurement is for August 9–12, 2012, located at http://www.gallup.com/poll/156698/Americans-Continue-Give-Obama-Low-Marks-Economy.aspx (accessed October 8, 2012).

3. From the "direction of the country" average at realclearpolitics.com for August 26, 2012.

REFERENCES

ABCnews. 2012. "Top 13 Quotes in Mitt Romney's Leaked Fundraiser Video." September 18, http://abcnews.go.com/Politics/OTUS/top-13-quotes-mitt-romneys-leaked-fundraiser-video/story?id=17264969 (accessed February 2, 2013).

American Enterprise Institute. 2012. "Debating Debate Impact." *AEI Political Report* 8 (7). http://www.aei.org/files/2012/09/13/-aei-political-report-september-2012_111308853467.pdf (accessed October 24, 2012).

Andrews, Wilson, Dan Keating, and Karen Yourish. 2012. "Mad Money: TV Ads in the 2012 Presidential Campaign." *Washington Post,* November 17. http://www.washingtonpost.com/wp-srv/special/politics/track-presidential-campaign-ads-2012/ (accessed December 3, 2012).

Blanton, Dana. 2012. "Fox News Poll: Most Voters Want Change, Even as Obama Holds Edge." FoxNews.com, September 27. http://www.foxnews.com/politics/2012/09/27/fox-news-poll-most-voters-want-change-even-as-obama-holds-edge/ (accessed October 3, 2012).

Byers, Dylan. 2012. "Nielsen: 59.2 Million Watch Last Debate." *Politico,* October 23. http://www.politico.com/blogs/media/2012/10/nielsen-million-watched-last-debate-139394.html (accessed October 24, 2012).

CBS DC. 2012. "Conservative Leaders: 'Out of Control' Media Bias for Obama Election." September 26. http://washington.cbslocal.com/2012/09/26/conservative-leaders-out-of-control-media-bias-for-obama-this-election/ (accessed October 3, 2012).

CBS News. 2012. "Obama Reverses on Super PACs, Seeks Support." February 7. http://www.cbsnews.com/8301-250_162-57372356/obama-reverses-on-super-pacs-seeks-support/ (accessed October 8, 2012).

CNN. 2012a. CNN/ORC Poll, September 9–12. http://i2.cdn.turner.com/cnn/2012/images/09/13/rel10c.pdf (accessed October 8, 2012).

CNN. 2012b. CNN/ORC Poll, October 3. http://i2.cdn.turner.com/cnn/2012/images/10/03/top12.pdf (accessed October 24, 2012).

CNN. 2012c. CNN/ORC Poll, October 11. http://i2.cdn.turner.com/cnn/2012/images/10/11/top13.pdf (accessed October 30, 2012).

CNN. 2012d. CNN/ORC Poll, October 22. http://politicalticker.blogs.cnn.com/2012/10/22/cnn-poll-who-won-the-debate/?iref=allsearch (accessed October 24, 2012).

CNN. 2012e. "Election 2012: Results." November 8. http://www.cnn.com/election/2012/results/main (accessed November 14, 2012).

Cillizza, Chris, and Aaron Blake. 2012. "President Obama's Real Opponent in 2012." *Washington Post,* September 18. http://www.washingtonpost.com/blogs/the-fix/

wp/2012/09/18/president-obamas-real-opponent-in-2012/?print=1 (accessed October 8, 2012).

Confessore, Nicholas. 2012. "Priorities USA Action Reports Record Monthly Donations." *New York Times,* September 4. http://thecaucus.blogs.nytimes.com/2012/09/04/priorities-usa-action-reports-record-monthly-donations/ (accessed October 3, 2012).

Cost, Jay. 2012. "Morning Jay: Will October Be a Bad Month For Obama?" *Weekly Standard,* October 5. http://www.weeklystandard.com/blogs/morning-jay-will-october-be-bad-month-obama_653661.html (accessed October 24, 2012).

Crabtree, Susan. 2012. "Obama Ground Game Won't Transfer to 2016, Aide Says." *Washington Times,* November 8. http://www.washingtontimes.com/blog/inside-politics/2012/nov/8/obama-ground-game-wont-transfer-2016-aide-says/ (accessed November 14, 2012).

Davenport, Coral. 2012. "Barbour: The Hurricane Is What Broke Romney's 'Momentum.'" *National Journal,* November 4. http://www.nationaljournal.com/sunday-shows/barbour-the-hurricane-is-what-broke-romney-s-momentum-20121104 (accessed November 14, 2012).

Eggen, Dan, and Philip Rucker. 2012. "Romney Camp Used $20M Loan to Cope with Summer Cash Flow Woes." *Washington Post,* September 18. http://www.washingtonpost.com/politics/decision2012/romney-camp-used-20m-loan-to-handle-summer-cash-flow-woes/2012/09/18/0794c824-020a-11e2-9367-4e1bafb958db_story.html (accessed October 3, 2012).

Fournier, Ron. 2012. "Obama Wins Third Debate but Romney Wins Debate Season." *National Journal,* October 23. http://www.nationaljournal.com/2012-presidential-campaign/obama-wins-third-debate-but-romney-wins-debate-season-20121022 (accessed October 24, 2012).

Gabriel, Trip. 2012. "Now Democrats Suggest Polling Is Flawed." *New York Times,* October 15. http://thecaucus.blogs.nytimes.com/2012/10/15/now-democrats-suggest-polling-is-flawed/ (accessed October 24, 2012).

Haberman, Maggie, and Alexander Burns. 2012. "Romney's Fail Whale: ORCA the Vote Tracker Left Team 'Flying Blind.'" *Politico,* November 8. http://www.politico.com/blogs/burns-haberman/2012/11/romneys-fail-whale-orca-the-votetracker-149098.html (accessed November 14, 2012).

Hartman, Margaret. 2012. "Democrats Beat Republicans in Convention Ratings, Michelle Trounces Everyone." *New York,* September 6. http://nymag.com/daily/intel/2012/09/democrats-beat-republicans-in-convention-ratings.html (accessed October 3, 2012).

Huffington Post. 2012a. "Obama Job Approval—Foreign Policy." http://elections.huffingtonpost.com/pollster/obama-job-approval-foreign-policy (accessed October 8, 2012).

Huffington Post. 2012b. "2012 General Election: Obama vs. Romney." http://elections.huffingtonpost.com/pollster/2012-general-election-romney-vs-obama#!minpct=40&maxpct=50&smoothing=less&showpoints=no&estimate=cus (accessed November 24, 2012).

Issenberg, Shasha. 2012. "A Vast Left Wing Competency." *Slate,* November 7. http://www.slate.com/articles/news_and_politics/victory_lab/2012/11/obama_s_victory_how_the_democrats_burned_by_karl_rove_became_the_party_of.html (accessed November 14, 2012).

Jones, Jeffrey M. 2012a. "Improving National Outlook Key to Obama Victory in 2012." Gallup.com, November 8. http://www.gallup.com/poll/158567/improving-national-outlook-key-obama-victory-2012.aspx (accessed November 14, 2012).

Jones, Jeffrey M. 2012b. "Obama's Challenge: Higher Likeability Than Approval." Gallup.com, September 6. http://www.gallup.com/poll/157292/obama-challenge-higher-likability-approval.aspx (accessed October 8, 2012).

Leahy, Michael, and Sean Sullivan. 2012. "Hurricane Sandy Helped Obama, Karl Rove Says." *Washington Post,* November 2. http://www.washingtonpost.com/blogs/the-fix/wp/2012/11/02/hurricane-sandy-helped-obama-politically-karl-rove-says/ (accessed November 14, 2012).

Lee, Kristin A. 2012. "Brutal Pro-Obama Ad Names Mitt in Cancer Death." *New York Daily News,* August 7. http://articles.nydailynews.com/2012-08-07/news/33087226_1_priorities-usa-ad-gst-steel-mitt-romney (accessed October 8, 2012).

Levinthal, Dave. 2012. "Koch-Backed Group, Romney Super PAC Lead Charge against Obama." *Politico,* August 17. http://www.politico.com/news/stories/0812/79841.html (accessed October 8, 2012).

Monmouth University. 2012. "National: Romney Leads in Monmouth Poll." October 22. http://www.monmouth.edu/assets/0/84/159/2147483694/0e2e970e-a544-4f4d-8659-6233705b8ae7.pdf (accessed October 24, 2012).

Moore, Martha T. 2012. "Romney Bring Autos Back to Center of Ohio Campaign." *USA Today,* November 2. http://www.usatoday.com/story/news/politics/2012/11/01/romney-auto-claim-criticized-ohio/1675067/ (accessed November 14, 2012).

Morales, Lyman. 2012. "U.S. Distrust of Media Hits New High." Gallup.com, September 21. http://www.gallup.com/poll/157589/distrust-media-hits-new-high.aspx (accessed November 14, 2012).

Noonan, Peggy. 2012. "Time for an Intervention." *Wall Street Journal,* September 18. http://blogs.wsj.com/peggynoonan/2012/09/18/time-for-an-intervention/ (accessed October 8, 2012).

Pew Research Center. 2012a. "Many Say Press Is Fair to Romney, Obama." September 28. http://pewresearch.org/pubs/2366/press-coverage-obama-romney-fair-unfair-easy-hard (accessed October 3, 2012).

Pew Research Center. 2012b. "Voters Divided over Who Will Win Second Debate." October 15. http://pewresearch.org/pubs/2389/romney-obama-second-presidential-debate-registered-voters-win-expectations (accessed October 24, 2012).

Romano, Andrew. 2012. "Why Mitt Romney Has the Worst Favorability Ratings in Memory." *Daily Beast,* September 6. http://www.thedailybeast.com/articles/2012/09/06/why-mitt-romney-has-the-worst-favorability-ratings-in-memory.html (accessed October 8, 2012).

Saad, Lydia. 2012. "Economy Is Dominant Issue for Americans as Election Nears." Gallup.com, October 22. http://www.gallup.com/poll/158267/economy-dominant-issue-americans-election-nears.aspx (accessed October 24, 2012).

Schier, Steven E., and Todd E. Eberly. 2012. "The New American Political System: Popular Discontent and Professional Government." *The Forum* 10 (2): 1540–1588.

Schier, Steven E., and Todd E. Eberly. 2013. *American Government and Popular Discontent.* New York: Routledge.

Sides, John. 2012. "The Perils of the Democrats' Euphoria or Why the 2012 Election Is Not a Realignment." *The Monkey Cage,* November 12. http://www. themonkeycage.org (accessed November 14, 2012).

Silver, Nate. 2012. "Par or Bogey?" *New York Times,* September 4. http://fivethirtyeight. blogs.nytimes.com/2012/09/04/sept-3-par-or-bogey/ (accessed October 8, 2012).

Temp, Henik. 2012. "Did Hurricane Sandy Get Obama Reelected?" *AEIdeas* (blog), American Enterprise Institute, November 14. http://www.aei-ideas. org/2012/11/did-hurricane-sandy-get-obama-reelected/ (accessed November 14, 2012).

Trende, Sean. 2012. "The Case of the Missing White Voters." RealClearPolitics, November 8. http://www.realclearpolitics.com/articles/2012/11/08/the_case_ of_the_missing_white_voters_116106.html (accessed November 14, 2012).

United States Election Project. 2013. "Voter Turnout." George Washington University, http://elections.gmu.edu/voter_turnout.htm (accessed February 1, 2013).

Vogel, Kenneth P. 2012. "The Billion Dollar Bust?" *Politico,* November 10. http:// www.politico.com/news/stories/1112/83534.html (accessed November 14, 2012).

Washington Post. 2012. "Obama Campaign Defends Big Spending during the Summer." August 21. http://www.washingtonpost.com/obama-campaign-defends-early- big-spending/2012/08/21/12067452-ebed-11e1-866f-60a00f604425_video. htm (accessed October 8, 2012).

5 Congressional Elections 2012

Roger H. Davidson

The context and character of the 2012 congressional elections contrast radically with the situation four years earlier. In many respects, they seem a photographic negative of the 2008 contests and their outcomes. The Democratic Party in 2006 captured both houses of Congress for the first time since 1992; its ranks swelled in 2008, matching Barack Obama's victory at the top of the ticket. Meanwhile, opinion surveys raised the prospect of a more progressive-minded electorate, propelled by the expected infusion of younger people and racial minorities within the civic culture (Pew Research Center 2007).

Obama's First Two Years

From the start, President Obama and his party faced a "perfect storm" of domestic and global policy crises—the most acute economic downturn since the 1930s; the perilous state of the financial markets; the collapse of a long-running home mortgage bubble; the near-meltdown of the nation's auto industry; numerous unmet domestic needs (e.g., in education, research, and infrastructure); soaring health care costs compared with lagging health outcomes; long-term wars in Iraq and Afghanistan; and natural and human disasters in Africa, Haiti, the Middle East, and elsewhere. Ironically, the very policy problems that ensured the Democrats' victories in 2008 led to the party's rejection two years later. Many of these crises were byproducts of the George W. Bush administration's failures of omission or commission. Now, however, Obama and his party "owned" the whole bundle of troubles.

Crafting legislation to deal with such contentious issues, Democratic leaders of the 111th Congress (2009–2011) were not in full control. The party's electoral victories in 2006 and 2008 were achieved in large part by the defeat of Republicans in moderate or even conservative states and districts. Ironically, the greater diversity in the Democratic caucuses' membership inevitably fostered greater resistance to the party's traditional progressive agenda. These Democratic newcomers naturally worried about holding their seats, which meant appealing to moderate voters. The House's "Blue Dog" group, composed of conservative Democrats, had 52 members in the 111th Congress. In both chambers, members from swing states or districts pushed back against activist policy initiatives, such as large financial bailout packages and single-payer health care plans. The 60 votes needed to overcome Senate filibusters could be obtained only with the support of all senators who caucused with the Democrats—including the two independents and several members from conservative states.

Citizens—whose generic call for "change" had put the Democrats in power in 2008—were unimpressed with the legislative products the party was able to achieve in the 111th Congress, which included an economic stimulus package, new financial regulations, bailouts for key industries, temporary help for car buyers and mortgage holders, and the Affordable Care Act of 2010, which its detractors dubbed "Obamacare." Seven months into the Obama administration, surveys recorded that despite the generalized support for reform, people harbored "growing doubts and worries about the rapid pace of the Democrats' ambitious policy agenda." Only 27 percent of citizens said that Obama's policies had improved the economic picture. Public trust and confidence in government actions—especially where Congress was concerned—had plummeted to a new low point by the spring of 2010 (Pew Research Center 2010).

On the eve of the 2010 elections, the Pew Research Center reported that people were still pessimistic about the U.S. economy—hardly a surprising finding. Fully 92 percent of the interviewees said that the nation's economy was only fair or poor (Pew Research Center 2010). More than 4 out of 10 Americans reported facing severe financial problems. The signs of a gradual economic recovery, moreover, were far from visible. "There was no evidence by the 2010 elections that things were getting better," recalled Sen. Sherrod Brown (D-Ohio). Nor were Democrats prepared to defend the recovery. "We let them [the GOP] get away with too much," Brown recalled (Dionne 2012).

Economic worries fostered rising pessimism about the government's capacity to cope with such issues. Seventy-seven percent of those interviewed said they were frustrated or even angry with the federal government. President Obama's approval numbers fell to less than 50 percent, below Bush's 2004 ratings. Even worse was the judgment about Congress: only 25 percent of those surveyed approved of its stewardship. Nor were the political parties to be trusted: the Democrats' rating was 38 percent, and the Republicans' was 37 percent (Pew Research Center 2011).

Thus, the 2010 midterm elections targeted the new majority: "Democrats no longer have the momentum they once possessed," campaign analyst Stuart Rothenberg wrote. "The landscape has shifted again, this time improving significantly for Republicans" (Rothenberg 2011, 9). Another nonpartisan commentator, Charlie Cook, observed that Democratic fortunes had "slipped completely out of control" (Brooks 2009, A29).

The Democrats' 2010 "Pasting"

Voters in the 2010 midterm elections—barely two years into the Obama administration—handed the Republicans control of the House and near-control of the Senate. The GOP's 242 representatives formed the party's largest caucus since the 80th Congress (1947–1949). The hapless Democrats—who in the two previous elections had gained a total of 52 House seats and 14 Senate seats—now lost 66 House seats (the greatest setback since the GOP's 71-seat loss in 1938) and 6 Senate seats. (The average midterm loss for presidential parties is 27.8 House members and 3.6 senators.) "It is an exaggeration, but perhaps a revealing one," analyst Michael Barone observed, "to say that the Republicans swept everything from the George Washington Bridge to the Donner Pass" (Barone and McCutcheon 2011, 2). This occurred despite Gary Jacobson's contention that legislative achievements during President Obama's first two years "made the 111th Congress among the most productive in many years, and . . . were fully consistent with promises Obama made during his successful campaign for the White House . . . In short, Obama had done what he might reasonably believe he was elected to do" (Jacobson 2011, 220–243).

The Democrats' 2010 "pasting" (Obama's term) was an unusually dramatic case of midterm election dynamics. The off-year electorate lacked many of the enthusiasts (independents, young people, and minority voters) that Obama had rallied to the polls two years before. Equally, the election served as a kind of true-false test about the first two years of Obama's presidency. Jacobson (2011) found that "the 2010 election was nationalized to an extraordinary degree and that the president was the primary focus." Inasmuch as Obama was not on the ballot, voters vented their anger and frustration on those whose names were on the ballots—Democratic incumbents seeking reelection to federal and state offices. The hapless Democrats were also linked to their unpopular congressional leaders: House Speaker Nancy Pelosi (D-CA) had only a 23 percent favorable rating (better than Senate Majority Leader Harry Reid, D-NV, who claimed a mere 8 percent) among people who had "heard enough" to respond at all (CBS News 2010).

Citizens were angry and confused over the issues that affected them: the weak economic recovery, massive losses of mostly middle-class jobs and home mortgages, mounting federal deficits and debt, and—for some people—images of a sinister, overweening federal assault on personal and states' rights. However understandable, such worries were magnified by citizens' own lack of information. Fewer than 4 out of 10 respondents in a Kaiser Foundation survey in March 2012, for example, claimed to understand how the Affordable Care Act would affect them personally; only 1 in 4 respondents were aware of the act's features already in force (Hiltzik 2012a, B1, B8). For their part, Obama's spokespersons and the act's congressional supporters failed to explain clearly the objectives of health care reform, much less the massive costs and mixed results of the existing system. In the 2010 campaigns, they allowed the act's detractors to define the terms of the debate. Nor did that strategy quickly change: only one sentence in the president's 2012 State of the Union message mentioned the Affordable Care Act; throughout the 2012 campaigns, he and most Democratic contenders tended to stress other issues (Garrett 2012, 44).

The Redistricting Thickets

The 2010 decennial census transformed the landscape of the 2012 elections. (The Senate, of course, is unaffected by the movement of populations. If the one person–one vote rule were applied to the Senate, California, for example, would command something like 14 seats.) Every state entitled to more than one House seat is obliged to establish district lines containing virtually equal numbers of people as defined by the new census numbers. Especially affected in the wake of a census are states that gain or lose seats due to the census results, according to their growth relative to others. Winners from the 2010 census were "sun-belt" states, most of which tilt toward the Republicans.[1] The losers were mainly so-called rust-belt states—northern and eastern industrial areas—where Democratic partisans tend to prevail.[2] Within a majority of these states, partisan control typically dictates how the districts are drawn, and thus the GOP's big 2010 gains in state legislatures and governors' mansions typically led to gerrymanders favoring the majority party.

Even within states whose House allotments do not change, intrastate population movements—as well as changes in the state's partisan control—drive the redrawing of district lines. Here again the Democrats were vulnerable in 2010. The contests that year brought the GOP no less than 675 state legislative seats and 5 governorships, awarding them control of both legislative chambers and governorships in 20 states, compared with the Democrats' 11 governorships. These landslides erased the advantages won by Democrats over the previous decade (Cooper 2010, A1, A3).

Despite the massive shift in the Republicans' favor, however, fresh gains from gerrymandered districts were not limitless. Two important Democratic-leaning states, California and Washington, joined several other states in delegating redistricting to nonpartisan commissions. Moreover, many of the most loyal red and blue states were already sending highly partisan House delegations to Capitol Hill. In many cases, then, gains from partisan line-drawing had arrived at least 10 years earlier, following the 2000 census. "There are limits to partisan gerrymandering," observed political scientist

Michael McDonald, "and so we saw mostly what the Republicans were doing this cycle was protecting the gains they had in 2010 rather than expanding the map with artful gerrymandering" (Wilson and Shepard 2012, 14–19).

Both parties' national committees began studying redistricting in the mid-2000s, focusing ahead on the 2010 state legislative and gubernatorial races that would shape the 2012 redistricting. Drawing the lines and awaiting the outcome of court challenges extended through April 2012. Redistricting is a tedious process for those involved and affected by it, including incumbents and would-be candidates. Patterns unique to every state were on display in the post-2010 redistricting battles. Two very different redistricting decision-making patterns were followed in California and North Carolina, neither of which gained or lost House seats.

The California Experiment

In California, state legislators had historically crafted the state's now 53 House districts—the largest House delegation—along with the state's Assembly and Senate districts (California's state legislators are term-limited). The districting process traditionally was geared toward partisan advantage and incumbent protection. Angered over excessive partisanship and legislative gridlock in Sacramento (where budget enactments require a two-thirds majority), voters in 2008 approved a new Citizens Redistricting Commission to redraw state Assembly and Senate districts; two years later, the voters expanded the commission's mandate to embrace congressional districts (McGreevy 2010, A1, A19). The law requires that the 14-member commission include five Republicans, five Democrats, and four independents.

Ethnic, geographic, and partisan diversity were among the reform's leading goals. The commissioners were instructed to honor "communities of interest." These are defined as "contiguous population[s]" that share "common social and economic interests." Work opportunities, media, transportation, race, ethnicity, and civic boundaries (i.e., cities and counties) are all taken into account. At the same time, the new districts were expected to yield more competitive elections. Finally, incumbents' home residences were to be ignored in the drawing of the new districts.

The result was the state's biggest political earthquake in two decades. (Of the 265 U.S. House contests since the 2000 census, only one of the state's incumbents who had run for reelection had been defeated.) As the *San Francisco Chronicle's* Carolyn Lockhead (2012, A4) reported, the new congressional map was "expected to yield more open seats, more competitive elections, and possibly three to five new Democrats."

The new map suggested that the state's Democrats had been underrepresented by previous districting. By September 7, 2012, more than 18 million Californians were registered—including 1.4 million new voters, half of whom used a new law allowing online registration. "While other states created illegitimate ways to suppress the vote, we found ways to increase the voters," declared state senator Leland Yee (D-San Francisco), author of the new law (McGreevy and Halper 2012, A1, A16). Democrats represented 48 percent of the registrants, and independents ("decline to state" and others) constituted 33 percent—both categories growing by 5 percent. Yet in 2012, only four independents ran in the state's 53 House elections. This is understandable, given the costs of running for office and the difficulties of arousing grassroots support.

The real losers were the Republicans, who dropped from 30 percent to 19 percent of registered voters. The state's Republican establishment, like its national core leadership, increasingly is seen as following a rigid far-right agenda. "California Republicans are out of touch with most voters," lamented longtime Southern California columnist Thomas D. Elias (2012, G1, G4). "Not only do its members of Congress display little or no independence from the party line, but that party line itself deviates considerably from what every poll shows the majority of the public wants."

Overall, the new congressional plan created 40 Democratic-leaning districts and only 13 Republican-leaning districts, according to party registration figures compiled by political analyst Ron Nehring (2012). Four Republican incumbents landed in Democratic-leaning districts (two of them decided to retire). Similarly, 12 Republican incumbents found themselves in competitive districts, compared to only six Democrats. So the immediate result of the new map was an unprecedented nine retirements—five Republicans and four Democrats. Allan Hoffenblum, publisher of the *California Target Book* (an analysis of legislative and congressional races), summarized the situation this way: "redistricting had more to do with the retirements than the desire to give up the seat" (Freking and Blood 2012, A6).

The major vortex of lagging Democratic representation lay in a group of formerly GOP districts in Southern California, all of them sites of a steady influx of Democratic-leaning people—especially Hispanics and Asian Americans. Newly drawn districts, explained Bruce Cain, director of the University of California's Washington, DC, Center, deprive incumbents of "their normal base of voters that know them" (quoted in Lockhead 2012, A4). Because advertising is so costly in media markets within the Los Angeles mega-basin, legislators must take to the streets and pursue personal campaigns. Rep. Jerry Lewis—whose 17 terms made him the state's longest-serving Republican and who was the former chair and ranking member of Appropriations—ended his career because after redistricting his home landed in the district of another Republican, seven-term representative Gary Miller. Sixteen-term representative David Dreier, chair of the House Rules Committee, quit because his former constituency was split into three newly drawn districts. Rep. Elton Gallegly (13 terms) bowed out when he was thrown into competition with Rep. Buck McKeon (10 terms), chair of the Armed Services Committee. Another GOP retiree was Rep. Wally Herger (13 terms), whose career on the Ways and Means Committee had stalled and who faced primary challenges from two other Republicans.

Of the four Democratic retirees, five-term representative Dennis Cardoza opted to withdraw rather than face his friend and fellow Democratic representative Jim Costa in a newly configured district. The two remaining Democratic retirees were Rep. Lynn Woolsey (10 terms) and Rep. Bob Filner (10 terms), the latter of whom—rather than compete in a heavily Hispanic district—ran in and won the San Diego mayoral race.

Another intra-Democratic contest found 15-term representative Howard Berman facing 8-term representative Brad Sherman—two liberals tossed into the same San Fernando Valley district. This race captured national attention and ample campaign funds, although the contest was more about the candidates and their supporters than about their political views. In an October 2012 debate the two "argued like kids in a schoolyard," with the debate ending in a physical shoving match that was stopped by a sheriff's deputy (Merl 2012a, A5). Another peculiarity was Berman's endorsements—not only from Democratic leaders, but also from GOP representative Darrell Issa, chair of the House Committee on Oversight and Governmental Reform, who stated, "Howard is in the race of his lifetime, and I want him back" (Merl 2012b, A1). In the end, Berman and his enviable legislative record lost out by 23 percentage points to Sherman—renowned for his constituency outreach and service.

In other districts, sharpened competition altered the pace and thrust of reelection campaigns. The 24th district added enough inland Republicans to dilute the safe Democratic district awarded to Democrat Lois Capps in 2001. The *Wall Street Journal* had branded the district as a "ribbon of shame" because it extended some 250 miles along the Pacific Coast—from Oxnard in the south to Morro Bay in the north. The district's plurality of registered Democrats shrank from almost 20 percent to less than 4 percent. Representative Capps, however, reached beyond her partisan base to win by a 10 percent margin. The new adjoining 26th district, once a safe GOP haven, also turned competitive—with a 4 percent Democratic registration advantage along with 19 percent independents; it covered most of Ventura County and blended affluent Republican suburbs northwest of Los Angeles with the heavily Democratic city of Oxnard. "It's going to be one of the closest races in the country," said the Democrats' campaign manager (Saillant 2012, AA1). Indeed, the Democratic candidate won by a margin of only 4 percent.

Another feature of the California reforms was the new possibility of "top-two" primary contests, in which the two candidates with the most votes, regardless of party affiliation, move on to the general election. Shaun Bowler of UC Riverside believes this feature might nudge the state's Republican Party toward the center of the ideological spectrum. Like the national party, the California GOP has, Bowler explains, "taken itself out of statewide races, and even in federal races, because it's become so extreme" (Simon and Willon 2012, A15).

Democrats, too, faced threats from the top-two rule. For example, Rep. Pete Stark (20 terms), who represented several eastern San Francisco Bay communities, was challenged by John Swalwell, a prosecutor and Dublin City Council member. Although born four years after Stark entered Congress, Swalwell prevailed by nearly 10,000 votes over Stark, whose "boorish and erratic" reputation was widely scorned (*San Francisco Chronicle* 2012).

North Carolina: Old-Fashioned Gerrymanders

Most states leave redistricting to their governors and state legislatures. Consider North Carolina, whose congressional apportionment, like that of California, was unchanged by the 2010 census—it maintained 13 seats, falling just short of gaining an additional seat. Unlike California, the redistricting, dominated by the Republican-led legislature, "seeks to unravel several decades of Democratic-led gerrymandering. Even the Democrats privately admit that the state GOP appears to have done a masterful job" (Miller 2011, 4–5). The hoary techniques of partisan gerrymandering aim at maximizing seats for the party in control while limiting those of the opposing party. North Carolina Republicans' 2012 goal was to flip the congressional ratio, from six Republicans and seven Democrats to at least nine Republicans and only three or perhaps four Democrats. The primary vehicles for accomplishing this are informally described as "cracking"—dividing the opposing party's voters among districts to prevent their reaching a majority—and "packing," which involves crowding the opposing party's voters into single districts, forcing them to waste the votes of their outsized majority. North Carolina, not incidentally, has since the 1970s been a battleground for political and judicial conflicts over partisan and racial gerrymandering (Davidson, Oleszek, and Lee 2011, chap. 3).

North Carolina boasts two majority-minority districts—that is, districts containing a majority or plurality of African Americans or Hispanics. One is the northeastern 1st district, whose fields produce tobacco, cotton, and a variety of edible crops. For 2012, the legislative drafters added some Democratic voters from the city of Durham and reattached a few heavily black areas (Miller 2011, 4–5). The incumbent is Rep. G. K. Butterfield, a black civil rights lawyer and former judge, who had an easy path to his fifth House term. The second majority-minority district is the 12th district, whose incumbent is 10-term Democratic representative Melvin Watt. Its new serpentine boundaries roughly follow Interstate 85, embracing African

American voters from Greensboro and Winston-Salem in the north to Charlotte in the south. Blacks make up 51 percent of the district's voters, making the district even safer for Democrats. The Republican legislature had ample incentives for cramming Democratic voters into such districts: with lopsided majorities, Democrats wasted many votes, whereas neighboring districts became safer for the majority Republicans.

Another pro-Democratic district is the 4th, centered in North Carolina's "Research Triangle" surrounding the cities of Raleigh and Durham. The incumbent is political scientist and lay Baptist minister Rep. David Price, first elected in 1986. His new district favors Democrats, embracing not only portions of his old district but also part of the old 13th—whose incumbent was Rep. Brad Miller, a Democrat first elected in 2002. Miller initially planned to run against Price in the new district but ultimately decided to retire. Although the odds-on favorite, Price nonetheless ramped up his campaigning and advertising to reach out to his new constituents.

Two other Democrats suffered from the 2012 redistricting. One was three-term representative Heath Shuler of the 11th district—a former Washington Redskins quarterback and a leader of the conservative Democratic "Blue Dogs." Shuler lost a big chunk of Democratic territory—including most of the city of Asheville, a conspicuous chunk on the map—and gained four very Republican counties. He faced primary opposition and a powerful general election opponent. Although some rated the race as a toss-up, Shuler decided to retire and resume his business career.

Finally, two endangered Democrats decided to buck the odds and seek reelection. Rep. Mike McIntyre in the 7th district and Rep. Larry Kissell in the 8th both faced districts that would have supported McCain in 2008. Although McIntyre, an eight-term veteran, fell into the new 8th district, he decided to fight it out in the 7th, his old territory, and he won by a razor-thin margin, the object of a recount. Kissell, first elected in 2008, was not so lucky; he lost by some 24,000 votes. Therefore, the GOP's gerrymander scheme was mostly successful: their share of House seats jumped from six to nine, and the number of Democrats shrank from seven to four—the victims of two retirements and one defeat.

These two states—California and North Carolina—handled congressional redistricting in vastly different ways, with equally different results. California reflects a recent trend toward empowering nonpartisan panels to do the job formerly left to politicians. North Carolina followed the traditional method of districting, leaving it to governors and state legislators. Both parties actively pursue strategic districting when they are in a position to do so—for example, Illinois Democrats in 2012. But with their statewide victories in 2010, Republicans were poised to shape the outcome of 2012 contests in a number of states. Although the GOP lost some eight House seats nationwide, their gerrymandering efforts—not only in North Carolina but also in Ohio, Pennsylvania, Virginia, and Wisconsin—insulated them from further losses.

Candidates: Retiring and Recruiting

Most candidates for congressional offices are strategic contenders (Schlesinger 1966). That is, they are individuals who calculate the pros and cons of seeking public office and who judge the opportune time to launch their candidacies. Many such men and women already hold public offices within their communities. Others are political amateurs who boast other valuable attributes: for example, athletes, media figures, successful business owners, or military veterans (Canon 1990). They must consider these central questions: What are my chances of getting the party's nomination? What are my chances for winning the general election? What will it cost me to succeed? What local or national trends can boost or impede my chances of success? And if an incumbent holds the post, what are his or her vulnerabilities? (Davidson, Oleszek, and Lee 2011; see especially chap. 3).

Candidacy decisions are often the most pivotal moments in the entire recruitment process. "Who runs, who does not run, how many candidates run. These questions set the stage for the campaigns themselves" (Maisel 1982, 34).

The Hill Campaign Committees

Although aspirants must decide for themselves whether and when to run, most serious office-seekers fall into the orbits of the two major parties, which carry the brand loyalties of a large majority of voters and also command impressive logistical and financial resources. Minor party candidates—who appeared on many 2012 ballots—may provide voters with alternatives, especially in cases where only one major party fields a candidate. Only a handful of such contenders—mainly from the Green or Libertarian parties—win a sizable number of votes, and only when they threaten major party candidates in close contests do political strategists or news media take these parties seriously.

The four campaign committees of the Capitol Hill parties—House and Senate Republicans and Democrats—are the major players in seeking out and supporting candidates.[3] Elections begin with fierce recruiting seasons, with both parties seeking lineups to win House and Senate majorities. Recruiting for 2012 began as soon as the 2010 contests ended. Party leaders start by studying the electoral maps and deciding where they need candidates. Open seats and those held by vulnerable opposition members are identified. Then the leaders and their staffs "reach out across the country in search of political talent. Like college football coaching staffs in hot pursuit of high-school prospects, they are . . . putting together the lineups of the future" (Walsh 1992, A1). Prospects can expect calls from the president, former presidents, governors, high-profile financial backers, and other notables.

The parties' four campaign committees followed different paths during 2010–2012. The GOP's Senate campaign committee (National Republican Senatorial Committee [NRSC]) was perhaps the least effective during those years. In 2012, the GOP's Senate campaign chair was John Cornyn of Texas—a state that is a financial mother lode for the party—but the committee took a hands-off approach to recruiting viable candidates. Conservative columnist Jennifer Rubin bitterly recounted the story. "The NRSC went into a crouch in 2010 and 2012," after grassroots activists rebelled when the committee backed candidates such as Florida's moderate Gov. Charlie Crist over Marco Rubio, a Tea Party favorite, in 2010 (Rubin 2012). But the NRSC's approach was also blamed for enabling such unelectable 2010 candidates as Sharron Angle of Nevada and Christine O'Donnell in Delaware (the NRSC supported nine-term Republican representative Michael Castle in the Republican primary, and O'Donnell lost Vice President Joe Biden's old seat to Democrat Christopher Coons, the New Castle County Executive) and such 2012 candidates as Todd Akin (Missouri) and Richard Mourdock (Indiana). Rubin also blamed the conservative party core: "Voters, grass-roots groups and . . . right-wing bloggers and talk show hosts have to decide if they want to keep selecting the unelectable to fritter away Senate seats in Colorado, North Dakota, Montana, Indiana, Missouri, and elsewhere, as they did in 2010 and 2012." Nonpartisan analyst Stuart Rothenberg states, "The fact of the matter is that in primaries, Republicans have a much more complicated grass-roots problem than do Democrats" (Rothenberg 2012, 20).

Senate Democrats faced their own problems in 2010, when they lost six seats. Both Majority Leader Harry Reid and New York senator Chuck Schumer—a prodigious fundraiser and political strategist—were running for reelection. The Democratic Senatorial Campaign Committee (DSCC) chair that year was New Jersey senator Robert Menendez, and though he was not everyone's favorite for the job, he was nonetheless able to tap New York's financial industry for funds.

For 2012, the DSCC chair was Sen. Patty Murray of Washington, who had chaired the committee in the 2002 election cycle. Murray's recruiting and fundraising efforts in 2002 were judged to be mostly successful, even though the party lost its Senate majority. In 2012, Senator Reid reportedly persuaded her to accept the job again after several other senators had turned it down. "She's a mechanic, not a visionary," reported the former head of Washington State's Republican Party. "And people have underestimated her for her entire career and they've always been wrong" (Barone and McCutcheon 2011, 1701). Her challenge in 2012 was daunting, considering the number of Democratic seats at risk and the number of retirements, but again her recruiting and fundraising skills—in tandem with the contributions of Senator Schumer, Sen. Dick Durbin of Illinois, and others—were remarkably successful. Also crucial was her choice of a veteran Hill staffer, Guy Cecil, to serve as the DSCC's executive director. The DSCC started earlier; built a bigger staff than the NRSC, including an in-house research shop; and aggressively helped candidates raise money. With vulnerable Democrats in several states where Mitt Romney won by double digits, "it was vital to turn each Senate race into a choice between the two candidates" (Trygstad 2012, 16). "If you really believe that these races are choices," Cecil explained, "all of a sudden recruitment takes on an elevated sense of importance." (For 2014—another crucial year for Senate Democrats—Guy Cecil will again be executive director, working with DSCC chair Michael Bennet of Colorado.)

The House Democrats' challenge in 2012 was even more fearsome: regaining the majority with 25 or more seats. After the party lost its majority status in 2010, Minority Leader Nancy Pelosi—the most effective booster and fundraiser among House Democrats—called on moderate New Yorker Steve Israel to chair the DCCC. Israel's fundraising prowess (he had reportedly brought in $1.9 million for the committee earlier) was a plus because the committee was at the time about $20 million in debt. Israel put the DCCC in the black and raised some $10 million more than the committee's GOP counterpart, and in 2011 he recruited 60 Democrats to run for Republican-held seats. "I do remind my colleagues," Israel said, "that we lost 63 seats in 2010 because swing voters swung away from us. Now . . . they're swinging back, because Republicans in this Congress have gone so excessively to the right" (Carney 2012). The Democrats won back a few seats, but because of retirements and newly drawn district lines, they fell far short of their goal.

Capitol Hill Restlessness in 2012

The 2012 electoral year saw an unusually large group of retirees in both chambers: 25 House members (14 Democrats and 11 Republicans) and 10 senators (6 Democrats, 3 Republicans, and 1 independent) vacated their seats on Capitol Hill. Eleven House members (6 Democrats and 5 Republicans) decided to run for the U.S. Senate. One representative (Dean Heller, R-NV) who had been appointed in 2011 to fill a Senate vacancy won a full term in 2012. Two others opted to run for other offices (Indiana governor, San Diego mayor). Others were simply ending long legislative careers—for example, 18-term Norm Dicks (D-WA), 15-term Edolphus Towns (D-NY), and senators such as 88-year-old Daniel Akaka (D-HI), 77-year-old Herb Kohl (D-WI), and 69-year-old Kay Bailey Hutchison (R-TX).

Several retirees professed weariness with Capitol Hill life. Sen. Olympia Snowe (R-ME), a three-term moderate, publicly denounced political polarization on the Hill. Sixteen-term representative Barney Frank (D-MA) was restless as the Banking Committee's ranking minority member and disdained campaigning in his newly drawn district. "It's been a privilege to fight for the quality of people's lives," the 71-year-old Frank explained, "but I'm ready to put a little more quality in my own life" (Goodnough 2011, A14). Redistricting halted the careers of 11 members of California's House delegation; gerrymandered redistricting in many states clouded incumbents' reelection calculations. The prevalence of Democratic retirees was surely an aftershock of the GOP's 2010 midterm triumphs. There was four-term representative Dan Boren (D-OK), a moderate in an otherwise fiercely red state, and two-term senator Ben Nelson (D-NE), who, despite his conservative record, faced an uphill battle in his state.

To maximize their number of seats, the parties' Hill campaign committees must perform several tasks: first, discourage members from retiring (because incumbents are safer bets than non-incumbents); second, support incumbents' reelection races; third, identify the best candidates for seats they want to capture (trying to "clear the field" for them at the nominating stage); and fourth, provide all their candidates with financial backing—from the committees' own funds, from friendly interest groups and other funding sources, and from the candidates' own resources and fundraising.

Democratic campaign committees in both chambers faced tough odds in 2012. House Democratic leaders (i.e., their floor leaders and the DCCC) had to recruit no fewer than 80 candidates (to account for 2010 losses plus 14 retirees in 2012). Senate Democrats (again, leaders and the DSCC) faced 12 vacancies and no less than 23 incumbent seats to defend (Democrats had enjoyed a banner year in 2006), compared to only 10 Republican incumbents' seats and 3 retirees (4, if one counts Nevada's John Ensign, who resigned from the Senate because of scandal). House Republicans, of course, had 66 freshmen—including the "Young Guns," those one-term Republicans whom the NRCC decided needed assistance.

The 2012 Political Landscape

Most all the experts held that the 2012 election would be fought over the sluggish recovery of the U.S. economy. House Speaker John Boehner (R-OH) opened nearly all of his press conferences with these words: "The American people are still asking: Where are the jobs?" (Newhauser 2012, 1). What was called "the Great Recession" was very much on voters' minds as they cast votes in 2012. According to exit polls, 6 out of 10 voters viewed the economy as the top issue—ahead of health care, the federal budget deficit, or foreign policy (Associated Press 2012). Voters cited years of high unemployment and rising prices as the biggest sources of concern.

But two sets of responses to the economy also affected voters' choices at the ballot box. Stubborn though the recession had been, financial recovery was palpable by autumn 2012. Having bottomed out, housing markets were showing signs of recovery; retail sales—especially in the auto industry—were increasingly robust; and even the sluggish job-creation picture, the so-called lagging indicator, was slowly trending upward. Unemployment had declined to 7.9 percent in October 2012, compared with 9.8 percent at the time of the 2010 midterm elections. Although 65 percent of citizens saw news about the job situation as mostly bad in September 2010, only 42 percent held that view by October 2012 (Pew Research Center 2012). "Americans are hearing less negative news about the nation's economy, and . . . perceptions of news about other economic sectors—notably, the job situation—have improved as well," researchers declared (Pew Research Center 2012). Summarizing the autumn surveys, David Lauter of the *Los Angeles Times* reported,

> Attitudes toward the economy have warmed in recent weeks. Measures of consumer confidence have begun to tick upward, voter outlook about future conditions has brightened after a slide during the summer, and the percentage of Americans who feel the country is on the "right track" has risen steadily—albeit slowly. (Lauter 2012, A1)

Four out of every 10 voters told exit interviewers that the nation's economy was recovering.

A second factor was that voters now tended to blame former president George W. Bush rather than Barack Obama and his Democratic allies for their economic woes. Almost four years after Bush left office, 53 percent of the voters in exit polls blamed Bush for the nation's economic problems, versus 38 percent who blamed Obama (Irwin 2012). Even 12 percent of Romney's voters blamed Bush for the economic situation. Some 37 percent of voters told exit interviewers that rising prices were the biggest problem they faced—compared to the 38 percent who named unemployment, the 14 percent who named taxes, and the 8 percent who named housing.

Other issues crowded into citizens' minds as they voted. The so-called GOP war on women added force to the gender gap: a long-term tendency for more women to vote for Democrats, whereas men tend to vote for Republicans. This gap expanded because of campaign gaffes by two GOP Senate hopefuls. Rep. Todd Akin of Missouri claimed that women who are victims of "legitimate rape" rarely become pregnant. Richard Mourdock of Indiana said in a debate that even if a fetus is the result of a rape, "it is something that God intended to happen." Abortion rights groups mounted fierce campaigns for pro-choice candidates, mostly Democrats. Elizabeth Warren, running against GOP senator Scott Brown in Massachusetts, pounced on Akins's comments with a television ad declaring, "[If] the Republicans control the Senate, they decide who sits on the Supreme Court and whether we could lose *Roe v. Wade*" (Seelye 2012, A15). Warren prevailed by eight percentage points over

Brown—the only GOP senator to be unseated. Akin and Mourdock both lost in their states by six percentage points.

Campaign Finances: Candidates, Party Committees, and "Super PACs"

An estimated six billion dollars was spent for the 2012 elections, the most costly in U.S. history. Campaign spending has risen steadily since the 1970s, when modern record keeping began. But the 2012 political landscape fostered extraordinary campaign spending for several reasons. First, many of the individual contests—from the flagship Obama–Romney rivalry down through congressional and local races—were expected to be very competitive. Although the GOP's House majority was never in serious danger, Democrats were determined to retake a number of the seats they had lost in 2010. Senate Democrats wanted to preserve their slim majority—53 to 47, counting the two independents who caucused with them. Observers initially agreed that this goal was a long shot, but in the end, Democrats actually expanded their margin to 55–45, again assuming that two independents (one newly elected) were allies. Second, 37 states had placed policy questions—weighty or trivial—before their voters. Four state contests over same-sex marriage attracted financial support, for and against, from interest groups throughout the country. California, a pioneer in what is called "direct democracy," placed no less than 11 ballot measures before the voters in 2012, attracting some $350 million in campaign spending (Hiltzik 2012b, B1, B4).[4]

The final impetus for uncontrolled campaign money came from the U.S. Supreme Court. From the time the Court first encountered campaign finance reforms in the 1970s, the justices expressed skepticism and not a little bewilderment. After issuing a series of decisions limiting campaign finance statutes, in 2010 the Court, in *Citizens United v. Federal Election Commission* (558 US 310), struck down all limits on contributions from corporations, labor unions, and nonprofits (Davidson, Oleszek, and Lee 2011, chap. 3). The controversial five-to-four decision opened floodgates of funds, not only from the aforementioned groups but also from wealthy individuals and organizations—even some that were exempted from identifying their donors and that ignored the barriers between promoting legitimate causes and supporting individual candidates by name. The Court majority reasoned that unfettered spending, in whatever amounts, fell within the First Amendment's free speech guarantee (in short, spending money equals free speech). The majority's high-minded view, expressed by Justice Anthony Kennedy, was that "prompt disclosure of expenditures can provide shareholders and citizens with the information needed to hold corporations and elected officials accountable." The minority, led by Justice John Paul Stevens, argued that the ruling "threatens to undermine the integrity of elected institutions across the nation."

A ruling from the D.C. Circuit Court of Appeals later the same year (*Speechnow.org v. FEC,* 99 F.3rd 686, 2010) held that PACs organized only to make independent expenditures—and not to contribute directly to candidates—are not subject to contribution caps. Thus were born the "Super PACs"—able to receive unlimited donations from individuals, labor unions, and corporations.

The Court majority's optimistic faith in the transparency and incorruptibility of unfettered campaign finance has not been borne out by subsequent events. Shadowy groups whose supporters are anonymous and whose addresses may be just postal boxes have attacked candidates. An unusually transparent 2012 case involved not candidate funding but an $11 million donation from an Arizona group attacking California governor Jerry Brown's tax-hike plan, Proposition 30, and favoring Proposition 32, limiting unions' political spending. State regulators forced the group to disclose the identities of its contributors. (Although the group could have fought the case in court, it apparently knew that its disclosures would convey very little.) As two journalists explained,

> The money started with the Virginia-based "Americans for Job Security" and then transferred to a group called "Center to Protect Patient Rights." Over the course of a few days in October it was sent to the Arizona group, "Americans for Responsible Leadership," and then transferred again to California. (Megerian and Halper 2012, A1, A9)

The recipient California organization, the "Small Business Action Committee," doubted that the funds were helpful. "At the end of the day," a spokesperson for the recipients said, "[the money] was a significant distraction that took us off our campaign message" (Megerian 2012, AA 1). The donor groups, so it appears, were erected solely to launder funds from anonymous donors—their names were meaningless, their purposes vague, and their supporters unknown. The state's voters eventually rejected the donors' viewpoints on both propositions. Many 2012 candidates and causes, representing both parties and all political persuasions, found themselves victims of such "drone attacks."

Senate candidates themselves raised $767 million for their 2012 campaigns, and House candidates raised some $1,074 million (all figures are from Center for Responsive Politics 2012a). As always, incumbents outspent challengers by large amounts. The average Senate incumbent raised $11.3 million, whereas challengers averaged almost $1.3 million, and candidates for open seats averaged almost $2.6 million. House candidates' numbers followed the same pattern: incumbents' average spending was $1.5 million, challengers' was $244,000, and open-seat candidates spent an average of $453 million. Spending levels ranged widely: some incumbents spent very little; others broke the bank, so to speak. For the record, the costliest Senate race—more than $70 million—occurred in Massachusetts, where Democrat Elizabeth Warren upended Scott Brown, the GOP incumbent. Spending in the Connecticut and Texas Senate races topped $50 million. The most expensive House race occurred in Minnesota, where Republican Michele Bachmann—a loud voice from the Tea Party movement and a 2012 presidential hopeful—fought off a challenge from Democrat Jim Graves. Bachmann spent more than $11 million to bring out a bare majority of the 174,241 votes cast—at a cost of $65 per vote (MPR News 2012). Both these races were magnets for contributions nationwide. More than $10 million was spent in California's 30th district, where Democrats Berman and Sherman battled each other.

We might expect Republican candidates—with their ties to corporate and financial supporters—to outspend their Democratic foes. However, in 2012 that held true only for House candidates. In Senate contests, Democratic contenders raised on average about $9.2 million, whereas their Republican foes averaged $7.5 million. This might be one reason for the party's unexpected success in protecting its incumbents and capturing GOP seats. The parties' national and Capitol Hill committees raised and spent their own funds, and in many cases, candidates' spending was overrun by money from the Super PACs. Republicans were bankrolled by American Crossroads, Crossroads GPS (both associated with GOP operative Karl Rove), and the U.S. Chamber of Commerce; Democrats benefited from such allied groups as Majority PAC and Patriot Majority USA. Such groups behave as investors: that is, they want to support winners or those who could win in tight races

One of the lessons buried in the 2012 financial numbers, however, is that although candidates must command *enough* money to broadcast their message, they don't necessarily have to spend *more* than their opponents do. Indeed, some of the largest donors of the year were found to have wasted their money. The top 20 Super PACs supporting individual congressional candidates lost 15 races and won only 5 (Center for Responsive Politics 2012b). Perhaps the rest of us can take some comfort in learning that these billionaires made poor political investments, allowing their enthusiasms to outrun their common sense.

As noted, some Super PACs focused on individual congressional races. The American Sunrise PAC raised $250,000 to support Patrick Murphy, a Democrat in Florida's 22nd district who challenged Rep. Allen B. West, who received $1 million from the Treasure Coast Jobs Coalition. "We don't have the kind of budget to go in with million-dollar TV buys," said the Democratic PAC's organizer. "We think that's a blunt instrument, where we can go in with a scalpel" (Confessore and McGinty 2012, A1, A12). Murphy won in a very close contest.

New York mayor Michael Bloomberg, a billionaire and a registered independent, announced one Super PAC that surfaced late in the campaign season. He planned to spend from $10 million to $15 million on "a flurry of advertising" to support candidates, regardless of party affiliation, who supported his three major policy concerns: legalizing same-sex marriage, tougher gun laws, and reforming public schools (Hernandez 2012). Although his commitment came only two weeks before the November balloting, the Mayor and his aides were "betting that his financial support [could] make a major difference in especially close contests" (Hernandez 2012).

The Outcomes

On the surface, the congressional races in 2012 reinstated the status quo established only two years before: Democrats held on to their control of the Senate, and Republicans continued to have the majority in the House. There were important differences, however. Democrats won two more Senate seats, which—with the two independents who caucus with them—gave their party a potential 55–45 majority for the 113th Congress, a more solid position than in the 112th Congress. The party was able to defend its incumbents' seats in 15 states, along with replacing retirees in five states—Hawaii, New Mexico, North Dakota, Virginia, and Wisconsin. Only in deep-red Nebraska did the Democrats fall short of replacing their retiree. In addition, they gained seats from Republicans in Indiana and Massachusetts and from an independent in Connecticut. Two independents will caucus with them— reelected Vermonter Bernie Sanders, the chamber's only professed Socialist, and a newcomer who replaced a moderate Republican: Maine's Angus King, who had served two terms as the state's governor, also as an independent.

In the House, Republicans retained their majority, with Democrats gaining only eight seats. The final count was 234 Republicans and 200 Democrats.[5] Despite the Democrats' efforts to unseat Republicans of the 2010 class, only 11 were defeated (and 2 by GOP rivals in the primaries). Though their majority shrank, the Republicans still won their second-largest majority in 60 years and their third-largest since the Great Depression. However, all six nonvoting delegates are Democrats.[6] Fewer minor parties seemed to have traction in 2012.

House Democrats took scant comfort in the fact that they appeared to have attracted more of the popular vote than their GOP counterparts did. According to numbers compiled by a *Washington Post* statistician, Democrats won roughly 49 percent of the House vote, compared to 48.5 percent for Republicans. "Redistricting drew such a GOP-friendly map that, in a neutral environment, Republicans [had] an inherent advantage . . . Without the friendly map, Democrats would have likely gained significantly more than the . . . seats they will add" (Blake 2012). The margin varies depending on whether unopposed candidates or same-party candidates who faced off (as happened in several California districts) are counted. But any way the votes are counted, the Democrats came out slightly ahead.

The major reason for the votes-to-seats gap was aggressive GOP-controlled districting in such states as Florida, North Carolina, Ohio, Pennsylvania, and

Virginia. In Pennsylvania, President Obama won 52 percent of the votes, and Sen. Bob Casey defeated his Republican rival by 8 points, but Democrats won only 5 of the 18 House seats—though all by large margins. Only one of the 13 Republican winners pulled more than 65 percent of the vote. (That is, Democrats who won in districts by large margins tended to waste their party's votes.) In Ohio, Obama won by 2 points, and Sen. Sherrod Brown by 5, but Democrats emerged with only 4 of the state's 16 seats. In Wisconsin Obama won by 7 and Democratic Senate candidate Rep. Tammy Baldwin by 5, but only 3 of the state's 8 House members were Democrats. Similar patterns appeared in Florida and Virginia.

Democrats, of course, happily engage in creative districting when they have the power to do so as well. After a party-controlled districting plan in 2011, Illinois Democrats picked up 5 House seats with the new boundaries, to hold 12 of the state's 18 seats. On the other hand, this was President Obama's home state, which he carried by a 17-point margin in 2012. So it might be argued that the party's advantage reflected the state's partisan balance.

The Democrats are victims of a second phenomenon: what might be termed a demographic "silent gerrymander." They tend to live in crowded places: large and medium-sized cities and bustling inner suburbs. Republicans are more likely to be entrenched in small towns and rural areas. Therefore, more than creative districting by the GOP is at play in placing Democrats at an overall disadvantage.

California offers another model of a more accurate measure of partisan preferences: its districts, for the first time in 2012, more closely reflect their voters' competitive ranks. Democrats hold 38 of the state's 53 seats in the 113th Congress—a delegation that includes 5 Asian Americans, 9 Hispanics, and 18 women. This division reflects the state's diversity and apparently its political inclination: President Obama carried the state by 21 points, and Sen. Dianne Feinstein won by 23. (Presidential candidates made no campaign stops in the state, although they visited to raise funds. Californians avoided the deluge of presidential messages, but they endured blizzards of media messages from state and local candidates, as well as ads for and against state and local propositions.)

Ten days after the balloting, the last of three longtime GOP notables, six-term representative Brian Bilbray, conceded to Democrat Scott Peters after a hard-fought race in San Diego's 52nd district. Bilbray's old 50th district had enjoyed a 10-point GOP edge; the Citizens Redistricting Commission cut the advantage in the new 52nd down to three points—35 percent Republican, 32 percent Democratic, 27 percent independent (Perry 2012, AA3). Other notables defeated in 2012 were nine-term representative (and former state treasurer and gubernatorial candidate) Dan Lungren and seven-term representative Mary Bono Mack of Riverside, who first won her seat in 1998 after the death of her husband, pop music celebrity Sonny Bono. However, as already noted, such results mainly reflect the state's current balance of power.

To sum up, the 2012 congressional elections would seem, like the presidential race, to ratify the status quo ante: Democrats continue to rule the U.S. Senate—but with two added seats, still not a filibuster-proof supermajority. In the House, the Republicans still dominate—though with eight fewer seats and the absence of a popular-vote mandate. Yet lying beneath these returns indicating little overall change, we discover a dizzying range of individual candidates and their stratagems, various levels of partisan activity, and the varying impact of campaign financing. All of these colorful details represent layers of political life far beyond the lofty presidential contests.

NOTES

1. Texas, which gained four seats, was the biggest winner; Arizona and Florida gained two each, and five other states (Georgia, Nevada, South Carolina, Utah, and Washington) gained a single seat.
2. Losing two House seats were New York and Ohio. Ten others lost one apiece (Illinois, Iowa, Louisiana, New Jersey, Massachusetts, Michigan, Minnesota, Missouri, Ohio, and Pennsylvania).
3. For the record, the House committees are the Democratic Congressional Campaign Committee (CC or DCCC, spoken as "D-triple-C") and the National Republican Campaign Committee (NRCC). The Senate counterparts are the Democratic Senatorial Campaign Committee (DSCC) and the National Republican Senatorial Committee (NRSC). The parties' national governing bodies aid them: the Democratic and Republican National Committees (DNC and RNC, respectively).
4. Same-sex marriage had been before voters no less than 32 times and had been rejected every time. In 2004, 11 states placed measures opposing same-sex marriage on state ballots; all were adopted. One objective of these was to mobilize conservative voters who would also vote to reelect President George W. Bush; the Ohio turnout proved decisive for Bush's victory. By 2012, however, six states and the District of Columbia had legalized same-sex marriage. In all of the states where the issue was on the ballot in 2012—Maine, Maryland, and Washington—same-sex marriage won approval. Minnesota voters rejected an amendment that would have placed a definition of traditional marriage in the state constitution.
5. Rep. Jesse Jackson Jr. (D-IL) resigned for health reasons following his reelection, and a runoff between two Republicans was scheduled in Louisiana's 3rd district.
6. These delegates are from the District of Columbia and the insular territories: American Samoa, Guam, the Northern Mariana Islands, Puerto Rico, and the Virgin Islands.

REFERENCES

Associated Press. 2012. "Exit Poll: Many Still Blame Bush for Bad Economy." November 7.

Barone, Michael, and Chuck McCutcheon. 2011. *The Almanac of American Politics, 2012.* Chicago: University of Chicago Press.

Blake, Aaron. 2012. "Democratic House Candidates Winning the Popular Vote, Despite Big GOP Majority." *Washington Post,* November 9.

Brooks, David. 2009. "The Obama Slide." *New York Times,* September 1, A29.

Canon, David T. 1990. *Actors, Athletes, and Astronauts: Political Amateurs in the United States.* Chicago: University of Chicago Press.

Carney, Eliza Newlin. 2012. "DCCC Works to Make Democrats Competitive." *Roll Call,* June 11, 4.

CBS News. 2010. "Poll: Low Favorability Ratings for Pelosi, Reid." March 22.

Center for Responsive Politics. 2012a. "Incumbent Advantage." OpenSecrets.org. November 9.

Center for Responsive Politics. 2012b. "Single-Candidate Super PACs Post Mixed Record in Congressional Races." OpenSecrets.org. November 8.

Confessore, Nicholas, and Jo Craven McGinty. 2012. "New 'Super PACs' Alter Landscape for House Races." *New York Times,* October 9, A1, A12.

Cooper, Michael. 2010. "Statehouse Gains Could Give GOP Edge on Redistricting." *New York Times,* September 8, A1, A3.

Davidson, Roger H., Walter J. Oleszek, and Frances E. Lee. 2011. *Congress and Its Members.* 13th ed. 53–58, 84–87.

Dionne, E. J. 2012. "Sherrod Brown's Lessons for Obama." *Washington Post,* October 10.

Elias, Thomas D. 2012. "Vote against Transparency Helps Explain GOP Plight." *Santa Barbara News-Press,* April 1, G1, G4.

Freking, Kevin, and Michael R. Blood. 2012. "Retirements Caused by Redistricting Will Affect Races." *Santa Barbara News-Press,* January 11, A6.

Garrett, Major. 2012. "Soft Sell." *National Journal* 44 (March 24): 44.

Goodnough, Abby. 2011. "Barney Frank a Top Liberal, Won't See Election." *New York Times,* November 28, A14.

Hernandez, Raymond. 2012. "For Bloomberg, a 'Super PAC' of His Own Making." *New York Times,* October 18, A1, A25.

Hiltzik, Michael. 2012a. "Here's What You Don't Know about Health Care Reform." *Los Angeles Times,* March 25, B1, B8.

Hiltzik, Michael. 2012b. "Initiative Process a Waste of Money." *Los Angeles Times,* November 4, B1, B4.

Irwin, Neil. 2012. "What Do Voters Really Think about the Economy: Three Lessons from Exit Polls." *Washington Post,* November 8.

Jacobson, Gary C. 2011. "Legislative Success and Political Failure: The Public's Reaction to Barack Obama's Early Presidency." *Presidential Studies Quarterly* 41 (2): 220–243.

Lauter, David. 2012. "Voters' Shifting Attitudes Weaken Romney Strategy." *Los Angeles Times,* October 25, A1.

Lockhead, Carolyn. 2012. "California Congressional Delegation Faces Shakeup." *San Francisco Chronicle,* January 13, A4.

Maisel, Louis Sandy. 1982. *From Obscurity to Oblivion: Running in the Congressional Primary.* Knoxville: University of Tennessee Press.

McGreevy, Patrick. 2010. "State Begins New Era in Redistricting." *Los Angeles Times,* November 19, A1, A19.

McGreevy, Patrick, and Evan Halper. 2012. "Number of State Voters Sets Record." *Los Angeles Times,* November 1, A1, A16.

Megerian. 2012. "Effect of Secret Funds Weighed." *Los Angeles Times,* November 13, AA1.

Megerian, Chris, and Evan Halper. 2012. "Naming Donors Fails to Disperse the Fog." *Los Angeles Times,* November 6, A1, A9.

Merl, Jean. 2012a. "Howard Berman Gets a Thumbs-Up from—Darrell Issa?" *Los Angeles Times,* April 5, A5.

Merl, Jean. 2012b. "Race Gets Rough and Tumble." *Los Angeles Times,* October 13, A1.

Miller, Joshua. 2011. "Race Ratings: GOP Looks for Major N. C. Gains." *Roll Call,* August 8, 4–5.

MPR News. 2012. "Bachmann Spends Most Per Vote among MN Congressional Hopefuls." November 12. http://www.mprnews.org.

Nehring, Ron. 2012. "California Congressional Districts, 2012–2022." http://www.ronnehring.com.

Newhauser, Daniel. 2012. "House Members Fight on Message." *Roll Call,* July 23, 1.

Perry, Tony. 2012. "ReBilbray Concedes Defeat." *Los Angeles Times,* November 17, AA3.

Pew Research Center. 2007. "Trends in Political Values and Core Attitudes: 1987–2007." http://www.people-press.org/2007/03/22/trends-in-political-values-and-core-attitudes-1987-2007/.

Pew Research Center. 2010. "Distrust, Discontent, Anger, and Partisan Rancor: The People and Their Government." April 18.

Pew Research Center. 2011. "Pessimism about National Economy Rises, Personal Financial Views Hold Steady." June 23.

Pew Research Center. 2012. "Public Less Negative about Economic News." October 10.

Rothenberg, Stuart. 2009. "Sizing Up the 2010 Senate Contests in the Summer of 2009." *Roll Call,* August 3, 9.

Rothenberg, Stuart. 2012. "Perfect Storm for Democratic Pickups." *Roll Call,* November 15, 20.

Rubin, Jennifer. 2012. "Will They Reject the Next Todd Akin or Sharron Angle?" *Washington Post,* November 19.

Saillant, Catherine. "Race Is Tight for House Seat in Ventura County." *Los Angeles Times,* October 15, AA1.

San Francisco Chronicle. 2012. "Stark's History of Burned Bridges." August 17.

Schlesinger, Joseph A. 1966. *Ambition and Politics: Political Careers in the United States.* Chicago: Rand McNally.

Seelye, Katharine Q. 2012. "Another Senate Race Seizes on Rape Remark." *New York Times,* August 23, A15.

Simon, Richard, and Phil Willon. 2012. "More House Seats Up for Grabs." *Los Angeles Times,* January 13, A15.

Trygstad, Kyle. 2012. "Cecil Says Strong Candidates Helped DSCC Win." *Roll Call,* November 15, 16.

Walsh, Edward. 1992. "In Every Campaign, There Is a Recruiting Season." *Washington Post,* November 12, A1.

Wilson, Reid, and Steven Shepard. 2012. "Drawn and Quartered." *National Journal* 44 (March 31): 14–19.

6 The Effect of the 2012 Elections on Party Polarization

Sean M. Theriault and Megan M. Moeller

The 2012 elections are best understood when described within the historical context in which they were conducted. Beginning with the 1968 election, it seemed as though the Democrats were severely disadvantaged in presidential elections. The overwhelming victories of Nixon, Reagan, and George H. W. Bush were only briefly interrupted by Carter's victory in the wake of Watergate. Republican success in Congress was slower to be realized. Republicans achieved a majority in the Senate only in 1980 (and lost it six years later); House Republicans would have to wait an additional 14 years to become a majority.

The elections that emerged in the 1990s and beyond had a different flavor than those preceding them. In the first section of this chapter, we analyze one of the most important characteristics of both congressional and presidential elections—the intense competition to win. After laying this groundwork, we discuss party polarization in various political arenas, including the electorate, member's congressional districts, the states, and finally Congress itself. We end our chapter by speculating about the future of party polarization in the United States.

Intense Party Competition

As the United States was recovering from the Great Depression and World War II, the Democrats were forging an electoral coalition that included Southerners, union members, Catholics, African Americans, and urban dwellers, a coalition that would come to be known as "the New Deal Coalition." In helping to bring about the 1932 realigning election, this coalition became the dominant electoral formation that delivered to Democrats both the White House and Congress for much of the next 50 years (Stanley and Niemi 1991; Carmines and Stanley 1992). Even as the New Deal Coalition began breaking down in presidential contests, it remained unified behind Democrats until the Civil Rights Act of 1964 and the Voting Rights Act of 1965 forced such internal tensions within the coalition that the ideological fissures between the disparate groups became too great for one party to manage.

The tensions within the Democratic Party took time to become visible fissures with electoral consequences. In the 1964 election, for example, the Democrats had 130 more seats than the Republicans in the House and 30 more seats in the Senate. Although these margins are particularly large, they are similar to the margins that the Democrats enjoyed as late as the 1970s.

Except for two congresses—the 80th (1947–1948) and 83rd (1953–1954)—the Democrats were a majority in the House and Senate from 1933 until 1980. With the Democrats safely in the majority, representing an ideologically diverse set of constituencies, Republicans understood that the way they could most influence policymaking in Congress was to constructively engage the majority. Because Democrats had so many conservative members and because the Republicans had so many moderate-to-liberal members, Republicans frequently found ideological counterparts in the majority party to help them work their will or, at a minimum, influence policies or even the process itself. So long as the Republicans did not mind not being chairs of the committees, policymaking in Congress did not regularly decay into partisan warfare.

Republicans achieved majority party status at different times in the different chambers. Heading into the 1980 election, most pundits thought the presidential election between the incumbent, Jimmy Carter, and his Republican challenger, Ronald Reagan, would be exceedingly close. No one thought that the Republicans had a prayer of becoming a majority party in either the House or the Senate. From the 89th to the 96th Congresses (1965–1980), the Democrats, on average, had held a 20-seat margin over the Republicans in the Senate. When Americans awoke on the day after the 1980 election, Reagan's landslide not only had delivered him 44 states in the electoral college but also had delivered to the Republicans 12 additional seats in the Senate, which was enough to give them a six-seat majority (see Figure 6.1 for the margin size of the majority party in both chambers).

Prior to 1994, the Democrats' lock on the House was as great as it had been on the Senate before the 1980 election. From the 89th to the 103rd Congress (1965–1994), the Democrats held an average of 263 House seats—an average margin of 91 seats. Only a handful of people in the United States thought that the Republicans could win a House majority in 1994, and most of them worked for House Minority Whip Newt Gingrich (R-GA). Gingrich's national strategy—embodied by the "Contract with America"—paid off when the Democrats went from a majority of 82 seats to a minority of 26 seats in what became known as the Republican Tsunami of 1994.

Since the Republicans became competitive in each chamber, the majority size for either party has been almost two-thirds smaller in both chambers. In the 17 congresses since the 1980 election, the majority has held, on average, fewer than 54 seats, which is one fewer than the seats the Democrats will control in the 113th Congress. In the nine congresses since the Republicans became a majority in the House (1995–2012), the majority has held an

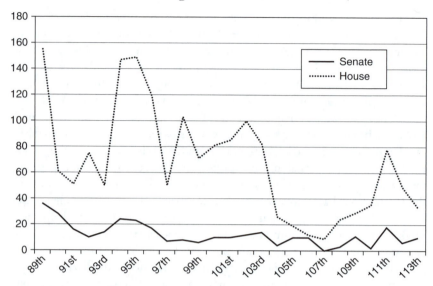

Figure 6.1 Margin Size for the Majority Party in Congress, 89th–113th Congresses (1965–2014)

average of 233 seats, resulting in a 31-seat majority, which is a bit less than the margin they will have in 2013. With perhaps only the 2008 and 2012 elections as exceptions, the future majority party in both chambers of Congress has been in doubt on the morning of Election Day.

Although the American electoral landscape may be shrinking over time (Shaw 2006), the stakes have drastically risen for the districts and states that remain electorally competitive for both parties. This phenomenon has consequences not only for electoral politics, but also for how Congress operates internally. The legislative process and the chamber floors have increasingly become arenas for electoral politics, which has contributed to some of the lowest congressional approval numbers in history.

The intense party competition in Congress has been mirrored in our presidential elections. In all but two of the seven presidential elections from 1964 to 1988, the winning candidate enjoyed an electoral college victory of more than 300 votes (see Figure 6.2). Since then, no candidate has enjoyed such a margin. The average margin since 1992 has been 130 votes, which is only four votes greater than Obama's victory in 2012.

Such close election results in the presidential and congressional races gives evidence to minority parties that their chance to enter majority party status is just an election away. The increased probability of winning—and losing—a majority has happened at the same time that the parties have grown increasingly polarized in every arena of American politics. We now turn to that polarization.

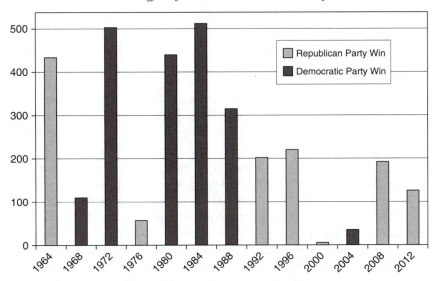

Figure 6.2 Electoral College Victory Margin, 1964–2012

Party Polarization of the Electorate

Along with the rise of intense party competition over the last several decades, the ideologies of the political elite have increasingly diverged. Since the 1970s, party activists, members of Congress, and party leadership in both parties have gradually moved toward their respective ideological poles (Rohde 1991; Sinclair 2006; McCarty, Poole, and Rosenthal 2006; Theriault 2008). Not only have Republicans moved to the right and Democrats to the left, but members within each party are more and more ideologically and politically unified as well. By almost any definition, elite polarization has been widely recognized by scholars and pundits alike. Since elite cues can powerfully affect mass behavior (Zaller 1992), polarization among politicians has had dramatic consequences for the electorate.

The *American Political Science Review* released a special report in 1950 titled "Toward a More Responsible Two-Party System." The authoring task force bemoaned the lack of clearly differentiated policy positions between the Democratic and Republican parties and the inadequate cohesion within parties at the time. Without clear distinctions between the parties, the report reasoned, voters had a difficult time making meaningful decisions in the voting booth. In that era of committee government, many conservative voters as well as liberal voters elected various breeds of Democrats: some liberal, some more conservative than many Republicans. Similarly, Republicans elected to Congress spanned the ideological spectrum, with some more liberal than many Democrats. In the modern era, however, polarized parties present voters with a notably discrete choice. The criticisms of the 1950 report seem foreign in today's political climate. We next outline the various ways in which the electorate has polarized.

Partisan Polarization

As the parties have ideologically diverged, the electorate has become increasingly sorted by party—what scholars have termed "partisan sorting" (Fiorina 2005; Abramowitz and Saunders 1998). Partisan sorting began in the South with conservative voters who had been electing conservative Democrats to Congress. As the distinctions between Democratic and Republican parties became clearer, conservative Southerners began electing Republicans instead. Over time, voters from both sides of the ideological spectrum have continued to "sort" themselves by voting for the presidential candidate from the party that better matches their ideology. Said another way, liberals are voting for Democratic presidential candidates, and conservatives are voting for Republicans more often than they have in the past (see Figure 6.3).[1]

Although the rate of liberals voting for Obama in 2012 was slightly lower than in 2008, the liberal vote for Obama exceeded the liberal vote for Kerry in 2004 as well as that vote for the Democratic candidate in any election between 1992 and 2012. It is also worth noting that although self–identified conservatives have not voted for Republicans at quite as high of rates as liberals vote for Democrats (except for 2000), conservatives in each election account for between 9 percent and 13 percent more of the electorate than liberals; thus, their greater voting heterogeneity is not surprising.

This phenomenon is not unique to presidential elections. Figure 6.4 illustrates that in House elections too, the rates of conservatives voting for

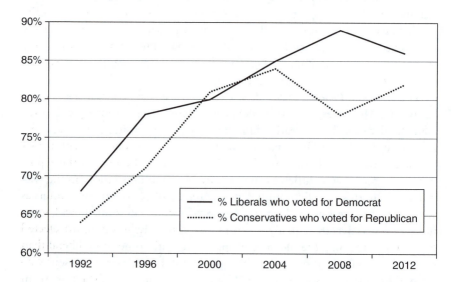

Figure 6.3 Partisan Sorting in Presidential Elections

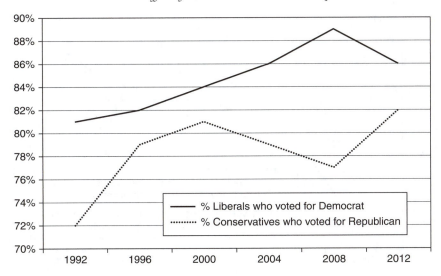

Figure 6.4 Partisan Sorting in House Elections

Republican representatives and of liberals voting for Democratic representatives have increased markedly over the last 20 years. House Republican candidates never secured a higher proportion of conservatives' votes than they did in 2012. But in the 2008 elections, Democrats had never secured as high a proportion of liberals' votes as they did in House elections.

One natural consequence of partisan sorting is that individual voters' choices for president and congressional representative display heightened agreement (Hetherington 2008). Figure 6.5 indicates that in 1992, among people who voted for a Democratic representative, 84 percent also voted for the Democratic presidential candidate. By the 2012 elections, that percentage had risen to 93 percent. Those who voted for a Republican representative displayed an even starker increase in their vote consistency; the percentage of those voters who also cast their ballots for the Republican presidential candidate rose from 76 percent in 1992 to 92 percent in 2012.

The increased party competition resulting from elite polarization means that parties have more to gain from an electoral victory and more to lose from an electoral loss. Unsurprisingly, parties have recently escalated their mobilization efforts in order to maximize their vote share in as many races as possible, and voter turnout has correspondingly increased (Hetherington 2008). Not only are ideological voters turning out at a higher rate; Hetherington finds that moderates and non-ideologues are turning out in higher rates as well. Despite voters' insistence that they dislike partisan fighting (Hibbing and Theiss-Morse 2002), voters have not disengaged from the political process as a result of polarization. In fact, elite polarization seems to have stimulated political participation among the electorate. The United States Elections Project at George Mason University reports that among the

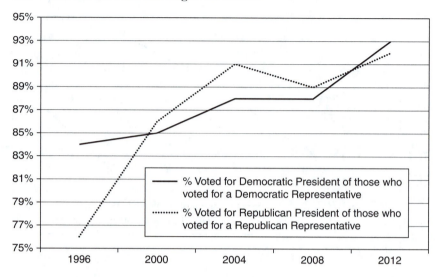

Figure 6.5 House and Presidential Vote Matches

eligible voters, turnout has increased each presidential election, from 52 percent in 1996 to 61.6 percent in 2008. Exit polls indicate that the estimated turnout rate for 2012 remains elevated at 58.7 percent—a slight slip from the high in 2008.

For all the effects of elite polarization, the percentages of voters who identify as Democrats, Republicans, and independents have remained relatively constant over the last six presidential elections. From 1992 to 2012, the percentage of voters who identify as Democrat hovered between 37 percent and 39 percent in each presidential election. Republican identifiers made up between 35 percent and 37 percent of the electorate from 1992 to 2004, but in 2008 and 2012, Republican voters' share of the electorate dropped slightly to 32 percent. Independents, on the other hand, made up 26 percent to 27 percent of the electorate from 1992 to 2004 and actually jumped slightly to 29 percent in 2008 and 2012. Clearly, party polarization has not affected the mass public to the extent of spurring increased partisan identification. Some disagreement remains, however, regarding the extent to which elite polarization has engendered ideological polarization among the electorate.

Ideological Polarization

Although there is widespread agreement that the electorate has undergone partisan sorting, such sorting does not necessarily imply that the ideological distribution of voters has changed at all. Since the 1960s, scholars have demonstrated that Americans do not know or care very much about politics (Campbell et al. 1960; Delli Carpini and Keeter 1996). Those in the electorate who do know and care about politics tend to be ideologues, whereas those who know and care little are more likely to identify as moderate (Converse 1964). Although elite polarization has increased party efforts to mobilize voters—including moderate voters—these mobilization efforts are not necessarily capable of shifting voters' moderate ideological preferences to extreme preferences. Using data from the National Election Study (NES) through the 2004 election, Fiorina (2005) shows that, indeed, a plurality of Americans remain moderate and are not nearly as ideologically disparate as the news media make them out to be. Even with regard to cleavage issues such as abortion, most Americans hold moderate attitudes. In 2012, for example, only 42 percent of voters took an absolutist position toward abortion, with 13 percent saying abortion should always be illegal and 29 percent saying it should always be legal. The majority of Americans believe in some varying degrees of restriction on abortion, rather than holding an ideologically extreme position. Fiorina argues that unlike the elites, the electorate has undergone very little *ideological* polarization, in which the policy preferences of the electorate shift from a centered, unimodal distribution to a bimodal distribution concentrated at the poles.

The exit polls from the 2012 elections, however, indicate that the rates of self-reported moderates have declined recently, as rates of conservatives and liberals have increased. Figure 6.6 illustrates that the percentage of voters who identify as liberal rose from 20 percent in 1996 to 25 percent in 2012. Similarly, the percentage of voters who identify as conservative increased from 30 percent in 1992 to 35 percent in 2012. Moderates, who constituted a full 50 percent of the electorate in 2000, have dwindled down to 41 percent of the

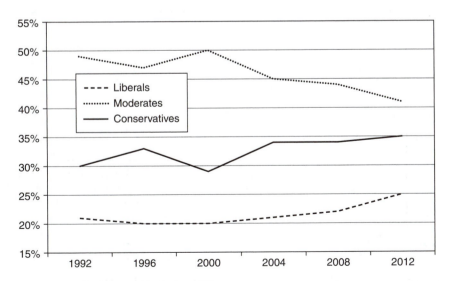

Figure 6.6 Self-Reported Ideologies of Voters

electorate but continue to account for a plurality of voters. It is worth noting that in each of the last five presidential elections, a plurality of self-identified moderates have voted for the Democratic presidential candidate, including 2012, in which 56 percent of moderates voted for Obama.

Demographic Polarization

One of the most noted aspects of the 2012 elections is the extent to which the partisan divide has taken on a demographic slant. In 2012, Obama won the vast majority of votes of the two fastest-growing demographics in the country. Figure 6.7 indicates that Obama achieved 71 percent of the Hispanic vote, up from 67 percent in 2008. He also gained 73 percent of the Asian American vote, an increase of 11 points from 62 percent in 2008. Although the Hispanic and Asian American vote constitute only 10 percent and 3 percent of the electorate, respectively, the Census Bureau reported that these two demographic groups both grew by more than 40 percent between 2000 and 2010, compared to the nation's growth rate of less than 10 percent. In 1992, only 2 percent of voters were Hispanic, and 1 percent were of Asian descent. Hispanic voters' share of the electorate quintupled in last 20 years, to make up 10 percent of voters in 2012, and Asian American voters tripled to 3 percent.

In 1992, 87 percent of voters were white, and 8 percent were African American. By 2012, the percentage of white voters had dropped 15 points to 72 percent. Conversely, African American voters gained five points of the vote share, making up 13 percent of voters in 2012. African Americans have consistently voted for the Democratic Party at greater rates than any other

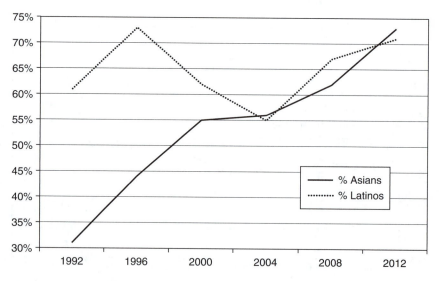

Figure 6.7 Percent of Group Voting for Democratic Presidential Candidate

demographic group. In fact, Republican presidential candidates have failed to secure more than 12 percent of the African American vote in the last 20 years. During that time period, white voters have accounted for a steadily declining percentage of the voting population while remaining the only major demographic group that supports Republican presidential candidates at greater rates than Democratic presidential candidates. In no presidential election since 1992 have more than 44 percent of white voters cast their ballots for the Democratic candidate. The 2012 presidential election not only reaffirmed the trends of most white voters opting for the Republican candidate and most non-white voters choosing the Democratic candidate; it magnified the trends among the demographic groups that are growing the most.

These results were also borne out in the House elections, with whites supporting Republicans at the same rate at which they supported Romney and Asian Americans supporting Democrats at the same rate at which they supported Obama. African Americans' and Hispanics' support for Democratic representatives was two to three points lower than their support for Obama, but remained overwhelmingly in favor of the Democrats. The stark partisan divide in the quickly expanding segments of the electorate has led to speculation among pundits and scholars alike about the sustainability of the Republican platform and its mass appeal, especially to Hispanic voters.

Comparing the 1996 election, when Clinton was reelected, to the 2012 election, when Obama was reelected vividly shows the demographic divide between the parties. In 1996, 93 percent of Republican candidate Bob Dole's votes came from Caucasians—the remaining votes came from African Americans (3 percent), Hispanics (2 percent), and others (2 percent). In 2012, Romney's numbers were almost exactly the same—90 percent of his votes came from Caucasians, 1 percent from African Americans, 6 percent from Hispanics, and 3 percent from others. The change from Clinton to Obama, however, is remarkable. Whereas Clinton got 74 percent of his votes from Caucasians, Obama got only 55 percent. Both Hispanic and African American voters made up seven additional percentage points of Obama's votes versus Clinton's (going from 17 percent to 24 percent for African Americans and 7 percent to 14 percent for Hispanics). The last 7 percent of Obama's votes came from the other racial groups, an increase of five percentage points over Clinton.

The 2012 election also demonstrated that the partisan divide remains relatively gendered. The gender gap refers to the difference in the percentage of women and the percentage of men voting for a given candidate. A gender gap in which a greater proportion of women than men prefer the Democratic candidate has persisted in each presidential election since 1980 and remained apparent in 2012. Although the gender gap is popularly attributed to women's attitudes diverging from those of men, women's attitudes have remained fairly constant over time. In truth, the gender gap is the result of men's ideological movement to the right (Kaufman and Petrocik 1999). Not only have women consistently voted for the Democratic presidential candidate at a rate hovering between 51 percent and 56 percent since 1996; they also have turned out at a higher rate than men by between four and eight points. Although women's support of Obama in 2012 dipped by a single percentage point from 2008, the women's vote played a critical role in Obama's victory.

Until 2008, exit polls categorized responses only by race *and* gender into white and non-white categories, making it difficult to make comparisons about the gender gap for any non-white demographic groups. Exit polls from 2008 and 2012, however, reveal that in both elections, white women, African American women, and Hispanic women voted more Democratic than their male counterparts. Further, the gaps were much more pronounced in 2012, especially among African American and Hispanic voters, for whom the gender gaps increased from 1 to 9 points and from 4 to 11 points, respectively. Although Hispanic men remained virtually unchanged in their support for Obama between 2008 and 2012, Hispanics increased their support for Obama by a full eight points. In fact, Hispanics were the only demographic or gender group to vote for Obama at a higher rate in 2012 than in 2008. African American men, on the other hand, held the distinction of being the demographic/gender group that displayed the greatest decrease in support for Obama between 2008 and 2012, dropping eight points from a support rate of 95 percent to 87 percent. African American women's support of Obama remained unchanged. White women's support for Obama dropped by four points between 2008 and 2012, and white men's support for Obama decreased by six points. As a result, the gender gap between white men and white women increased from five to seven points. Even though white women remain more likely to support Obama than white men, a majority of white women in both elections (53 percent in 2008 and 56 percent in 2012) joined their male counterparts in voting for the Republican presidential candidate. White women were the only racial or ethnic group of women to vote predominately Republican.

Party Polarization of Members' Constituencies

As Lyndon Johnson won reelection in 1964, Democrats were expanding their domination on Capitol Hill. They captured more seats in the House (295) and Senate (68) than they have in any Congress since. As a consequence of their greater than two-to-one ratio in both chambers, the Democrats were representing a wide diversity of constituencies. In fact, Johnson's Republican opponent, Barry Goldwater, received a higher percentage of the two-party vote in states represented by Democrats in the Senate than in states represented by Republicans. Furthermore, Goldwater did less than one percentage point better in Republican representatives' districts than he did nationwide and approximately four percentage points worse in Democratic representatives' districts.

The 1966 House elections provided even more puzzling results for the partisanship of the constituencies than the 1964 elections. The Democrats lost 47 seats, but those losses primarily came in the North, where Goldwater had been trounced; the party remained dominant in the South, where Goldwater had performed better. The partisan difference between the Democratic and Republican representatives' districts became even smaller.

To measure the underlying partisanship of members' districts and senators' states systematically, we calculate the Republican presidential vote advantage (RPVA) in each district. This statistic, which is sometimes called the normalized vote, measures the difference between the Republican presidential candidate's two-party vote in the district and the candidate's nationwide percentage. For example, 2008 Republican presidential candidate John McCain received 67 percent of the vote in Wyoming but only 47 percent of the vote nationwide, making Wyoming's RPVA 20 percent.

Figure 6.8 shows the difference in the districts' partisan tilt represented by Democrats and Republicans in the House of Representatives and Senate since the 89th Congress (1965–1966). In the 1960s, Democrats represented districts where, on average, the Republican presidential candidate did about 10 percentage points worse than in the districts represented by Republicans. During the same time period, the difference between Democratic

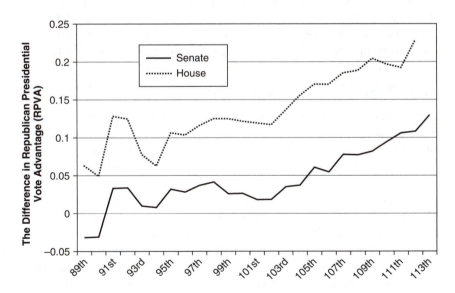

Figure 6.8 The Partisan Difference between Democratic and Republican Constituencies, 89th–113th Congresses (1965–2014)

presidential candidates and the Democratic senators was about half as much. Within thirty years, both numbers would double. In the 112th Congress (2011–2012), House Republicans represented districts that were 23 percent more Republican than the districts represented by Democrats.[2] The difference in the Senate was about half as much. Following the 2012 elections, the Senate Democrats' states were 13 percent less Republican than the Senate Republicans' states.

Political scientists have pointed to a number of reasons that the constituencies represented by Democrats and Republicans are increasingly distinct, including the design and implementation of partisan redistricting plans (Hirsch 2003; Carson, Engstrom, and Roberts 2007), the geographic sorting of constituents into like-minded neighborhoods (Oppenheimer 2005; Bishop 2008), the ideological sorting that has occurred within parties (Fiorina 2005), and the extremism of party activists (Fiorina 2005; Brady, Han, and Pope 2007). The disputes between the proponents of these arguments, though illuminating, are immaterial for our purposes in this chapter—all of these studies agree that the districts are becoming increasingly distinct.

The growing gap between the two major party constituencies not only tells an electoral story but also can provide clues to an institutional story. If the constituencies that Democrats represent are increasingly distinct from the constituencies that Republicans represent, the members' decisions over whether to side with their constituents or with their parties are increasingly rare. If members' partisan identification and constituencies' partisan tilt point in the same direction, so too do their primary voting considerations, thus decreasing the number of difficult votes members face and increasing the proportion of votes in which the parties are internally consistent and externally divergent (Rohde 1991; Aldrich 1995; Aldrich and Rohde 2001).

Party Polarization among the States

Not only are the constituencies that Republican members of Congress represent increasingly distinct from the constituencies that Democratic members of Congress represent, but so too have the states become increasingly distinct. Over time, both liberal and conservative voters have migrated to live near others who share their political persuasions. In tandem with voters' partisan sorting, the electorate has progressively sorted itself geographically as well (Oppenheimer 2005). Much of this sorting has occurred at neighborhood, county, and district levels. Given the prevalence of "red state, blue state" rhetoric in the political sphere, it should be no surprise that some degree of sorting has occurred on a state level as well. Some, such as Fiorina, would dispute that red states are brimming solely with those who frequently search Google for "founding fathers quotes," "clean jokes," and "flag clipart" or that every single citizen of a blue state spends his or her nights googling "top

Table 6.1 Presidential Victory Margins by State

Year	Mean victory margin	Mean victory margin for GOP	Mean victory margin for Democrats
1992	9.7%	7.6%	10.8%
1996	13.1%	8.8%	15.7%
2000	15.2%	16.0%	14.0%
2004	16.1%	18.0%	13.0%
2008	18.1%	16.6%	19.2%
2012	17.2%	20.1%	14.6%

chef" and "mos def." The voting patterns of states, however, have indisputably transformed in the last several decades.

One of the most notable aspects of states' voting behavior over time is the change in distribution of Democratic and Republican presidential votes within states. Since 1992, the party that ultimately carries a state in the electoral college has won the popular vote in that state by increasingly wider margins. For example, Bush won Texas in 1992 by a margin of only 3 percent. By 2012, Romney won Texas by a margin of 16 percent, a drastically more definitive victory. As Table 6.1 shows, the average margin of victory for the presidential candidate who wins a given state has grown from 10 percent in 1992 to 18 percent in 2008. In 2012, the average margin of victory of Obama in the states that Obama carried and of Romney in the states that Romney carried was 17 percent, a rate slightly lower than in 2008 but still the second-highest in the 1992 to 2012 time period. Table 6.1 also indicates that from 1992 to 2008, the candidate who ultimately won the electoral college unsurprisingly received stronger margins of victory in the states he carried than his challenger won in the states that his challenger carried. This trend was broken, however, in 2012, when the average margin of victory Romney achieved in red states was 20 percent, but the average margin of victory Obama obtained in blue states was just less than 15 percent. Red states in 2012 voted against Obama at a higher rate than blue states voted for him.

Corresponding to an increase in average victory margins over the last six presidential elections, the number of states in which one candidate has won the state in a landslide has markedly grown. In 1992, only one state was decided by a margin of greater than 20 percent—a standard reached by 20 states in 2012. Similarly, the number of states decided by a margin of 3 percent or smaller has shrunk from 11 states in 1992 to only 4 states in 2012. These trends hold for other definitions of "landslide" and for smaller margins of victory. In 1992, only 19 states were decided by a margin of 10 percent or greater. In 2008 and 2012, that number climbed to 38 states. Likewise, from 1992 to 2000, seven states were decided by a margin of 2 percent or less, but in only two states in 2012 was the result so close. The extent to which these changes can be attributed to ideological polarization, partisan sorting, or geographic sorting among the electorate remains unclear. It is clear, however, that as elite polarization has grown, both Democratic and Republican presidential candidates have been winning states by stronger margins, more frequently. Even if the distribution of ideological preferences among the electorate remains moderate, partisans within states are voting more and more alike over time.

Partisans within states have also been incredibly consistent with their vote from election to election as partisans between states have been increasingly heterogeneous in their votes. In 31 states, plus the District of Columbia, the same party has won at least a plurality in each of the last six presidential elections. Said another way, 31 states have not changed their electoral college vote over the last 20 years. In the last four presidential elections, 40 states, plus the District of Columbia, have solidly remained in the hands of the same party. During this time, the Democratic and Republican candidates have equally shared only five states: Virginia, Ohio, Nevada, Florida, and Colorado. Between 2008 and 2012, the states were so consistent in their electoral college choices that only two, Indiana and North Carolina, changed parties. Since standard deviation is a measure of variation, we can measure the heterogeneity between states by the standard deviations of the two-party vote that the Republican presidential candidate received (RPV). A standard deviation of 0 indicates a complete lack of variation. For example, if every state had given Romney 47 percent of its two-party vote, the standard deviation of the RPV would be 0 (Theriault 2008). Larger standard deviation values reveal increased dispersion among the individual data points. The standard deviations of the RPV measured by state have generally increased over time, from 0.064 in 1992 to 0.105 in 2012, just slightly smaller than the standard deviation of 0.115 in 2008. This means that since 1992, states have become increasingly different from each other in their allocation of presidential votes. As elite polarization has grown, the states have undeniably displayed heightened intrastate homogeneity as well as heightened interstate heterogeneity in their electoral college votes.

Party Polarization in Congress

The recent congressional elections have brought about the most polarized Congress since at least the early 1900s. We analyze DW-NOMINATE data in this section to show how polarized the parties inside Congress have become (Poole and Rosenthal 1997). These data, which are generated from all non-consensual roll-call votes in both the House and the Senate, range from –1 for extremely liberal members to 1 for extremely conservative members.[3]

The congresses after the 1964 election and into the 1970s were some of the least polarized in modern history. In the congresses during the Johnson administration, the House Republicans were less conservative than the House Democrats were liberal. By Reagan's reelection in 1984, though, they had become more polarized than the Democrats. In the 112th Congress (2011–2012), the Republicans' votes were a remarkably 187 percent more conservative than they were in the days after Johnson's reelection in 1964. The Democrats, though still becoming more ideological, moved much more slowly to their ideological pole. The Democrats serving after the 2010 elections cast votes that were only 55 percent more polarizing. Such disparity in the parties gives credibility to the arguments offered by Hacker and Pierson (2006) and Mann and Ornstein (2012) that the Republican members are primarily responsible for the growing divide between the parties in Congress.

Although the parties have not polarized as much in the Senate, the gap between the polarization rates of Democrats and Republicans is similar. Since Johnson's reelection in 1964, the Senate Democrats have become only 27 percent more polarizing—the Senate Republicans, on the other hand, have become more than 70 percent more polarizing. This disparity gives credibility to Theriault's (2013) argument that the Republicans, primarily the Gingrich senators, have driven the parties apart in the Senate.

Both parties in both chambers are heading toward their ideological endpoint, but they are not all moving at the same rate. For every step that the Senate Democrats are taking, the House Democrats are taking two steps, the Senate Republicans are taking three steps, and the House Republicans are taking seven steps!

Expected Polarization in the 113th Congress (2013–2014)

Incumbents were the big winners in the 2012 elections: Barack Obama was reelected president, only 2 senators were defeated, and only 39 House members lost. The incumbency win rate was a bit higher than normal for the Senate and slightly lower for the House. Given the continuity between the officeholders before the 2012 election and after, the polarization between the parties should continue along the same path we have seen since the mid-1960s.

Expected Polarization in the House

The shocking result from the 2012 election was not that 39 House members were defeated, but that *only* 39 House members were defeated. Although 39 members is about 50 percent more than the average in elections since 1988, the confluence of factors at play in 2012 should have seen many more incumbent defeats.

First, congressional approval was at an all-time low. Although Congress rarely enjoys the support of the American public, it seldom has seen approval numbers so low. Members of Congress would give themselves a similar rating—perhaps even lower. When House Minority Whip Steny Hoyer (D-MD) was told of the 16 percent approval, he commented,

> I want to talk to the 16 percent and find out what they are thinking. The Congress is not meeting hopefully its own expectations for itself, and I think the American public are right to be distressed, disappointed, anxious, angry about the failure of the Congress to address the serious problems confronting our country. (Milligan 2012)

When Congress suffers such low esteem among the American public, it usually pays a price at the ballot box (Jones and McDermott 2009).

Second, the 2012 elections came after a wave election for the Republicans in 2010. After the 2010 elections, the Republicans enjoyed the largest margin that they have had in the House since 1950. Their 242 seats were more than 50 seats greater than their average seat number of 190 since the 1964 election and 22 more seats than their average since they lost their "permanent minority" status in the 1994 elections. Such a good election as the Republicans had in 2010 "exposes" a party to defeat in the subsequent election. According to Jacobson (2012), many of the members who were swept into office in the wave should have been carried back to sea when the wave receded. Nonetheless, only 13 House Republicans lost in the 2012 general elections.

Third, the 2012 elections were the first election after the 2010 census. Usually such elections result in more incumbent defeats. As a result of states shifting their congressional district lines, incumbents are forced to campaign in front of voters whom they have never represented. Additionally, when states lose seats, two incumbent members are frequently forced to run against each other. These uncertain electoral circumstances usually increase the number of incumbent defeats.

Luckily for the Republicans, the combination of the 2010 wave election and the redistricting that came after it meant that they could lock in some of their incumbents who otherwise would have been swept to sea as a result of their exposure. The tale of just three states vividly shows how the House majority switched from Democrat to Republican in 2010 and how the Republicans consolidated their advantage with redistricting in 2012.

In 2008, Barack Obama won the critically important swing states of Pennsylvania, Ohio, and Florida on his way to winning the presidency. During that election, the three states sent an equal number of Democrats and Republicans to the House. In the 2010 wave election, the Republican advantage in just those three states grew to 26 representatives. In addition to winning 44 House seats in the 2010 elections (compared to 18 for the Democrats), the Republicans also won back the governorships in two of those three states from Democratic governors and increased their state legislature seats. Normally, such a good election year would be followed by a decline as the political landscape returned to normal. But because the Republicans controlled the levers of redistricting in these states, they were able to insulate some of their more vulnerable incumbents. In the 2012 elections, the three states sent 23 more Republicans than Democrats to the House despite the fact that, again, Obama carried all three states. Although Obama got 50.5 percent of the vote in Florida, 51.0 percent of the vote in Ohio, and 52.7 percent of the vote in Pennsylvania, the Republicans walked away with 73 percent, 75 percent, and 72 percent of the House seats in those states.

Because of the relatively little turnover in the 113th Congress, the polarization of the 112th Congress should continue without a hitch. Those members who left the House at the end of the 112th Congress came from across the ideological continuum. Although some moderates lost in the general election, two of the most ideological members did not return to the 113th Congress either. Jeff Flake (R–AZ), the fifth most conservative Republican, was promoted to the Senate, and Dennis Kucinich (D–OH), the most liberal Democrat, lost in a primary following the Republican gerrymander in Ohio, a state that lost two seats in the House because of reapportionment following the 2010 census.

The Republicans who have returned to the 113th Congress are, according to the DW-NOMINATE scale, 0.01 less conservative than the Republicans who left the House (0.67 compared to 0.68). The Democrats who left the House, on the other hand, are 0.04 more moderate than the Democrats who are continuing their service into the 113th Congress (0.37 compared to 0.41). By and large, the member-to-member transitions should not have a great effect on the overall polarization. The defeat of two Democratic incumbents illustrates these trade-offs. Pete Stark, one of the more liberal members in the Democratic caucus, lost to Eric Swalwell, who during the campaign promised to work across the aisle, in this Democrat-versus-Democrat race in California. On the other hand, in a Republican district in North Carolina, moderate Larry Kissel lost to Republican Richard Hudson, who will certainly cast more ideologically extreme votes than his predecessor. Across the 85 new members, such ideologically extreme transitions are likely to largely wash out.

Not only have the rank-and-file members stayed relatively similar in the House; so too have the party leaders. The entire Democratic Party leadership in the 112th Congress has continued into the 113th Congress. The top four Republican leaders are continuing in their 112th Congress roles. The only important party leadership position switch in the Republican ranks comes from the 112th Congress Republican conference vice chair, Cathy McMorris Rodgers (R–WA), becoming the conference chair in the 113th Congress.

Demographic Polarization in the House

The stark demographic divide between the parties that was present in the electorate is reflected in the House of Representatives. White men will continue to dominate the Republican House conference. Of the 234 Republicans who were sworn in, 209 were white men; the remaining Republicans include

18 white women, 4 Hispanic men, 1 Hispanic woman, 1 African American man, and 1 Native American man.

Although the face of the Republican Party has remained similar the last few election cycles, the face of the Democratic Party in the House continues to evolve. In fact, for the first time in history, white men will be a minority of its members. Nancy Pelosi, the party leader, will be joined with 61 other women (33 white women, 15 African American women, 7 Hispanic women, 5 Asian American women, and 1 Pacific Islander), constituting the largest bloc ever for Democratic women. They will be joined 44 non-white men (28 African American men, 12 Hispanic men, and 4 Asian American men). Only 101 other white men, making up just 49 percent of the Democratic caucus, will join Steny Hoyer, the minority whip.[4]

Expected Polarization in the Senate

Incumbents in the Senate also did exceedingly well in the 2012 elections. Just two senators were defeated in the 2010 elections. In Indiana, Richard Lugar lost in the primary to Richard Mourdock, who in turn lost to Joe Donnelly. And Elizabeth Warren defeated Scott Brown in Massachusetts. The other 22 incumbents who sought reelection were reelected. The changes brought about by these defeats and the other retirements are easier to analyze than the changes in the House for two reasons. First, two-thirds of the chamber was not up this election cycle, which sufficiently reduces the possible seat-to-seat transitions above and beyond the relatively smaller size of the Senate. Second, the Senate does not redistrict, so it is easier to follow seat changes than it is in the House, where some states gain seats as other states lose them. Third, several of the incoming senators were previously in the House, so we have a good idea of the kind of votes that they will cast in the Senate. One enduring finding of the House-to-Senate transitions is that members cast remarkably similar votes even when their constituencies greatly change (Theriault 2008), which is consistent with Keith Poole and Howard Rosenthal's (1997) finding that members "die with their ideological boots on."

The senators leaving the chamber were more concentrated in the middle of the ideological continuum—8 of the 12 departing senators had a DW-NOMINATE score between -0.3 and 0.3. To measure the effect of these transitions, we develop "extremism scores," which are simply the absolute value of their ideology scores as calculated by Keith Poole and Howard Rosenthal (1996) in the DW-NOMINATE algorithm. Extreme liberals and extreme conservatives will both have extremism scores near one. Ideological moderates will have scores around zero. The seven Democrats who left the Senate at the conclusion of the 112th Congress had an average extremism score of 0.28; the 46 Democrats who are continuing to serve in the 113th are a third more liberal with a score of 0.38. The gap among Republicans is even bigger. The four Republicans who left the Senate after the 112th Congress had 0.27 extremism scores, whereas the Republicans who have stayed are almost twice as conservative, with a score of 0.51.

We do not expect any of the 12 seat-to-seat transitions to result in a less polarized Senate. The one that may come closest is the Indiana transition from Lugar to Donnelly. Four other transitions should yield an insignificant change in polarization: Lieberman–Murphy (CT), Akaka–Hirono (HI), Bingaman–Heinrich (NM), and Conrad–Heitkamp (ND). Four transitions should see a more extreme member replacing a more moderate member: the extremely conservative Flake in Arizona replacing the middle-of-the-road conservative Kyl, the middle-of-the-road liberal King replacing the moderate Snowe in Maine, the middle-of-the-road liberal Kaine replacing the moderate Webb in Virginia, and the liberal Baldwin replacing the moderate Kohl in Wisconsin. Three transitions will offer senators with high extremism scores replacing moderates. In two of the states, the voters chose a senator of the party that more closely matches their presidential voting record: Warren should be much more extreme than Brown in Massachusetts, which is consistent with Massachusetts's voting record, and Nebraskans chose Sarah Palin favorite Deb Fischer, who will likely cast very conservative votes to replace the retiring Ben Nelson (D). The other big change should come from Texas, where Tea Party favorite Ted Cruz is replacing moderate Kay Baily Hutchison.

All of these seat-to-seat transitions will likely result in a Senate where Democrats are even further from Republicans than they were in the 112th Congress. Although a couple of the new members may occupy the space being vacated by Nelson, Snowe, Brown, and Lugar, fewer moderates will exist to try to bridge the bipolarity that characterizes the current Senate.

The growing demographic split between the parties that is present in the House is less obvious—or nonexistent —in the Senate. Although 76 white men serve in the Senate in the 113th Congress, they are split almost evenly between the two parties (39 Republicans and 37 Democrats). Twenty women now serve in the Senate. The same gender gap present in women's votes in the general election is reflected in the partisan composition of those 20 women— 16 are Democrats, and only 4 are Republicans. The two Asian American members are both Democrats, and two of three Hispanics are Republican.

Conclusion

At a minimum, the 2012 elections continued the recent trend of a growing partisan divide in the United States at every level. Partisan voters were more likely to line up behind their candidates in both the presidential and congressional races. Ideological voters were more likely to align with the party more closely tied to their preferences. States were more likely to cast overwhelmingly partisan ballots. Furthermore, congressional members were more likely to receive a disproportionate amount of partisan votes and represent constituents who disproportionately voted for the same presidential candidate. Several of these trends were more than simply the next step on existing trend lines, but were magnified by the 2012 elections.

The 2012 elections also revealed a bigger demographic divide in the United States. The Republican Party's demographic coalition has remained the same. Forty-five percent of Romney's votes came from white men, only a 3 percent decline from the percentage that Dole received in 1996. On the other hand, the Democratic Party has increasingly become the home for women and racial and ethnic minorities. Barack Obama got more votes from African Americans (both men and women) than he did from white men. Sixteen years earlier, Bill Clinton received almost twice as many votes from white men as he did from African Americans. This demographic divide is reflected in the House of Representatives, where white men make up less than a majority for the first time in history.

Nothing in the results from the 2012 election suggests that these polarizing trends—either by party or by demographic group—are likely to change in the near future. In the wake of these election results, the Republicans increasingly recognize that an electoral coalition built primarily on white voters is going to be exceedingly difficult to ride to victory. As they begin to sketch out a legislative and electoral strategy to expand their base into a governing majority, the party and demographic balance in the United States will certainly shift and change, just as it has since the minority vote in elections has become more prominent in the last few election cycles.

NOTES

1. All data from National Election Poll/Voter News Service unless otherwise cited. Member companies consist of ABC News, the Associated Press, CBS News, CNN, Fox News, and NBC News.
2. Regrettably, the redistricting caused by the 2010 census has delayed the computation of the presidential vote by congressional district. Early analysis strongly suggests that the underlying partisan composition of the districts represented by Democrats has become even more distinct from the districts represented by Republicans.
3. Poole and Rosenthal (1997) generate these data so that they are comparable across congresses within party systems. More care should be used in comparing these scores across chambers. The estimates for the 112th Congress are based on votes up until March 16, 2012; retrieved from Keith Poole on November 13, 2012.
4. These data include nonvoting delegates, all six of whom are Democrats. Of the six, three are women, two are Asian American men, and one is a Hispanic man. Excluding these delegates results in a Democratic House Caucus composed of 50.7 percent white men.

REFERENCES

Abramowitz, Alan, and Kyle Saunders. 1998. "Ideological Realignment in the American Electorate." *Journal of Politics* 60 (August): 634–653.

Aldrich, John H. 1995. *Why Parties? The Origins and Transformation of Political Parties in America.* Chicago: University of Chicago Press.

Aldrich, John H., and David W. Rohde. 2001. "The Logic of Conditional Party Government: Revisiting the Electoral Connection." In *Congress Reconsidered,* 7th ed., ed. Lawrence C. Dodd and Bruce I. Oppenheimer. Washington, DC: CQ Press.

Bishop, Bill. 2008. The Big Sort: Why the Clustering of Like-Minded America is Tearing Us Apart. New York: Houghton Miflin Company.

Brady, David W., Hahrie Han, and Jeremy C. Pope. 2007. "Primary Elections and Candidate Ideology: Out of Step with the Primary Electorate?" *Legislative Studies Quarterly* 32 (1): 79–106.

Campbell, Angus, Philip E. Converse, Warren E. Miller, and Donald Stokes. 1960. *The American Voter.* New York: Wiley.

Carmines, Edward G., and Harold W. Stanley. 1992. "The Transformation of the New Deal Party System: Social Groups, Political Ideology, and Changing Partisanship among Northern Whites, 1972–1988." *Political Behavior* 14: 213–237.

Carson, Jamie, Erik Engstrom, and Jason Roberts. 2007. "Candidate Quality, the Personal Vote, and the Incumbency Advantage in Congress." *American Political Science Review* 101 (2): 239–301.

Converse, Philip. 1964. "The Nature of Belief Systems in Mass Publics." In *Ideology and Discontent,* ed. David Apter. New York: Free Press.

Delli Carpini, Michael X., and Scott Keeter. 1996. *What Americans Know about Politics and Why It Matters.* New Haven: Yale University Press.

Fiorina, Morris P. 2005. *Culture War? The Myth of a Polarized America.* New York: Pearson Longman.

Hacker, Jacob S., and Paul Pierson. 2006. *Off Center: The Republican Revolution and the Erosion of American Democracy.* New Haven, CT: Yale University Press.

Hetherington, Marc. 2008. "Turned Off or Turned On: The Effects of Polarization on Political Participation, Engagement, and Representation." In *Red and Blue Nation?,* ed. David Brady and Pietro Nivola, vol. 2. Washington, DC: Brookings.

Hibbing, John R., and Elizabeth Theiss-Morse. 2002. *Stealth Democracy: Americans' Beliefs about How Government Should Work.* New York: Cambridge University Press.

Hirsch, Sam. 2003. "The United States of Unrepresentatives: What Went Wrong in the Latest Round of Congressional Redistricting." *Election Law Journal* 2 (November): 179–216.

Jacobson, Gary C. 2012. *The Politics of Congressional Elections*, 8th ed. Upper Saddle River: Pearson.

Jones, David R., and Monika L. McDermott. 2009. *Americans, Congress, and Democratic Responsiveness: Public Evaluations of Congress and Electoral Consequences.* Ann Arbor: University of Michigan Press.

Kaufmann, K. M., and J. R. Petrocik. (1999). "The Changing Politics of American Men: Understanding the Sources of the Gender Gap." *American Journal of Political Science* 43 (3): 864–887.

Mann, Thomas E., and Norman J. Ornstein. 2012. *It's Even Worse Than It Looks: How the American Constitutional System Collided with the New Politics of Extremism.* New York: Basic Books.

McCarty, Nolan, Keith Poole, and Howard Rosenthal. 2006. *Polarized America: The Dance of Ideology and Unequal Riches.* Cambridge: Massachusetts Institute of Technology Press.

Milligan, Susan. 2012. "Everybody Hates Congress." *U.S. News Weekly,* January 20, 4.

Oppenheimer, Bruce I. 2005. "Deep Red and Blue Congressional Districts." In *Congress Reconsidered,* 8th ed., ed. Lawrence C. Dodd and Bruce I. Oppenheimer. Washington, DC: CQ Press.

Poole, Keith T., and Howard Rosenthal. 1997. *Congress: A Political-Economic History of Roll Call Voting.* New York: Oxford University Press.

Rohde, David W. 1991. *Parties and Leaders in the Postreform House.* Chicago: University of Chicago.

Shaw, Daron R. 2006. *The Race to 270: The Electoral College and the Campaign Strategies of 2000 and 2004.* Chicago: University of Chicago Press.

Sinclair, Barbara. 2006. *Party Wars: Polarization and the Politics of National Policy Making.* Norman: University of Oklahoma Press.

Stanley, Harold W., and Richard G. Niemi. 1991. "Partisanship and Group Support, 1952–1988." *American Politics Quarterly* 19 (2): 189–210.

Theriault, Sean M. 2008. *Party Polarization in Congress.* New York: Cambridge University Press.

Theriault, Sean M. 2013. *The Gingrich Senators: The Roots of Partisan Warfare in Congress.* New York: Oxford University Press.

Zaller, John. 1992. *The Nature and Origins of Mass Opinion.* Cambridge, UK: Cambridge University Press.

7 Campaign Finance in the 2012 Election

Robert G. Boatright

Since accurate data became available on presidential campaign finance, every election has been more expensive than the one before it. The 2012 election was clearly no exception to this rule, but it is far more difficult to discern how much money was spent on the 2012 election—and who spent it—than in any other election of the past 40 years. The 2012 election featured the first presidential race held since the Supreme Court's *Citizens United v. Federal Election Commission* decision struck down limits on advocacy spending, and as a consequence we can measure only part of what was spent by outside groups. We do know, however, that measurable spending by nonparty outside groups totaled approximately $1 billion, a more than threefold increase over the 2008 total.[1] There are many ironies to this flood of unregulated money, however. During the presidential primaries, the spending of outside groups eclipsed the spending of the candidates themselves, arguably prolonging the Republican race and benefiting candidates with little appeal to traditional individual donors. President Barack Obama raised less money than he had in 2008, and although Mitt Romney raised more than John McCain had in 2008, he raised far less money than some had predicted. The results of the election also do not provide clear evidence that outside spending made a difference to the election outcome. Republicans and Republican-leaning groups outspent Democrats and their allies in the presidential race's competitive states, in competitive Senate races, and in competitive House races, yet the Democrats gained seats in each chamber. This does not mean that money did not matter in 2012, but means only that at some point there may be declining returns to campaign spending, particularly when much of that spending is devoted to television advertising.

The 2012 election was shaped by three developments that occurred long before campaigning began. First, the unraveling of the system of public financing for presidential elections, a system that had restrained spending from 1976 through 2004, was complete from the moment the 2008 election ended. The Revenue Act of 1971 and the Federal Elections and Campaigns Act (FECA) amendments of 1974, had established a system in which the first $250 of each contribution raised by major party presidential candidates was matched with public funds, with the condition that candidates accepted restrictions on their total campaign spending. FECA also offered candidates grants to cover general election expenses if they agreed not to raise money during that time. The primary and general election limits were indexed to inflation; in 2012, had anyone accepted public funds, the 2012 primary spending limit would have been $45.6 million, and the general election grant would have been $91.2 million. In 2000, George W. Bush became the first presidential nominee to have declined public matching funds during the primaries; in order to compete with Bush, 2004 Democratic nominee John Kerry followed suit. In 2008 most primary candidates declined matching funds. Barack Obama became the first nominee to decline the general election grant as well. In 2012 it was clear from the outset that all major party candidates would decline matching funds and that both nominees would decline the general election grant.

Second, the success of the 2008 Obama campaign at using the Internet to raise small contributions ensured that Obama's 2012 campaign, as well as those of his potential opponents, would be scrutinized for signs of the enthusiasm that had characterized his 2008 campaign. Success at raising money in small amounts has numerous advantages—it enables candidates to re-solicit donors; it has become, with the development of Internet and social media, relatively inexpensive; and it allows a candidate to create a movement-style, inclusive campaign. Obama's success in appealing to small donors was pivotal in his defeat of Hillary Clinton in the 2008 primaries and in his decision to forgo public financing in the general election.

Third, the 2012 presidential election was the first held since the Supreme Court's *Citizens United v. FEC* decision took effect. This decision, handed down in January 2010, overturned eight-year-old restrictions on election-related advertising by groups that accept corporate and labor funding. Moreover, the decision lifted the ban enacted in 1990 on explicit electoral advocacy (that is, exhorting citizens to vote for or against a candidate) by corporations. Two months later, the District of Columbia Circuit Court of Appeals held in the *SpeechNow.org v. FEC* decision that political organizations could solicit unlimited contributions from individuals and corporations if the organizations engaged only in independent expenditures and did not contribute money directly to candidates. These two decisions raised the specter that the efforts of a small number of wealthy individuals or corporations would influence the outcomes of the presidential race and congressional races. In 2010, the efforts of newly formed independent expenditure–only PACs, or Super PACs, made that year's congressional races the most expensive ever and likely ensured that many incumbents were defeated because of multimillion-dollar independent expenditures against them. It was hard, however, to separate the effect of the natural midterm backlash against the president's party from that year's spending.

The 2012 election year thus was fated to be an extraordinarily expensive one, and it was fated to be a year in which campaign money was a major subject of campaign coverage. With limits on contributions and expenditures in tatters, what remained of FECA's system of campaign finance regulations were the rules regarding disclosure. That is, most (though not all) of the spending in 2012 could be observed and measured. More than any other election in recent memory, discussions of the 2012 election focused on the money being spent to sway voters. This may have had a corrosive effect on citizens' views of the political system, but it is not clear how much of a difference all of this unrestricted spending made in the outcome of the election.

The Presidential Primaries

In one sense, the 2012 Republican presidential primaries unfolded in undramatic fashion. The early front-runner, in terms of elites' predictions about the race and in terms of fundraising, managed to knock out his rivals early in the year. Although he lost primaries in several Southern states, Mitt Romney became the de facto nominee by April—slightly later than he might have preferred, but early enough that he was able to spend far more time campaigning against his general election opponent than Barack Obama was able in 2008. As Table 7.1 shows, the Republican fundraising race was never close at any point in the election.

The Republican primary field was, according to many observers, weaker in 2012 than it had been in previous elections. This perceived weakness was borne out in the candidates' early fundraising. In 2008, Romney, the runner-up, raised over $100 million in a campaign that operated into February 2008, but $46 million of his money that year came out of his own pocket. Four Republican candidates in 2008 raised over $30 million, even though the 2008 race had effectively ended by March 2008. Only two Republicans in 2012, Romney and Ron Paul, raised over $30 million, and Paul's somewhat idiosyncratic fundraising success never made him a threat to Romney's nomination. The lack of financial competition in the Republican race was surprising in that during 2011 President Obama appeared to be as vulnerable as any incumbent president in the past two decades and in that Romney was not well liked by many Republicans.

As of June 31, 2011, Romney's edge over the rest of the Republican field was apparent. Romney had raised $18.4 million, whereas five opponents—Ron Paul, Tim Pawlenty, Michele Bachmann, Herman Cain, and Newt Gingrich—had each raised between $2 million and $4.5 million. As a Campaign Finance Institute (2011b) report noted, Romney actually raised less in the first half of 2011 than he had during the first six months of 2007, but Romney did not have serious financial opposition during the first half of 2011; there was no urgency to his fundraising appeals. Romney had a higher percentage of "maxed out" donors—donors who had given the maximum

Table 7.1 Presidential Primary Receipts

Candidate	December 31, 2011			March 31, 2012			August 31, 2012		
	Total receipts	Individual contributions	% small contributions	Total receipts	Individual contributions	% small contributions	Total receipts	Individual contributions	% small contributions
Republicans									
Romney	56.7	56.3	9	87.4	86.8	9	244.0	223.0	18
Paul	26.0	25.5	48	36.9	35.9	35	40.9	39.9	34
Gingrich	12.7	12.4	49	22.5	21.9	43			
Santorum	2.2	2.1	32	20.6	20.3	47			
Perry	20.1	19.8	5						
Cain	16.8	16.7	52						
Bachmann	9.3	9.2	60						
Huntsman	5.9	5.8	10						
Pawlenty	5.1	4.9	13						
Johnson	0.6	0.6	27						
Roemer	0.3	0.3	100	0.7	0.4	100			
McCotter	0.5	0.1	54						
Democrats									
Obama	118.8	118.8	48	183.6	183.6	44	426.9	426.9	34

Sources: Campaign Finance Institute (2012b, 2012e, 2012f).

Note: Receipts listed in millions of dollars, cumulative to the appropriate filing deadline. All Republican candidates are listed for December 31, 2011, filing, although Pawlenty and McCotter had dropped out. Only active candidates are listed for the March and August 2012 filings. Amounts listed are for primary contributions only; Obama and Romney's pre–convention general election contributions are listed in Table 7.3. The other candidates raised negligible amounts of general election funds.

permissible amount—than any other Republican candidate, and two of his opponents, Michele Bachmann and Ron Paul, were candidates with a history of success at raising contributions of $200 or less. Given the Obama campaign's ability to inspire small contributors to give again and again (and the inability of Romney's donors at that point to do so), the Romney campaign had reason, despite its massive fundraising advantage, to be concerned about what would happen were another candidate to jump into the race or were one of his competitors to catch fire.

Romney got just such a competitor in the next quarter when Texas governor Rick Perry jumped into the race. Perry entered the race on August 12, and by September 30 he had amassed $17 million. Romney raised only $14 million between July 1 and September 30. As 2011 wound down, however, it became apparent that Perry's initial fundraising largely reflected his established donor base in Texas; Perry would go on to raise less than $3 million during the rest of the campaign, and over half of the total money he raised came from Texas (Bravender 2011; Farnam 2011). Although Perry initially appeared to be the strongest conservative threat to Romney, he fared poorly in the debates and was not able to translate his initial fundraising strength into strong performances in the early primaries and caucuses.

As is recounted elsewhere in this book, there was then a series of boomlets of support in public opinion polls for several of Romney's opponents. At various times in 2011 and early 2012, surveys placed Perry, Michele Bachmann, Rick Santorum, Herman Cain, and Newt Gingrich ahead in early primary and caucus states or in nationwide polls of Republicans. These boomlets may have translated into short-lived fundraising successes for some candidates (Vogel and Philip 2012). Herman Cain, who surged briefly in polls of Republican voters in the fall of 2011, raised $11.5 million in the final quarter of 2011; Newt Gingrich, who also enjoyed greater public support during that quarter, raised $9.8 million during the last quarter of 2011 and $5.6 million during January 2012. Rick Santorum, the surprise winner of the Iowa caucus, raised $9.0 million during February 2012 alone, over 50 percent more than he had raised cumulatively through January 31 (Campaign Finance Institute 2011a, 2011b, 2012b, 2012c, 2012d).

All of these candidates raised large percentages of their money from small donors, indicating that Romney did indeed have a problem exciting the party rank and file. Through February 2012, Bachmann, Cain, Gingrich, Paul, and Santorum had all raised over one-third of their money from small donors, whereas Romney had raised less than 10 percent of his money from such contributors. Romney, moreover, spent his money at a fast clip; many news accounts during early 2012 noted that Romney's campaign funds were being exhausted by his need to compete with the rest of the Republican field, and his reliance on large donors raised the possibility that he would not be well equipped to continue to raise money to compete with Barack Obama during

Table 7.2 Super PAC Receipts during the 2012 Presidential Primaries

Organization	Candidate supported	December 31, 2011		March 31, 2012		August 31, 2012	
		Receipts	Independent expenditures	Receipts	Independent expenditures	Receipts	Independent expenditures
Restore Our Future	Romney	30.2	4.1	52.3	41.2	96.7	84.6
Endorse Liberty	Paul	1.4	0.4	5.3	3.9		
Winning Our Future	Gingrich	2.2	0.9	24.2	17.2		
Red White and Blue Fund	Santorum	0.9	0.7	8.5	7.7		
Make Us Great Again	Perry	5.4	3.8				
9-9-9 Fund	Cain	0.6	0.4				
Our Destiny Fund	Huntsman	2.7	2.3				
Priorities USA Action	Obama	4.4	0.3	9.0	0.7	35.6	33.2

Sources: Campaign Finance Institute 2012b, 2012e, 2012f; Center for Responsive Politics.

Note: All amounts listed in millions of dollars. Amounts listed are cumulative.

the spring and summer even if he wrapped up the Republican nomination quickly (Palmer 2012b; Rucker and Eggen 2012).

Romney's primary troubles, however, were not solely related to his own fundraising or the fundraising of his opponents. As Table 7.2 shows, seven Republican candidates (Cain, Gingrich, Paul, Perry, Romney, Santorum, and Jon Huntsman) had Super PACs raising and spending money on their behalf. Just as the Romney campaign raised two to three times as much as his competitors, his Super PAC also raised two to three times what any of the other Super PACs raised. As the early 2012 primaries unfolded, however, it became apparent that the dynamics of Super PAC fundraising or expenditures bore little relation to those of candidate fundraising and spending. The surge in small donor support for Romney's opponents is not reflected in Super PAC fundraising. Instead, the lack of limitations on what could be given to Super PACs ensured that individual donors could give a lifeline to candidates through large donations to their Super PACs. A series of *New York Times* explorations of the fundraising for Mitt Romney's Super PAC, Restore Our Future, showed that Romney's Super PAC was not heavily reliant on one large donor; instead, as many as 21 individuals, many with ties to Romney's former firm, Bain Capital, contributed to the Super PAC in 2011 (Confessore and Luo 2012; Schoenberg 2012). Newt Gingrich and Rick Santorum, on the other hand, were supported by Super PACs that drew heavily on only one or two contributors. Sheldon Adelson, owner of Sands Casino, and his family contributed $20.5 million to Winning Our Future, the Gingrich Super PAC (Confessore 2012a, 2012b; Levinthal and Vogel 2012). William Dore, an energy executive, and Foster Friess, an investment management firm owner and longtime supporter of evangelical causes, each provided over $2 million for the Red White and Blue Fund, a Super PAC supporting Rick Santorum (Eggen and Farnam 2012; Homans 2012). A case could be made that these contributions enabled Gingrich and Santorum to remain in the race far longer than they would have had they relied solely on their own campaign funds.

The advantage of Super PACs lies in their ability to quickly translate large donations into campaign activity. The biggest problem that the Republican candidates had with Super PACs, however, is that Super PACs have neither the organizational ability nor the financial stability to translate funding into on-the-ground campaign organizations (Gardner 2012; Vogel and Levinthal 2012). In many of the early primary states, Super PACs outspent the candidates; in Iowa, the *Washington Post* concluded that Super PACs spent twice as much as the candidates (Eggen 2012b). The Wesleyan Media Project conducted analyses of advertising expenditures in South Carolina and Florida, home of the second and third Republican primaries (Fowler 2012). Florida is a state with 11 different media markets, far more than any of the states that had previously voted, and it is generally considered a state where advertising is more essential than in other early primary states. Rick Santorum is reported to have done almost all of his Iowa campaigning in person, relying on his own automobile to barnstorm from one city to the next. This simply is not possible in Florida. Instead, the candidates invested heavily in advertising. An estimated $13.7 million was spent there by the candidates, with $7.3 million of that coming from the Romney campaign and the remainder split between four other candidates. Super PACs came to the aid of candidates who could not afford to go on the air themselves; Newt Gingrich, for instance, was vastly outspent by Romney, but Gingrich's Super PAC outspent the Gingrich campaign on ads by a 14 to 1 margin. The Super PAC did not enable Gingrich to come close to matching Romney's spending, but Gingrich did manage to make the race somewhat competitive, receiving 32 percent of the vote to Romney's 46 percent.

By the time it became evident that Mitt Romney would be the Republican nominee, Romney had raised $87.4 million, but had spent all but $10.1 million of that amount. Romney made it through the primaries without tapping into his own personal fortune. Although Romney has enough money of his own that he easily could have solved any financial problems during the campaign, he likely saw it as important for public relations purposes that he not rely as heavily on his own money as he had in 2008 (Mooney 2012).

Romney could also look forward to the so-called bridge period between the time he became the de facto nominee and when he would actually accept the Republican nomination in late August, with the knowledge that traditional Republican donors who either had given money to other candidates in the primaries or had not contributed at all would eventually contribute to him now that his nomination was inevitable (Eggen 2012a; Rutenberg and Zeleny 2011). Although Ron Paul chose to continue running up until the convention—and actually raised almost $4 million during the spring and summer—Paul's campaign largely receded from public view, and Romney could focus his attention on campaigning against Barack Obama.

Obama, meanwhile, raised money aggressively throughout the Republican primary season. This was no surprise. What was surprising, however, was that Obama spent the money he raised far more quickly than had previous incumbents. As of September 30, 2011, Obama had raised $89.5 million and had spent $28.1 million of that. Obama's fundraising and spending then picked up in the coming months; by the end of March 2012, Obama had raised an additional $113.9 million but had spent a total of $94.4 million. Obama was clearly building a campaign infrastructure, but he also used this money to attack Romney throughout the Republican primaries. This was a model that had been used by incumbents in the past—Bill Clinton, for instance, had raised money in the 1996 primaries despite having no opposition and then used that money to put Republican nominee Bob Dole on the defensive once Dole locked up the Republican nomination. George W. Bush had done the same in 2004, although John Kerry had managed to raise enough money after winning the Democratic nomination that he kept pace with Bush. Obama's fundraising success in 2008, however, signified that he had a large enough donor base to put Romney on the defensive if Romney did not manage to step up his fundraising.

Obama's fundraising operation was burdened with high expectations. Some early forecasters predicted that he would raise over $1 billion, an increase of about $250 million (or 33 percent) over his 2008 fundraising numbers (to put this in perspective, $1 billion is nearly three times as much as any other presidential candidate besides Obama had ever raised). Obama's early fundraising was also consistently compared to his 2008 fundraising—a misleading comparison given that his 2008 fundraising efforts were made in the context of a competitive and exciting primary race (Confessore 2011b; Eggen and Farnam 2011). In 2008, Obama had excelled at raising small contributions; his campaign had also excelled at creating an impression in the media that his campaign was fueled by small contributors, even though post-election analyses showed that his campaign was not in fact that much more adept at raising small contributions than the campaigns of George W. Bush and John Kerry had been (Campaign Finance Institute 2008). In 2012, running as an incumbent, the Obama campaign still touted its success among small donors, and the Obama campaign did rely more on small donors than the Romney campaign. Although the Obama campaign initially lagged behind its own 2008 numbers, by the end of August 2012, Obama had raised $432.2 million in primary contributions, only slightly less than the $466.8 million he had raised during the 2008 primaries. He was not on pace to raise $1 billion, but he did not have to spend any of this money running against other Democrats. Moreover, Obama raised $147 million in contributions of less than $200 and $289.9 million in contributions of less than $1,000. Romney's numbers for equivalent contributions were $39.5 million and $81.8 million. Obama had 50 percent more itemized donors than Romney and, presumably, three to four times as many unitemized donors.

Initially it appeared that Obama planned not to rely on large Super PAC contributions; early in the campaign he courted big donors old and new and again turned to some of the bundlers who had been integral to his 2008 campaign (Cummings 2011b; Palmer 2012a). Amid several news reports that Obama did not adequately cultivate large donors—news reports recounted several 2008 contributors' claims that Obama had not adequately thanked them—the Obama campaign team spent much of 2011 deliberating about whether to endorse the creation of a pro-Obama Super PAC (Bravender and Vogel 2012; Hamburger and Gold 2011). Obama had spoken out against the *Citizens United* decision, and many wealthy liberal activists had announced that they would not give to Super PACs. A pro-Obama Super PAC, Priorities USA, was formed in 2011, but the group struggled to raise money as the president kept his distance from the group (Cummings 2011a; Rutenberg 2011). Finally, on February 6, 2012, Obama campaign manager Jim Messina finally announced the Obama campaign's approval of Priorities USA, with a statement that the campaign "would not unilaterally disarm" (Messina 2012; Zeleny and Rutenberg 2012). Priorities USA raised money very slowly, however; by the end of March, it had raised $9.0 million, far less than the $52.4 million the pro-Romney Super PAC had raised—and for that matter, far less than the pro-Gingrich Super PAC raised.

Fundraising by the Obama and Romney campaigns picked up substantially in the summer of 2012. Romney had averaged slightly over $10 million per month during the primaries, but he raised $23.4 million in May and $33.8 million in June. Obama outraised Romney during each of these months, raising $39.8 million and $49.2 million in the same two months. As tends to be the case during the bridge period, Romney increased his fundraising from small contributors. The Romney campaign announced in June and July that if one combined the fundraising of the candidate committee, the RNC, and the joint party–candidate fundraising committee, it was outraising Obama and the Democrats. Despite the still-sizable Obama advantage in cash on hand, the Obama campaign was quick to use this as a fundraising ploy, sending e-mails to its supporters urging them to contribute, lest Obama be the first sitting president to be outraised by his opponent. Using the Romney campaign's combined metric, Obama and the Democrats narrowly outraised Romney and the Republicans in August.

Unsurprisingly, public financing played no role at all in the 2012 primaries. All major party nominees from 1976 through 2004 had accepted public funds in the general election, and almost all credible primary candidates had accepted federal matching funds—and the corresponding limits on spending—from 1976 through 1996. No serious candidates accepted matching funds in 2012; two minor Republican candidates (Buddy Roemer and Gary Johnson) did receive public funds, and two minor party nominees (Johnson, running as a Libertarian, and Green Party nominee Jill Stein) received small general election grants. It was clear as far back as 2000 that accepting matching funds and their accompanying spending limits was risky. Presumptive nominees who took public funds might well be out of money long before the convention. If one nominee took public funds and the other did not, the one who did not could attack the other, and the publicly funded candidate would be unable to respond until after the convention. Nonetheless, all of the Republicans save for Romney raised so little money that they would have been under the overall limit (if not the state limits) and thus would have raised more money with matching funds.

One of the rationales for matching funds and the general election flat grant had been that public financing gave candidates more time to campaign and reduced the amount of time they needed to spend soliciting money. Whatever the merits of public financing, it was apparent in the campaigns of Obama and Romney that the candidates had to spend time fundraising when they might otherwise be campaigning. In its effort to court small contributors, the Obama campaign created numerous contests for donors—a small contribution was the price of entry into a lottery to have dinner with celebrities such as Beyoncé Knowles and Jay-Z or President Obama and the First Lady themselves. Romney, meanwhile, suffered in early September from the release of a secretly recorded video of a fundraising dinner at which Romney told donors that 47 percent of the electorate would vote for Obama because they paid no income tax and were dependent on the federal government. A charitable take on Romney's comments might include a lament that the candidate had to spend as much time as he did courting wealthy contributors. In response to criticism from Republicans that Romney was spending too much time raising money, he responded that it was a consequence of Obama's decision not to accept public funds, saying, "I'd far rather be spending my time out in the key swing states campaigning . . . but fundraising is a part of politics when your opponent decides not to live by the federal spending limits" (Gibson 2012).

The disappearance of public funding for presidential candidates may have struck some as regrettable, but the candidates' own fundraising remained the most effectively regulated aspect of election financing. Super PACs occupied a much shadier section of the election law turf. In order to raise and spend unlimited amounts of money, Super PACs must disclose their donors and must not coordinate their efforts with the candidates whom they support. The disclosure requirements, widely misunderstood by the public and media commentators, ensured that eventually the public could find out who was providing the funds that buoyed the campaigns of Gingrich, Santorum, and Romney during the primaries. But the public did not always learn this information promptly; in the case of the Romney Super PAC, some donors provided only a post office box as an address and were difficult to track down (Confessore and Luo 2012). The Romney and Paul Super PACs also did not officially organize themselves for filing purposes until January 2012, thus ensuring that they would not file their information until January 31, 2012, and thus would not have their contributions scrutinized by the public until late February—after the early primaries had taken place (Levinthal 2012b; Levinthal and Vogel 2011). Whatever criticisms one might raise of the "megadonors" who financed the Gingrich and Santorum Super PACs, however, the largest contributors in 2012 were not shy about announcing and explaining their contributions to the public.

The coordination restrictions on Super PACs were difficult to rigorously enforce. Coordination restrictions have long governed the actions of PACs and 501(c) organizations, and such groups have operated using winks and nudges to candidates—a candidate may infer a group's strategy from its public announcements of its campaign activities, or vice versa, without coordination having technically taken place. Candidates could not directly be involved in discussing Super PAC strategy or soliciting donations, but campaign staffers could leave the campaign to take positions at the candidate Super PACs, and campaign surrogates could raise money both for the campaign and for the Super PAC (Confessore 2011a; McIntire and Luo 2012). Super PACs are not privy to information about the campaigns' grassroots organizing, but they proved in 2012 that they could engage in advertising that was virtually indistinguishable from candidate advertising except that it was slightly more negative (Fowler 2012).

The Presidential General Election

Once the parties' conventions had passed, the allied forces backing the two main contenders raised and spent roughly similar amounts of money. The synchrony of the candidates' own campaign fundraising, fundraising by the party committees, and fundraising by the Super PACs supporting both candidates was evident in media coverage of the campaign; accounts of monthly fundraising totals tended to aggregate funds raised by all of these organizations, tallying money raised by "the blue team" and "the red team." Table 7.3

Table 7.3 Presidential General Election Receipts for Candidates, Parties, and Their Main Super PAC Supporters

	Cash on hand August 31	September 1–31	October 1–17	October 18– November 26	General election total	Election cycle total
Obama campaign account	88.8	126.1	77.3	88.1	380.2	733.5
Democratic National Committee	7.1	20.3	13.8	22.0	63.2	289.4
Priorities USA	4.8	15.3	13.1	15.2	48.4	79.0
Democratic total	*100.7*	*161.7*	*104.2*	*123.3*	*491.8*	*1,101.9*
Romney campaign account	30.4*	77.7	51.8	65.6	225.5	451.8
Republican National Committee	76.6	48.4	19.8	20.4	165.2	371.4
Restore Our Future	6.2	14.8	20.2	22.1	63.4	153.8
Republican total	*113.2*	*140.9*	*91.8*	*108.1*	*454.1*	*977.0*

* Excludes a $20 million loan from the candidate.

Source: Federal Election Commission.

Note: All amounts listed in millions of dollars. Monthly totals are *not* cumulative. Funds given to the candidate and party committees from the joint fundraising committees are included in the candidate and party totals.

shows fundraising during the general election, by month and by organization, for the two candidates and the rest of their "team." On the one hand, the total money raised by all of these organizations ensured that 2012 would be different from 2008 in that neither candidate would have to worry about running low on money. On the other hand, however, the differences in who was receiving money and where that money was coming from would arguably be consequential in the later days of the election. As had been the case in 2008, the Republican National Committee substantially outraised the Democratic National Committee. The Romney Super PAC established an early lead on the Obama Super PAC, although the Obama Super PAC (Priorities USA) caught up to its pace in the last weeks of the campaign. Most importantly, however, the Obama campaign committee had more money than the Romney campaign; this enabled Obama to spend his money more efficiently than the Republican National Committee or Republican-leaning Super PACs could.

Before we discuss the implications of these differences, however, a few notes on Table 7.3 are in order. The first column of numbers in the table shows the cash-on-hand balance for both sides as of August 31. Some studies of the election have argued that the general election campaign truly began in April, once Romney's final opponent had stepped aside. Federal campaign finance law, however, treats the primary and general election campaigns as separate election cycles; this distinction has lost some of its importance now that public funding is inconsequential, but I keep it here in part to show that Obama went into the general election campaign with a substantial cash advantage, stemming from his ability to raise general election funds during the primary. Romney was thus at a disadvantage in terms of his own campaign funds, but the Republican "team" had a slight advantage. The combined Romney, RNC, and Romney Super PAC totals had exceeded those of the Democrats during much of the summer, but Obama pulled ahead in the fall, in large part because large Democratic donors finally began to contribute. Obama's fundraising success in September and October came as a surprise to many. The numbers here do not, however, include spending by outside groups other than the parties or the candidates' Super PACs; outside groups, as we see later in this chapter, tilted Republican by a substantial margin.

Let us return, however, to the similarities and differences between the two campaigns' fundraising. As for similarities, the 2012 election featured near-universal agreement on which states were in play. The closeness of the race ensured that both campaigns anticipated limited opportunities to win 270 electoral votes, so for most of September and October, nine states were regarded as pivotal in the election. Agreement on these states meant that there was little need for coordination, whether actual or de facto, between the candidates and the organizations seeking to help them. This stood in contrast to 2008; in that election, Barack Obama's fundraising advantage enabled him to put the McCain campaign on the defensive, spending money in states such as Georgia and Arizona that were not necessarily in play but that served as distractions to the cash-strapped McCain campaign. McCain was outspent substantially in many competitive states, focusing much of his money on a small number of states, including some that were likely hopeless for the campaign. Until the final week of the 2012 campaign, the Obama and Romney campaigns exclusively paid attention to the nine states that both agreed were competitive. In the last week, the Romney campaign invested some money in states that had not previously been viewed as competitive, such as Pennsylvania, Michigan, and Minnesota. This was presented by the Romney campaign as a sign that it was going on the offense and by the Obama campaign as either a feint or a sign of desperation. The earlier focus on just nine states, however, ensured that media markets in each of these states were saturated with advertising. In addition, several of these states had competitive Senate, House, or gubernatorial races, adding to the advertising overload. If one looks at polls in these states, it is difficult to argue that spending affected the result; the only changes in polling are more easily explained by the debates or by other factors.

As for salient differences in the two campaigns' fundraising, let us first consider the sizable advantage of the Obama campaign in the number of contributors and the number of small donors. By many metrics, there was less enthusiasm surrounding the Obama campaign in 2012 than there was in 2008. However, the large number of people who contributed to the Obama campaign meant that, just as in 2008, Obama was able to re-solicit the same donors throughout the campaign. Romney, of course, could do this not only with his small contributors but also with wealthier Super PAC donors (he couldn't do this himself, but the Super PAC itself could). The Obama campaign had, in addition, been able to use its fundraising list in 2008 to encourage donors to volunteer, and it made even more of an effort to do this in 2012, developing web-based get-out-the-vote programs and encouraging donors to make calls to swing-state voters. Romney had the ability to do the same thing, but logic would dictate that a campaign that has more donors has a larger pool of people to turn to for volunteer work. Because campaigns are not required to report the names of people who contribute less than $200, there is no way to know exactly how many donors each campaign had. As of August 31 the Obama campaign had over 400,000 itemized donors in comparison to slightly less than 200,000 for Romney. The Obama campaign claimed in September that it had over four million donors, and the amount of money given in unitemized contributions makes this a plausible claim. Both candidates reportedly had to take time off from campaigning in order to court donors, but news reports indicated that Romney had to spend more time doing this than did Obama (Confessore, McGinty, and Willis 2012; Levinthal 2012c). Conversely, both candidates bombarded supporters with pleas for small donations in the waning months of the campaign, but Obama reportedly did better at this than Romney (Levinthal 2012a). As was the case in the primaries, the absence of public financing arguably worked to President Obama's advantage but clearly cut into the time that both candidates would have otherwise spent on the hustings.

In addition, the president also surprised many observers by winning the television advertising wars during the general election. Many people expected that the Romney campaign and its allies would have a substantial advantage in the number of advertisements they were able to afford (see, e.g., Ferguson 2012), yet this never happened. There is a legal reason for this. Federal campaign finance law treats candidate campaign committees differently from party campaign committees or other political organizations. Since 1971, federal law has required television stations to charge political candidates what is known as the "lowest unit rate," the lowest price the network charges for advertising comparable to what the candidate seeks. In other words, television stations must charge candidates the same rates charged to year-round, high-volume advertising clients (Hagen and Kolodny 2008; Taylor and Ornstein 2002). Television stations are not, however, required to offer similar low prices to political parties or interest groups. Most of the pro–Obama advertising in the general election was paid for by the Obama campaign, which qualified for the lowest unit rate; most of the pro–Romney advertising was paid for by the RNC and by Super PACs, which did not qualify. Weekly reports during September and October cataloged Obama's advantage in the number of ad airings, despite Republican parity or dominance in ad spending (see, e.g., Eggen 2012c). Even in the last weeks of the campaign, partisans on both sides spoke of an upcoming surge in Republican spending, but by the end of the campaign, Obama still maintained an advantage in advertising in 10 of the 15 largest media markets in the battleground states and in a substantial majority of all media markets in these states (Baum 2012). If one aggregates spending during the April through October period by the campaigns and the groups supporting them, this pattern is evident: according to the Wesleyan Media Project's October 29 data, Obama and groups supporting his campaign spent approximately $319 million on the purchase of television advertising time, and Romney and his allies spent approximately $380 million. There were, however, a total of 572,000 ads supporting Obama in comparison to 525,000 ads supporting Romney.[2]

Campaign committees have other, extralegal advantages over Super PACs—and possibly over party committees as well—in what they can do with their money. The Obama campaign outspent the Romney campaign on a variety of "ground game" activities, just as it had outspent McCain in 2008. There were far more Obama field offices in the swing states than there were Romney offices, and these offices were also, according to media observers, better staffed and more active in their communities (Ball 2012; Sides 2012). This is in part a matter of money—the Obama campaign was able to spend money during the primaries to seed these offices, whereas the Romney campaign could not. The Obama campaign committee also had the ability to use information gathered about voters over the past several years to develop a field operation; the Romney campaign and its allied supporters had no such institutional memory to fall back on. Academic research has consistently found that personal contacting methods are a more effective means of winning votes than are media advertisements (see, e.g., Green and Gerber 2008).

In sum, there was an unprecedented amount of money spent in the 2012 presidential election, and perhaps more consequentially, much of this money was raised for organizations that could not legally have existed in previous presidential elections. This spending arguably took a toll on the residents of the nine states that mattered in 2012 and, some would say, on American democracy more generally. Despite this, however, there is no clear evidence that all of this spending had noticeable consequences for the outcome of the 2012 election.

The 2012 Congressional Elections

Although many open seats were created by redistricting, there was little change in the partisan composition of Congress in 2012. Excluding incumbent versus incumbent races, 15 House incumbents lost their seats in 2012—11 Republicans and 4 Democrats. Democrats captured one Republican open seat, and Republicans won five Democratic open seats. Democrats captured a majority of the newly created seats, but the party also had held a majority of the seats that were eliminated in redistricting. The end result of all of this was an eight-seat Democratic gain. Democrats also won virtually all of the close races in the Senate, unseating one Republican incumbent and gaining a total of two seats. These changes are in line with historical trends—the party that wins the presidency traditionally gains seats in Congress—but they came in the face of substantial spending by outside groups that supported Republicans. Just as it is difficult to understand the 2012 presidential election merely by looking at candidate spending, so it is difficult to appreciate the results of congressional elections without accounting for Super PAC spending.

The first section of Table 7.4 shows the average total receipts and individual contribution receipts by party and by candidate type. The totals here are unremarkable in comparison to previous elections. In 2008, the average incumbent raised between $1.2 million and $1.3 million; the average open-seat candidate raised approximately $1.4 million, and the average challenger raised slightly over $500,000. Four years later, the average incumbent and the average challenger did slightly better, and the average open-seat candidate in 2012 in fact raised less than the average open-seat candidate in 2008. Given the idiosyncrasies of which seats become open, it is hard to make too much of these changes; one could, however, speculate that redistricting in 2012 ought to have produced greater competition and hence more spending, particularly in open-seat races.[3]

The real story of the 2012 House elections, however, can be told by looking at the second section of the table. It is customary in analyses of congressional elections to separate out competitive and uncompetitive races, using pre-election forecasts or the target lists of the party campaign committees. Conveniently, in 2012 outside groups largely did this for us. Almost all competitive House races featured spending by outside groups. What is most remarkable here is that among the six different candidate types here, only one group (Republican incumbents) improved on its 2008 averages. In other words, even the strongest 2012 candidates appeared (as of October 17) to raise less, on average, than the strongest candidates in previous years. Outside groups, however, spent far more than they had previously; there was more spending, and perhaps just as consequentially, there were more races with substantial outside spending than in past years. The 2010 House elections, according to Paul Herrnson (2013, 26), featured slightly under $100 million in independent expenditures by nonparty groups. In 2012, there was slightly over $177 million. Sixty-seven different candidates benefited from over $2 million in outside spending on their behalf; only eight of these candidates raised more money on their own than what was spent on their behalf by outside organizations. Competitive challengers, as shown in Table 7.4, raised, on average, little more than a third of what was spent on their behalf.

Table 7.4 Campaign Finance in the 2012 House of Representatives Elections

	Number of candidates	*Net receipts*	*Individual contributions*	*Total independent expenditures*	*Party independent expenditures*	*Nonparty independent expenditures*
All races						
Democrats						
Incumbents	157	1,331,920	660,470			
Challengers	174	656,498	464,260			
Open seats	35	1,120,180	706,129			
Republicans						
Incumbents	208	1,849,082	996,139			
Challengers	130	515,032	341,186			
Open seats	29	975,980	679,181			
Totals						
Incumbents	365	1,626,631	851,755			
Challengers	304	596,003	411,630			
Open seats	64	1,054,799	693,918			
Races with independent spending						
Democrats						
Incumbents	31	2,033,470	1,082,940	1,095,211	367,021	728,190
Challengers	49	1,657,540	1,174,069	1,748,231	786,236	961,995
Open seats	12	1,539,588	891,670	1,152,354	703,316	449,038
Republicans						
Incumbents	47	2,867,968	1,850,213	1,933,589	721,911	1,211,679
Challengers	35	1,380,661	902,046	1,664,287	695,964	968,323
Open seats	10	1,129,839	778,402	1,572,249	451,395	1,120,864
Totals						
Incumbents	78	2,536,309	1,545,271	1,600,388	580,865	1,019,523
Challengers	84	1,542,174	1,060,726	1,713,254	748,623	964,632
Open seats	22	1,353,339	840,201	1,343,215	588,802	754,413

Sources: Federal Election Commission; Campaign Finance Institute.

Note: Candidate totals through October 17; independent expenditure data through November 7. All dollar amounts listed are averages.

Senate races, summarized in Table 7.5, tell a similar story. Few political experts believed that control of the House would change, but for much of the election cycle, many expected that the Republican Party had a good chance of gaining control of the Senate. In fact, during the late summer, as

Table 7.5 Campaign Finance in the 2012 Senate Elections

	Number of candidates	Net receipts	Individual contributions	Total independent expenditures	Party independent expenditures	Nonparty independent expenditures
All races						
Democrats						
Incumbents	16	9,852,712	7,276,253	2,495,160	909,922	1,585,238
Challengers	4	13,464,620	12,257,726	7,032,961	2,302,296	4,730,665
Open seats	11	6,279,679	5,289,483	6,904,964	2,576,235	4,328,729
Republicans						
Incumbents	6	10,100,566	7,009,522	2,540,259	538,907	2,001,352
Challengers	17	4,860,553	3,163,797	4,286,992	505,366	3,781,626
Open seats	10	10,656,716	5,139,006	8,317,464	1,981,792	6,335,672
Totals						
Incumbents	22	9,920,309	7,203,508	2,507,460	808,736	1,698,724
Challengers	21	6,499,423	4,895,974	4,810,034	847,638	3,962,396
Open seats	21	8,363,982	5,217,827	7,577,583	2,293,167	5,284,416
Races with over $2 million in independent spending						
Democrats						
Incumbents	4	14,857,553	11,920,595	9,341,368	3,639,358	5,702,011
Challengers	3	17,819,373	16,261,206	9,359,591	3,069,727	6,289,864
Open seats	7	8,656,014	7,358,122	10,304,083	3,835,498	6,468,585
Republicans						
Incumbents	2	17,535,589	13,337,494	7,611,916	1,616,721	5,995,195
Challengers	6	10,684,844	6,227,155	11,600,752	1,408,535	10,192,217
Open seats	7	6,510,520	4,895,437	11,526,191	2,829,751	8,696,440
Totals						
Incumbents	6	15,750,232	12,392,894	8,764,884	2,965,145	5,799,739
Challengers	9	13,063,020	9,571,838	10,853,698	1,962,266	8,891,433
Open seats	14	7,583,267	6,126,780	10,915,137	3,332,624	7,582,513

Sources: Federal Election Commission; Campaign Finance Institute.

Note: Candidate totals through October 17; independent expenditure data through November 7. All dollar amounts listed are averages.

Mitt Romney's prospects for winning the presidency appeared to dim, some prominent Republicans argued that wealthy Republican donors should turn their attention to Senate contests. Competitive Senate candidates raised, on average, well over $10 million, and interest groups poured a total of $231.5

million into independent expenditures for Senate candidates, more than double what they spent on Senate races in 2010. The year's marquee Senate race, the Massachusetts race between Republican Scott Brown and Democrat Elizabeth Warren, however, was noteworthy for the candidates' successful effort to prevent interest groups and parties from purchasing advocacy advertisements. Under the terms of their pact, a candidate who was the beneficiary of advocacy advertisements would contribute a sum equal to half the cost of the advertisements to a charity of the other candidate's choice. Warren was perhaps the most successful Senate candidate in 2012 at raising money in small contributions and from out-of-state donors; the race wound up being the most expensive Senate race in history that featured neither a self-funded candidate nor Hillary Clinton. Interest group spending in the race, however, was limited to direct mail and get-out-the-vote efforts.

Many analyses of outside spending in the 2012 congressional elections were quick to claim that outside spending did not make a difference in the outcomes of the races (Confessore and Bidgood 2012). There was an overall pro-Republican tilt to outside spending in 2012, and Republican incumbents had a hefty financial advantage in many congressional races, with or without outside help. Yet Democrats fully joined the Super PAC game as well; 9 of the 20 biggest beneficiaries of outside expenditures in the House were Democrats. It may be, as well, that some Republican Super PACs made poor choices about where to spend their money or that Republicans faced a challenging environment in congressional races. There are also many concerns one might raise about the consequences of outside spending for the quality of campaigns, the tone of campaigns, the ability of citizens to make informed choices, and so forth. Many of these concerns are well beyond the scope of this chapter, but it is important to note that the financing of 2012 congressional races was qualitatively different than in years past and that the relatively unremarkable outcomes of many races should not be taken to mean that the 2012 congressional elections were not unusual.

The activities of outside groups in the 2012 congressional races were reminiscent of 2010 in that they arguably expanded the playing field. Organizations such as Karl Rove's American Crossroads had deep enough pockets that they could invest heavily in congressional races, in some instances outspending the candidates and the parties. The Young Guns Action Fund, a Super PAC associated with House Majority Leader Eric Cantor, also spent heavily on several House races. As in 2010, in some instances Super PAC spending preceded party spending, and outside groups were able to draw the attention of the party committees to races they had previously ignored. One noteworthy difference between 2010 and 2012, however, is that 2012 featured a much larger number of candidate-specific groups. Many House candidates, including Illinois Republicans Joe Walsh and Judy Biggert, Florida Republican Allen West, and Utah Democrat Jim Matheson, were the beneficiaries of groups that had only one major donor and that spent all of their money on behalf of only one candidate (Confessore and McGinty 2012; Davis 2012). Other idiosyncratic "boutique PACs" included the Campaign for Primary Accountability, which spent money against incumbents of both parties in the primaries, and Friends of Democracy, a Super PAC that spent money in opposition to incumbents who had spoken in favor of the *Citizens United* decision and the creation of Super PACs. Although not as closely aligned with their favored candidates as the presidential Super PACs, these groups clearly frightened many incumbents of both parties, and by the end of the election, incumbents of both parties were reportedly working on legislation to limit the role of such groups in future races (Steinhauer and Weisman 2012).

Where the Money Came From: Wealthy Donors, Interest Groups, and Party Committees

One of the main fears raised by the *Citizens United* decision was that there would be a flood of anonymous money into the 2012 elections. Although the preceding discussion makes it clear that there was a substantial increase in spending, many of the biggest spenders in 2012 allowed themselves to be identified and in some instances actually sought to discuss their reasons for spending money. The *Citizens United* decision permitted corporations to engage in express advocacy, but most corporations that did engage in political activity sought to do so through umbrella organizations such as the U.S. Chamber of Commerce or through Super PACs; the same was true of individuals. 501(c) groups such as the Chamber, Americans for Prosperity, and Karl Rove's Crossroads GPS are not required to disclose their donors; Super PACs, on the other hand, are required to do so. According to Center for Responsive Politics data, 85 individuals contributed $1 million or more to nonparty groups; these individuals gave a total of $186.6 million to Republican-leaning groups and $74.0 million to Democratic-leaning groups. Three individuals (and their spouses) contributed over $98 million, all of it going to Republican groups. These three individuals—casino magnate Sheldon Adelson, real estate developer Robert Perry, and Texas businessman Harold Simmons—had long been supporters of conservative politicians and causes. Adelson in particular was very open about his actions. Some reporters speculated that despite their deep pockets, even donors such as Adelson understood that they could not singlehandedly influence the election, and their openness about how much they were giving and what the groups they supported were doing with their money was aimed at encouraging others to give (Vogel 2012). Super PACs and 501(c)(4) groups like the Koch Brothers' Americans for Prosperity also openly discussed strategy, with the aim of assuring donors that their money had been well spent.

Adelson, Perry, and Simmons are not, however, household names, nor are their businesses. Although *Citizens United* raised the specter that any large business could play in American elections, in reality few well-known businesses made contributions that could be traced. A very public incident in 2010 in which the Target Corporation was attacked by the liberal group MoveOn.org for supporting a politician who had made antigay statements forced Target to apologize for its actions and to contribute money to gay rights causes (Palmer and Phillip 2012). Although a relatively minor flap, this incident served as a reminder to corporations that there could be a harsh public backlash if they became too involved in partisan politics. More traditional political action committees remained an important part of candidate fundraising, but they were no more consequential than in previous elections; direct contributions from PACs to federal candidates totaled slightly over $400 million, approximately the same as in 2008 and about $20 million less than in 2010.[4] Corporations and wealthy individuals had the option of contributing to 501(c) groups such as the Chamber of Commerce. The Chamber did spend over $50 million, a large number (the largest in the group's history) but not a surprising one given that the group had spent over $30 million in 2010. Other traditional corporate, labor, and advocacy groups were heavily involved in the 2012 election, but even in instances where such groups increased their spending over their 2008 or 2010 totals, they were not able to compete with Rove's two Crossroads groups—a Super PAC and a 501(c)(4), which together spent $215.8 million—or other large Super PACs.

The candidate-sponsored Super PACs received much attention from the news media. Although some Super PAC contributors were clearly unhappy about receiving attention, nothing particularly out of the ordinary was turned up in any of these analyses. What did become clear, however, was that there was effectively no way for the parties, the candidates, or the media to discipline Super PACs. Some Super PACs supported candidates whom the party campaign committees had abandoned, and others employed advertising strategies that the parties and traditional interest groups would not touch.[5] David Keating, president of the Center for Competitive Politics (a group opposed to campaign finance restrictions), noted,

> There's been all this critique of Super PACs—"there's too much coordination, they're just arms of the campaigns." In a lot of cases, these independent campaigns do things the campaigns don't want them to do. They're often seen as loose cannons and there isn't even a lot of gratitude for what they're doing. (Burns 2012)

At the outset of this chapter, I noted that the *Citizens United* decision had, among other things, eliminated restrictions on political advertising by corporations and labor unions. These restrictions had been one of the two major components of the Bipartisan Campaign Reform Act (BCRA), which took effect for the 2004 election cycle. The other major component of BCRA was a prohibition on "soft money" fundraising by political parties. Prior to BCRA, party campaign committees had been permitted to receive contributions in unlimited amounts provided these contributions were used for "party building" purposes—that is, they were not permitted to use these contributions to directly advocate for the election or defeat of a candidate. Despite predictions that the parties would be harmed by BCRA, the six party campaign committees quickly adapted and developed extensive grassroots fundraising efforts. In 2012, the parties raised slightly less than they had in 2008; two of the three Republican committees (the National Republican Senatorial Campaign Committee and the National Republican Congressional Committee) raised somewhat more than they had in 2008, as did the Democratic National Committee, whereas the other three raised less. The Republican National Committee, which had been plagued by mismanagement following the 2008 election, rebounded to the point that it was able to play a constructive role in the Romney campaign (as Table 7.3 shows). And the Democratic Party House and Senate committees, although they raised less than in previous cycles, outraised their Republican counterparts; the two Democratic committees raised a total of $266.1 million, whereas the two Republican committees raised $235.8 million. All of these developments, however, did not clearly mean that the party committees were able to play the dominant role they had played in so many congressional races in previous cycles. As a Campaign Finance Institute (2012a) press release noted, even a modest increase in fundraising would put the parties at a competitive disadvantage simply because of the greatly expanded role of nonparty groups. Such developments led many of those who had advocated for the soft money ban early in the decade to rethink their position. Restrictions on party spending, in other words, appear to have made more sense when nonparty groups were also restricted in similar ways.

Conclusion

The 2012 election was clearly more expensive than past elections. Estimates have pegged overall spending on the presidential and congressional elections at approximately $6 billion, an increase of more than $700 million since the 2008 election (Center for Responsive Politics 2012). More importantly, however, the role of money in 2012 dominated public discussion of the race, as wealthy contributors discussed their goals, Super PACs dominated the airwaves, and the presidential candidates frequently detoured from their swing-state campaign stops to court wealthy donors. The story behind these developments, however, is complicated. The *Citizens United* decision clearly played a role in the surge in campaign money, yet so did changes in the technology candidates use to raise money and the increasing irrelevance of presidential public-funding mechanisms. One might argue, further, that the increases in overall spending and the fact that some of this money is difficult to trace were unintended consequences of the early-2000s changes in campaign finance law.

As the 2012 election took shape, many Democrats publicly fretted that the onslaught of corporate money *Citizens United* had unleashed would doom the party. The status quo result of the 2012 election shows that this was not the case—that both parties have begun to adapt to the new, less regulated campaign finance regime. Perhaps it merely means that there are enough wealthy contributors on the political left to provide some sort of balance. The 2012 election showed that campaign finance deregulation has not been demonstrably harmful to two-party competition (yet). Still, which party wins and loses is not the only metric for judging the fairness of our campaign finance laws. In the next few years there will certainly be much debate about the consequences of our nation's new campaign finance arrangements for public policy and, more generally, for the well-being of the American voters.

NOTES

1. Here, as elsewhere in the chapter, estimates for total spending and for spending by sector are drawn from data compiled by the Center for Responsive Politics and the Sunlight Foundation; individual candidate data are taken from the Federal Election Commission website unless otherwise noted. Presidential data include the full election cycle. Congressional general election data are taken from October 17 preprimary filings and do not reflect receipts between October 17 and Election Day.

2. This is not the only explanation that has been provided for the lower cost per ad for Democrats. Another common explanation has to do with the shows on which the Obama campaign advertised; Scherer (2012) argues that the Obama campaign's microtargeting efforts led it to advertise on less popular television shows that reached small subsets of voters that its research had indicated were persuadable.

3. This comparison uses data for the full 2008 election cycle, but only fundraising numbers through October 17 for the 2012 candidates. Fundraising during the final weeks of the 2012 campaign may well have increased totals for the different candidate types somewhat, but it is unlikely that it increased these totals to the point that there was a substantial increase over 2008.

4. Again, we are comparing data through October 17, 2012, with full cycle data for 2008 and 2010.

5. Edsall (2012) discusses some of these tactics. See also Center for Responsive Politics (2012).

REFERENCES

Ball, Molly. 2012. "Obama's Edge: The Ground Game That Could Put Him Over the Top." *The Atlantic,* October 24.

Baum, Laura. 2012. "Presidential Ad War Tops 1M Airings." Middletown, CT: Wesleyan Media Project. http://mediaproject.wesleyan.edu/2012/11/02/presidential-ad-war-tops-1m-airings/ (accessed November 28, 2012).

Bravender, Robin. 2011. "Texas Key in Perry Fundraising." *Politico,* October 15.

Bravender, Robin, and Kenneth P. Vogel. 2012. "Democrats' Most Wanted Donors." *Politico,* February 25.

Burns, Alexander. 2012. "Dems, GOP Fear Bomb from Outside Groups." *Politico,* May 21.

Campaign Finance Institute. 2008. "CFI Analysis of Presidential Candidates' Donor Reports: Reality Check—Obama Received about the Same Percentage from Small Donors in 2008 as Bush in 2004." November 24. Washington, DC: Campaign Finance Institute.

Campaign Finance Institute. 2011a. "CFI Analysis of September 30th Presidential Reports: Romney and Perry Financially Separate from the GOP Pack; President Obama Raises the Bulk of His Money from Small Donors." October 17. Washington, DC: Campaign Finance Institute.

Campaign Finance Institute. 2011b. "Presidential Campaign Reports for June 30, 2011: Three of This Year's Top Four Presidential Fundraisers So Far Are Relying on Small Donors." July 19. Washington, DC: Campaign Finance Institute.

Campaign Finance Institute. 2012a. "The National Parties Are Holding Their Own Financially at the Eighteen-Month Mark." July 30. Washington, DC: Campaign Finance Institute.

Campaign Finance Institute. 2012b. "Presidential Campaign Finance Reports through Dec. 31: 48% of President Obama's 2011 Money Came from Small Donors—Better Than Doubling 2007. Romney's Small Donors: 9%." February 8. Washington, DC: Campaign Finance Institute.

Campaign Finance Institute. 2012c. "Presidential Campaign Finance Reports for January 2012: 88% of Obama's Itemized Donors in January Were Repeaters; 40% of Romney's Donors Have Maxed Out." February 22. Washington, DC: Campaign Finance Institute.

Campaign Finance Institute. 2012d. "Presidential Campaign Finance Reports for February 2012: Obama's Small-Dollar Percentage Down Slightly in February; Santorum's Stayed High; Romney's Stayed Low." March 22. Washington, DC: Campaign Finance Institute.

Campaign Finance Institute. 2012e. "Presidential Campaign Finance Reports for March 2012: Obama and Romney Each Have Their Best Months So Far, Gearing Up for the General Election." April 24. Washington, DC: Campaign Finance Institute.

Campaign Finance Institute. 2012f. "Presidential Campaign Finance Reports for August 2012: Obama's Long-Term Small-Donor Strategy Begins to Show Dividends against Romney in August." September 24. Washington, DC: Campaign Finance Institute.

Center for Responsive Politics. 2012. *2012 Election Spending Will Reach $6 Billion, Center for Responsive Politics Predicts.* Washington, DC: Center for Responsive Politics.

http://www.opensecrets.org/news/2012/10/2012-election-spending-will-reach-6.html (accessed February 3, 2013).

Confessore, Nicholas. 2011a. "Lines Blur between Candidates and PACs with Unlimited Cash." *New York Times,* August 27.

Confessore, Nicholas. 2011b. "Small Donors Are Slow to Return to the Obama Fold." *New York Times,* September 24.

Confessore, Nicholas. 2012a. "GOP Campaigns Grow More Dependent on 'Super PAC' Aid." *New York Times,* February 20.

Confessore, Nicholas. 2012b. "'Super PACs' Supply Millions as GOP Race Drains Field." *New York Times,* March 20.

Confessore, Nicholas, and Jess Bidgood. 2012. "Little to Show for Cash Flood by Big Donors." *New York Times,* November 7.

Confessore, Nicholas, and Michael Luo. 2012. "Secrecy Shrouds 'Super PAC' Funds in Latest Filings." *New York Times,* February 2.

Confessore, Nicholas, and Jo Craven McGinty. 2012. "New 'Super PACs' Alter Landscape for House Races." *New York Times,* October 8.

Confessore, Nicholas, Jo Craven McGinty, and Derek Willis. 2012. "Low on Cash, Romney Tries to Rally Donors for Final Phase." *New York Times,* September 20.

Cummings, Jeanne. 2011a. "New Dem Money Group to Take on GOP." *Politico,* April 29.

Cummings, Jeanne. 2011b. "Team Obama's 2012 Cash Challenge." *Politico,* January 14.

Davis, Susan. 2012. "Boutique PACs Making a Big Splash." *USA Today,* October 8.

Edsall, Thomas. 2012. "Billionaires Going Rogue." *New York Times,* October 28.

Eggen, Dan. 2012a. "2012 GOP Contest Shaping Up to Be Cheapest Race in Years." *Washington Post,* March 12.

Eggen, Dan. 2012b. "Are Iowa Caucuses Harbinger of the Super-PAC Era?" *Washington Post,* January 3.

Eggen, Dan. 2012c. "With More Control over Campaign Cash, Obama Gets More Discounts on Advertising." *Washington Post,* September 26.

Eggen, Dan, and T. W. Farman. 2011. "Obama Outpaces GOP Rivals—and His Own 2008 Results—in Small Donations." *Washington Post,* November 18.

Eggen, Dan, and T. W. Farnam. 2012. "Super PAC Donors Revealed: Who Are the Power Players in the GOP Primary?" *Washington Post,* February 22.

Farnam, T. W. 2011. "GOP Candidates' Third-Quarter Funding: Most of Perry's Money Came from Texas." *Washington Post,* October 15.

Ferguson, Thomas. 2012. "Massive Surge of Republican Money in Last Ditch Effort to Sink Obama." *Alternet,* November 1.

Fowler, Erika. 2012. "Outside Group Involvement in GOP Contest Skyrockets Compared to 2008." Middletown, CT: Wesleyan Media Project. http://mediaproject.wesleyan.edu/2012/01/30/group-involvement-skyrockets/ (accessed November 28, 2012).

Gardner, Amy. 2012. "Pro-Gingrich Super PAC Builds a Shadow Campaign." *Washington Post,* January 24.

Gibson, Ginger. 2012. "Mitt Romney: President Obama at Fault for Fundraising Focus." *Politico,* September 24.

Green, Donald P., and Alan S. Gerber. 2008. *Get Out the Vote.* 2nd ed. Washington, DC: Brookings Institution.

Hagen, Michael G., and Robin Kolodny. 2008. "Finding the Cost of Campaign Advertising." *The Forum* 6 (1): article 11.

Hamburger, Tom, and Matea Gold. 2011. "Obama Campaign Team Courts Wealthy Donors." *Los Angeles Time,* June 25.

Herrnson, Paul S. 2013. "A New Era of Interest Group Participation in Federal Elections." In *Interest Groups Unleashed,* ed. Paul S. Herrnson, Christopher J. Deering, and Clyde Wilcox, 9–30. Washington, DC: Congressional Quarterly Press.

Homans, Charles. 2012. "Can the Republican Party Survive Its Billionaires?" *Washington Post,* February 24.

Levinthal, Dave. 2012a. "The Fight for the $5 Donation." *Politico,* October 1.

Levinthal, Dave. 2012b. "Pro-Paul Super PAC Ducks Disclosure." *Politico,* January 9.

Levinthal, Dave. 2012c. "Romney's Small Donor Decline." *Politico,* September 20.

Levinthal, Dave, and Kenneth P. Vogel. 2011. "Super PACs Go Stealth." *Politico,* December 30.

Levinthal, Dave, and Kenneth P. Vogel. 2012. "Adelsons Gave Big to Pro-Newt PAC." *Politico,* February 20.

McIntire, Mike, and Michael Luo. 2012. "Fine Line between 'Super PACs' and Campaigns." *New York Times,* February 25.

Messina, Jim. 2012. "We Will Not Play by Two Sets of Rules." Press release, Obama for President, February 6. http://www.barackobama.com/news/entry/we-will-not-play-by-two-sets-of-rules/ (accessed November 28, 2012).

Mooney, Brian C. 2012. "With Donors Tough to Find, Romney Faces Dilemma." *Boston Globe,* March 16.

Palmer, Anna. 2012a. "Bye-Bye to Bragging about Bundling." *Politico,* February 14.

Palmer, Anna. 2012b. "Romney Calls in the Cash Cavalry." *Politico,* March 9.

Palmer, Anna, and Abby Phillip. 2012. "Corporations Not Funding Super PACs." *Politico,* March 8.

Rucker, Philip, and Dan Eggen. 2012. "Mitt Romney, Facing Money Challenges, Aggressively Seeks Donations." *Washington Post,* February 29.

Rutenberg, Jim. 2011. "Groups Form to Aid Democrats with Anonymous Money." *New York Times,* April 29.

Rutenberg, Jim, and Jeff Zeleny. 2011. "Big GOP Donors Adopt Wait-and-See 2012 Tack." *New York Times,* May 7.

Scherer, Michael. 2012. "Inside the Secret World of Quant and Data Crunchers Who Helped Obama Win." *Time,* November 19, 56–60.

Schoenberg, Shira. 2012. "Super PAC Backing Romney Fueled by Financial Industry." *Boston Globe,* February 2.

Sides, John. 2012. "Mapping Romney and Obama Field Offices." *The Monkey Cage.* http://themonkeycage.org/blog/2012/11/06/mapping-romney-and-obama-field-offices/ (accessed November 28, 2012).

Steinhauer, Jennifer, and Jonathan Weisman. 2012. "Mauled by Attack Ads, Incumbents Weigh Tighter Rules." *New York Times,* October 23.

Taylor, Paul, and Norman Ornstein. 2002. "The Case for Free Air Time: A Broadcast Spectrum Fee for Campaign Finance Reform." Washington, DC: New America Foundation.

Vogel, Kenneth P. 2012. "Playing to Donors, GOP Groups Spill Some Secrets." *Politico,* October 19.

Vogel, Kenneth P., and Dave Levinthal. 2012. "Campaigns Reject Super PAC Take-over." *Politico,* January 29.

Vogel, Kenneth P., and Abby Philip. 2012. "Santorum Donations Soar after Wins." *Politico,* February 20.

Zeleny, Jeff, and Jim Rutenberg. 2012. "Obama Yields in Marshalling of 'Super PAC.'" *New York Times,* February 7.

8 Public Opinion and the Presidential Election

Christopher Wlezien

The 2012 presidential election turned out to be strikingly predictable.[1] This was all too clear at the end of the campaign, when various "quants" successfully predicted the result in 49 or 50 states (see, e.g., Bartlett 2012). The most celebrated was Nate Silver of the *New York Times* blog *FiveThirtyEight,* but there were numerous others, including Simon Jackman at Pollster.com, Drew Linzer of Votamatic, and Sam Wang of Princeton Election Consortium. Much of their success at the end of the campaign was due to the pre-election polls themselves, with basic RealClearPolitics averages of poll results from the last few days correctly predicting the winner in 49 of the 50 states, narrowly missing (by 0.3 of a percentage point) Florida. However, there is value in taking seriously how to combine polls from different survey organizations, or "houses" (Erikson and Wlezien 1999; Jackman 2005).

The Election Day result actually was foreseeable much earlier in the year. The Pollyvote website (http://pollyvote.com) provided updates and summaries of different forecasting methods throughout the election year. Included there are a wide variety of approaches, among the most compelling of which are the following six: (1) averages of pre-election polls asking how respondents would vote if the election were held today, (2) the projections of the vote from these pre-election polls based on their historical relationships, (3) polls of the public asking about who will win, (4) surveys of political science experts, (5) election prediction market prices, and (6) the political science models. For information about the different approaches and about combining them to forecast elections, see the Pollyvote website.[2]

In January of the election year, the forecasts were mixed. Poll-based methods and the prediction markets indicated a toss-up, whereas the others gave Obama a very slight advantage. By April, all six approaches pointed to Obama, but in each case only by a little. This advantage remained until the end of the campaign. The specific forecast did change as the campaign unfolded and as events played a role, most notably, the Democratic convention and the first presidential debate. The former gave Obama a bump, and the latter allowed Romney to pull even in the polls, but even at that time the other forecasts continued to point to Obama. The president won and with a bare majority (51.1 percent) of the vote, pretty much as forecasters had expected all along. That the result was close and yet predictable is a paradox of sorts. It also is understandable, as we will see.

Elections ask voters to stay the course or change. Political scientists have learned that presidential elections in the United States mostly are a referendum on the sitting president. Has the president done a good job? What do I think of his policies? How about conditions in the country? Although answers to these questions matter, so does the choice of candidates. Voters consider whether the promise of the alternative is better than the record of the incumbent. In 2012, the voters chose to stay the course. This chapter considers why.

The Partisan Context

Party identification is of primary importance to voters on Election Day. Individuals who identify with a party are very likely to support the party's candidate for president. This has been known for a long time (Campbell et al. 1960). The balance of partisans in the electorate thus matters on Election Day. When more people identify with one party than the other, the candidate of the favored party benefits. When the balance shifts, moreover, the candidate's share changes accordingly. This also is well known (Erikson, MacKuen, and Stimson 2002).

Party identification in the United States has changed over time. Figure 8.1 plots the percentages of people who identify with the two main political parties along with those who consider themselves independent. The data are for each presidential election from 1952 to 2012 and come from American National Election Studies (http://www.electionstudies.org/). These surveys ask, "Generally speaking, do you usually think of yourself as a Republican, a Democrat, an Independent or what?" In Figure 8.1, we can see that Democrats have held an advantage throughout the period, though the advantage declined some and leveled off in recent election years. The Republican share has remained stable. The percentage of independents has increased.

The numbers in Figure 8.1 are to some degree deceiving. Most notably, the percentage of independents misrepresents attachment over time. That is, most independents lean toward one of the two parties, and these leaners behave like expressed partisans. In 2012, a Pew survey conducted right before the election (October 31–November 3) found that 40 percent of voters called themselves independents, but most of these—29 percent of all voters—leaned toward either the Democrats or the Republicans. Taking into account leaners, 50 percent of the electorate identified with the Democratic Party, and 39 percent identified with the Republicans. Only 11 percent were "pure" independents. This figure has dropped steadily from 16 percent in 1976. The number was

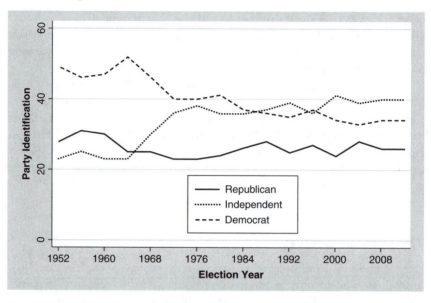

Figure 8.1 Party Identification in Historical Perspective, 1952–2012

Sources: American National Election Study, 1952–2008 (http://electionstudies.org/nesguide/toptable/tab2a_1.htm); Pew survey of adults, October 31–November 3, 2012 (http://www.people-press.org/files/legacy-pdf/11-4-12%20Election%20Weekend%20Release.pdf).

much lower in the 1950s and averaged 7–8 percent. For details, see the American National Election Studies website (http://www.electionstudies.org/).

Expressed identification with parties is only half of the story because its importance to voters can vary over time. Scholars have learned that party identification matters more on Election Day in the present than it did in the past. In other words, people who identify with a party are more likely to support that party's candidate today than in earlier elections (Bartels 2000). In 2012, 92 percent of Democrats reported voting for Obama and 93 percent of Republicans for Romney. By comparison, in the 1976 and 1980 elections, approximately 85 percent of partisans voted for their party's candidate; the number was lower still in 1972, when about 75 percent did so. Despite the growth of independents, the electorate actually is more partisan now than it has been in the last 40 years—there are more leaners, and those who identify with or lean toward a party are more likely to vote for the party's candidate.

What did this mean in 2012? There was a partisan advantage for the Democrats, perhaps a little less than they enjoyed in 2008. The advantage was lower still on Election Day, given that Democrats are less likely to vote. The national exit poll found that 38 percent of voters identified with the Democrats, 32 percent identified with the Republicans, and 29 percent identified as independents. (As usual, there were more partisans and fewer independents in the voting electorate than in surveys of the adult population before Election Day—see Figure 8.1.) Though small, Obama's edge was relatively solid, partly because of partisan intensity. There are fewer "floating" voters up for grabs (Zaller 2004). This limits the swing from election to election. Still, election results do change. Consider that President Obama's share of the vote in 2012 was approximately 1.5 percent below what he received in 2008. It also appears from Figure 8.1 that the difference was not due to changing party identification.

The President's Record

Presidential elections largely are referenda on the sitting president (see, e.g., Gelman and King 1993; Holbrook 1996; J. Campbell 2000; Erikson and Wlezien 2012b). Though this is true even when the president is not running for reelection, there is reason to suppose that the president's record is a more reliable predictor when the incumbent is on the ballot. In 2012, President Obama was running. How did his record figure into his reelection?

Presidential Approval

Survey organizations frequently ask people about whether they approve or disapprove of the job the president is doing. The responses tell us a lot about voters' electoral preferences (Brody and Sigelman 1983; Abramson, Aldrich, and Rohde 2007). This is clear in Figure 8.2. The figure plots the incumbent party's share of the two-party vote—ignoring third-party candidates—by the approval rating in the three months before the election. Also shown is the line relating approval and the vote. Here we can see a strong positive relationship. When approval is high, voters tend to stay the course and support the candidate of the incumbent party; when approval is low, voters change course.

Though strong (the Pearson's correlation equals 0.86), the relationship between approval and the vote is not perfect, especially when approval is high. That is, sometimes voters elect to change course even when presidential approval nears 60 percent, as in 1960 and 2000. These were years when the incumbent was not running, which may help explain what happened in those years. (Consider that approval has never erred in predicting the winner when the incumbent was running—see Figure 8.2.) But approval did predict well in each of the other years without incumbents—1952, 1968, 1988, and 2008. Indeed, the vote in those years was right on or extremely close to the line predicting the vote from approval. Thus, what we can say for sure is that high approval rates are not a sufficient condition for incumbent party return to the White House—that is, they don't guarantee it.

Just as high approval rates are not sufficient for election, neither are they necessary. The 2012 election is a case in point. President Obama's average

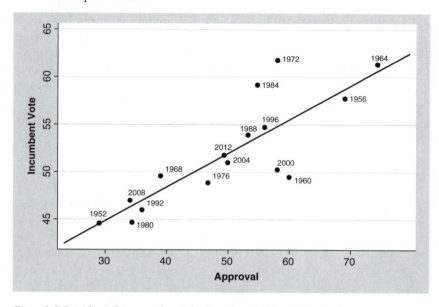

Figure 8.2 Presidential Approval and the Presidential Vote, 1952–2012
Sources: Data for 1952–2008 are from Erikson and Wlezien (2012b); data for 2012 are from Pollster.com.

approval rating during the fall campaign was 49 percent, though it drifted up to just below 50 percent by Election Day. Of course, he did win and secured approximately 51 percent of the vote to former governor Romney's 47.2 percent. From Figure 8.2 we can see that the vote Obama received was exactly what we expect based on his approval rating alone. Much the same was true in 2004, when President George W. Bush won just less than 51 percent of the vote despite an approval rating of almost 50 percent. These two cases suggest an incumbency advantage of sorts—that presidents can win reelection despite not having the approval of a majority of voters. It is not perfectly clear how low presidential approval can go and still offer the incumbent party candidate an edge, however. The line in Figure 8.2 indicates that a 45 percent approval rating predicts a 50–50 split, but this was not enough for President Ford in 1976. There are no other cases when approval leading up to Election Day was above 40 percent (but below 50 percent). In all five of the cases when it was below 40 percent, the incumbent party candidate lost, and whether the incumbent president was running did not matter.

The Economy

The economy is of special importance in presidential elections. It structures the campaign and can be decisive on Election Day (see, e.g., Gelman and King 1993; Holbrook 1996; J. Campbell 2000; Erikson, MacKuen, and Stimson

2002; Vavreck 2009; Erikson and Wlezien 2012b). The connection has been the subject of political science research for decades and was popularized by Bill Clinton's campaign advisor James Carville during their successful 1992 campaign: "It's the economy, stupid." Although everyone agrees that the economy has an impact on what voters do, why and how it matters is the subject of scholarly debate. Consider that politicians have little direct control over the economy and that, even to the extent they do, the president is just one actor among others, including Congress and the Federal Reserve Board. Although it has been the subject of a good amount of research, the psychology by which voters respond to the economy remains unclear.

Part of the economy's impact on the vote is through presidential approval and party identification itself—when the economy is going well, the public tends to approve of the job the president is doing and is more likely to identify with the party of the president (Erikson, MacKuen, and Stimson 2002). This benefits the incumbent party candidate, as we have seen. When the economy is not going well, by contrast, it bodes badly. How did the economy matter in 2012?

The economy was uppermost in the minds of the American public throughout the 2012 election cycle. This is not at all surprising given the depth of the recession and the protracted emergence from it. At the beginning of the election year, the unemployment rate was 8.5 percent. Conditions improved thereafter, and the unemployment rate dropped to 7.8 percent, but economic issues remained dominant on Election Day. This is clear from the responses people gave to the common question asking about the "most important problem" facing the nation. Results of the Gallup poll from mid-October in Table 8.1 are typical. Here we can see that an astounding 69 percent of survey respondents mentioned economic issues. A distant second was the federal budget deficit, mentioned by 12 percent of respondents, and keep in mind that this too is an economic issue of sorts. Foreign affairs and defense were further down the list, at 9 percent. The economic context in

Table 8.1 2012 Public Opinion about the Most Important Problem Facing the Country

What do you think is the most important problem facing the country today?			
Economy	69	Ethics and morality	4
Federal budget deficit	12	Immigration	2
Foreign and defense	9	Care for elderly/Medicare	2
Government	9	Taxes	2
Health	7	Welfare	2
Education	5	Fuel/oil prices	2

Note: Numbers are percentages of respondents; the percentages sum to more than 100 because many respondents give more than one response. The source is the October 15–16, 2012, Gallup poll of 1,004 adults.

Table 8.2 Economic Perceptions in 2012

Do you think the condition of the national economy is:	
Excellent	2
Good	21
Not so good	45
Poor	31
Is the U.S. economy:	
Getting better	39
Staying the same	29
Getting worse	30

Note: Numbers are percentages of respondents. The source is the 2012 national exit poll.

2012 looked to be much like that in 1992, and some observers pointed back to 1980, when the economy actually shrank, seemingly dooming incumbent president Jimmy Carter to defeat.

Although the public thought the economy was a problem for the country, it is not clear that it was a problem for President Obama's reelection. To be sure, conditions were not good. They were getting better, however, and voters perceived the trend. This is evident in Table 8.2, which reports responses to questions about the economy from the 2012 exit poll. Fully 76 percent of voters said that conditions were either "not so good" or "poor," and only 23 percent said that the economy was "good" or "excellent." At the same time, 39 percent said that the economy was "getting better," and only 30 percent said that it was "getting worse."

Economic circumstances were bad but getting better, and the latter is what matters most on Election Day (Hibbs 1987). Voters mostly care about the answer to the question "what have you done for me lately?"—putting special weight on what happens during the election year.[3] The 1980 and 1984 elections are illustrative. In 1980, with an unemployment rate of 7.5 percent, incumbent Jimmy Carter lost in a landslide to Ronald Reagan. In 1984, with a virtually identical unemployment rate of 7.4 percent, Reagan won reelection in a landslide. The difference between the two years is the "slope" of the economy: things were declining in 1980 and booming in 1984. In contrast to what many observers and commentators thought, therefore, the economy in 2012 really was not a disadvantage for the president. Did it give President Obama an advantage? If so, how much?

Figure 8.3 shows how public perceptions of the economy relate to the presidential vote based on data from 15 elections between 1956 and 2012. (In contrast with presidential approval, economic perceptions have been collected only since the early 1950s, so our time series must begin with the 1956

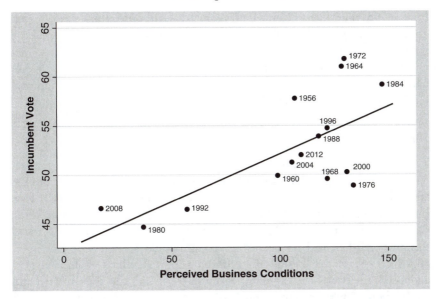

Figure 8.3 Perceived Business Conditions and the Presidential Vote, 1956–2012
Source: University of Michigan Survey of Consumers.

election.) The figure plots perceptions of business conditions, collected by the University of Michigan as part of its Survey of Consumers—specifically, the question asks whether "business conditions have gotten better or worse over the last year." Responses to this question are particularly important to voters on Election Day (see Erikson and Wlezien 2012b).[4] The figure demonstrates a clear, positive relationship between economic perceptions and the incumbent party vote. The more the public thinks conditions have improved, the better for the incumbent party candidate. The relationship is weaker (Pearson's correlation equals 0.70) than what we saw for approval, which is understandable given that the latter includes noneconomic things that are important to our evaluations of presidents and on Election Day. There are some similarities, however.

Just as we saw when approval levels are low, perceptions of a worsening economy—as in 1980, 1992, and 2008—have doomed the incumbent party candidate. As when approval is high, an improving economy gives the in-party an advantage, but is no guarantee of reelection. Perhaps most importantly, given the circumstances in 2012, middling economic perceptions, like middling approval rates, are not a disadvantage for the in-party. When equal numbers of people think the economy is getting better and getting worse, which is indicated by a score of 100, the incumbent party candidate is expected to receive about 52 percent of the two-party vote. This is precisely what Obama received in 2012, and it is a little less than we would have predicted given perceptions in 2012, which were positive on balance—recall Table 8.2 and see Figure 8.3. Although the economy was a major problem in 2012, the economic fundamentals actually favored the incumbent, if only a little.[5] Other scholars using gross domestic product (GDP) growth concluded much the same (J. Campbell 2012; Sides 2012a). This growth in the GDP presumably helped elevate the president's approval rating leading up to Election Day.

Foreign Policy

The economy is not the only important issue to voters. Other issues also matter, including foreign affairs. Indeed, the two aspects of "security"—economic and national—have been leading issues to voters on a recurring basis, at least since scholars began conducting election studies in 1952 (see Asher 1992; Claggett and Shafer 2010). This may have been especially true in 2012, given that the president had inherited big economic and foreign problems upon taking office in 2008. Besides the economic context, which we have already addressed, there was the ongoing legacy of 9/11 and the wars in Iraq and Afghanistan. These occupied much of President Obama's attention during his first term, and there were notable foreign policy successes: the weakening of al-Qaeda, the killing of Osama Bin Laden, and the end of the war in Iraq. The commitment in Afghanistan continues, though it changed and continues to change as Obama begins his second term. What did the public think of his performance on foreign affairs leading up to Election Day?

We know that pollsters ask people about their overall approval of the president's performance, and this has been true for a long time. We also have seen that this approval matters for the vote. In recent elections, pollsters have asked about approval on the "economy" and "foreign policy." Table 8.3 displays the percentages that approved and disapproved of the president in 2012. The numbers are the Pollster.com summaries of results from various polls conducted near the very end of the election cycle. At that time, 50 percent of the public approved of President Obama's performance overall, and 47 percent disapproved. This provided the president with an advantage, as we already have discussed. Table 8.3 shows that the advantage was not based primarily on public evaluations of performance on the economy, given that only 46 percent of the public approved, and 51 percent disapproved. Recall

Table 8.3 Presidential Approval in 2012

	Overall	Economic	Foreign policy
Approve	50	46	50
Disapprove	47	51	44

Note: Numbers are percentages of respondents. The source is Pollster.com.

from earlier discussion that this level of (overall) approval would predict an electoral coin flip. The numbers were better for Obama on foreign policy. Here, 50 percent approved, and only 44 percent disapproved, very close to what we see overall.

It may be tempting to conclude from Table 8.3 that foreign policy dominated the economy in the public's overall evaluation of the president. This may be true, but a more likely explanation is that most people relied on their economic assessments and that a small number of others cared more about foreign policy and approved of the president in that area despite disapproving of his performance on the economy. Because these people cared more about foreign policy, their overall assessment reflected their approval of the president in that area. Yet another possibility is that Obama's overall approval reflected public opinion on other noneconomic non-foreign issue areas. Let us see whether and the extent to which this is true.

Policy Mood

Public preferences for policy matter in presidential elections. If the public shifts in a liberal direction, the shift tends to benefit Democratic candidates; likewise, if the public shifts in a conservative direction, it tends to benefit Republicans. This is highly intuitive and is well established (Zaller 1998; Erikson, MacKuen, and Stimson 2002; Erikson and Wlezien 2012b). Thanks to work by James Stimson (1999), it is possible to measure public policy preferences in a general way, across issues. He averages across hundreds of political survey questions to create an overtime measure of the public's policy mood. This measure of policy mood is of particular interest because it correlates nicely with policy outputs in all three branches of U.S. government (Erikson, MacKuen, and Stimson 2002). It also correlates with the presidential vote.

Figure 8.4 plots Stimson's measure of mood over the last 16 presidential elections. Higher values indicate liberalism. To be clear, the measure taps "relative" liberalism, the degree to which the public wants more (or less) policy than they currently are getting. This is because survey organizations commonly ask people about their relative preferences—whether they think government should "spend more" or "do more"—and these items tend to dominate the others over time. Thus, mood is "thermostatic." It reflects both the public's underlying preferences for policy and policy itself—that is, whether the public thinks the government is doing too little or too much (Wlezien 1995; Erikson, MacKuen, and Stimson 2002). A low mood score, like that in 1952, indicates that the public wants the government to do less; a high score, like that in 1992, indicates that the public wants the government to do more.

The figure demonstrates that the public's policy preferences change over time. Mood began at its conservative extreme in 1952 and then shifted in a liberal direction through 1964 before rebounding in a conservative direction,

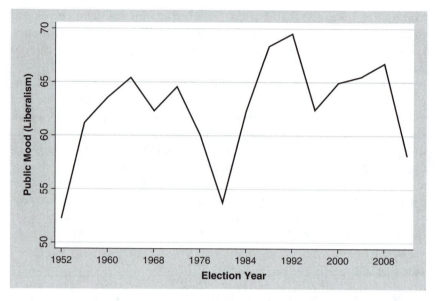

Figure 8.4 Public Policy Mood in Historical Perspective, 1952–2012
Source: James Stimson.

hitting bottom in 1980. Public opinion then shifted sharply in a liberal direction under Reagan, leveled off under George H. W. Bush, and then dropped under Clinton before leveling off once more. Between 2008 and 2012, public opinion again shifted sharply, though this time in a conservative direction. It is the third biggest conservative jump over the last 60 years and is equal to the liberal shifts during Eisenhower's and Reagan's first terms.

The 2012 mood score is the third most conservative on record, next only to 1952 and 1980. In each of these years, Democrats held the White House. The three most liberal scores occurred in years—1988, 1992, and 2008—that the president was a Republican. This makes sense, given that mood taps relative preferences and is thermostatic. Democratic presidents tend to drive policy in a liberal direction, which causes the public to become less supportive of doing more; Republican presidents push policy in a conservative direction, which leads the public to become supportive of doing more (Soroka and Wlezien 2010). This is important because it reveals that the public actually notices and responds to what policymakers do. How does it matter on Election Day? What effect did it have in 2012?

Public mood influences election outcomes. Consider that Republican candidates won in the two most conservative years—Eisenhower in 1952 and Reagan in 1980. Democratic candidates also did better in liberal years, but here things are messier. Although the Democrat Bill Clinton won his first election in the peak liberal year, 1992, Republican George H. W. Bush won in the second most liberal year, 1988. Democratic President Obama won in the third most liberal year, but Republican George W. Bush, who won reelection in the next most liberal year, preceded him. The public's policy opinions matter, but they are not sufficient or even necessary to guarantee victory. Like the economy and foreign policy, mood gives one candidate or the other an advantage.

As we have seen, Obama faced the third most conservative electorate in 2012. What may be most striking is that he began office with the third most liberal electorate on record. This suggests that the policies of the Obama administration were particularly liberal or that the public reacted in a particularly strong way, perhaps owing to the passage of the Affordable Care Act, aka Obamacare. It is important to recognize that there have been a number of election years with very similar scores—especially 1956 and 1976 but also 1968, 1984, and 1996. In these years, moreover, no party had a real advantage. Republicans and Democrats split the first two, with Eisenhower winning in 1956 and Democrat Carter winning in 1976. In the remaining three, Republicans won two and Democrats won the other. The public's policy sentiment was not an advantage to President Obama in 2012, but it was not a major disadvantage either. It may have been even less of a disadvantage because of the obstructionist behavior of the Republican-controlled House of Representatives during the preceding Congress. After all, elections are a choice, and perhaps the president's positions were preferable to the Republican alternative. To assess this directly, we need to compare Obama and his opponent, former governor Mitt Romney.

On Choice

Thus far, we have seen that presidential elections are largely about the incumbent, even if the incumbent is not running. To a large extent, voters decide whether to stay the course or change. In 2012, economic and political conditions tended to favor the incumbent, if only a little. However, the election is not simply a referendum because the choice candidates offer also matters. This is clear from the massive literature on presidential voting behavior; also consider that prediction models including the polls outperform those relying only on "exogeneous" variables, such as the economy and incumbency (see Erikson and Wlezien 2012b). In 2012, voters received a substantial choice, given that Obama and Romney proposed different policy directions. Did the public notice these differences? Which candidate benefited and to what extent?

Ideology

Much voting behavior research demonstrates that candidate proximity matters, where voters tend to support the candidate whose positions are closer to their own. The literature originates with Downs's (1957) classic work and is immense—for a recent, excellent review and analysis, see Jessee (2012). Some of the research focuses on very general "ideological" positions, where voters are asked about their own liberal–conservative position and those of the candidates. YouGov did this on a weekly basis during the 2012 election year. Specifically, they asked respondents to place themselves, Obama, and Romney on a five-category scale ranging from "very liberal" to "very conservative."

The YouGov surveys showed a number of things (Sides 2012b). First, people were more likely to place themselves on the conservative side—the average score on the five-point scale was 3.2. This hardly changed during the election year. Second, in early 2012, people were more likely to place Romney closer to the average self-placement—3.7 on average for Romney and 2.0 for Obama. Third, people increasingly placed both candidates away from the average over the year, and this was especially true for Romney. In mid-October, on the eve of the election, he still was closer to the average self-placement, with a score of 3.9 compared to 1.9 for Obama and 3.2 for the public. This implies a proximity advantage for Romney heading into the last weeks of the campaign.

The proximity advantage for Romney is surprising for two reasons. First, he staked out a variety of conservative positions in the process of securing the Republican nomination, among the most notable of which related to immigration and taxes. On the former, the candidate promised to veto the Dream Act, which provides a path to citizenship for some children of undocumented immigrants, and he said that he favored that undocumented immigrants "self-deport." On taxes, Romney advocated across-the-board cuts of 20 percent, or $5 trillion over 10 years, which would mostly benefit high-income earners and complicate his deficit reduction math. The resulting narrative was that he was "too conservative" (see, e.g., Salam 2012). Second, the Romney proximity advantage surprises because it contrasts with what we would expect if placements reflected support for the candidates. That is, much research shows that people tend to place candidates they favor closer to their own placement and candidates they oppose further away. (For a recent installment, see Lenz 2012.) Given that Obama led in most polls throughout the fall campaign and ultimately won, we might have expected people to place him closer or at least not farther than Romney. Of course, it may be that Obama's relatively liberal position owed to policy shifts during his first term, recalling Figure 8.4 and the surrounding discussion.

It is not clear exactly how much difference Romney's ideological proximity advantage made in 2012. First, the meaning of liberal–conservative placement is not straightforward. Although it is tempting to think of the placement as a (weighted) summary of positions on various issues, this is not what it mostly represents. Many years ago, Converse (1964) showed that ideological labels mean different things to different people, and they are meaningful indicators of policy attitudes for but a small fraction of the electorate. More recently, Ellis and Stimson (2012) have revealed a substantial mismatch between ideological identification and policy preferences. For example, self-placed "conservatives" do not reliably hold conservative positions, and many so-called conflicted conservatives actually hold liberal positions. Second, even to the extent ideological placements do capture information about the proximity of candidates to the median voter, they seemed to have little impact in 2012. Recall that the vote was exactly as we expected given presidential approval and economic conditions leading up to Election Day. Obama might have done better were it not for his liberal–conservative proximity disadvantage, though presumably not that much better.[6]

Specific Issues

It may be that positions on specific issues mattered more than broad ideological placements (see Hillygus and Shields 2008). Unfortunately, we do not have placements on particular issues. We do have assessments of performance, however. Survey organizations frequently ask about which candidate "would better handle" different issue areas. The exit poll asked voters about the economy, the federal budget deficit, and Medicare. Table 8.4 summarizes the results.

In the table, we can see that voter assessments of the candidates varied across domestic issues. (This variation is important because the projection of voter preferences that we discussed previously regarding ideological placements cannot easily explain it.) On the economy, voters were pretty much split: 48 percent said Obama would do a better job, and 49 percent said Romney would. This contrasts some with what we showed earlier, in that it implies that the economy may not have been an advantage for the president on Election Day. That is, had voters acted solely on their comparative assessments of the two candidates on the economy, the election seemingly would have been much closer. Things were much the same on the federal budget deficit, though here Romney held a slight 49–47 percent advantage. Had voters voted solely on these evaluations, the race not only would have been close; Romney would have won.

Other issues may have mattered in the 2012 election, of course. Of these, the exit poll asked only about Medicare. On this issue, in contrast with the economy and budget deficit, Obama held a clear advantage, 52–44 percent.

Table 8.4 2012 Public Opinion about the Best Candidate on Various Issues

	Obama	*Romney*
Who would better handle the economy?	48	49
Who would better handle the federal budget deficit?	47	49
Who would better handle Medicare?	52	44

Note: Numbers are percentages of respondents. The source is the 2012 national exit poll.

Voters evidently did not act solely on these assessments on Election Day, or the result would have been much more lopsided. The assessments may have played a role, however. Let us assume that voters based their decisions on their combined assessments of the economy, the federal budget deficit, and Medicare. Let us further assume that they weighted each issue equally. This almost certainly is not right because voters surely considered other issues and weighted some more than others. It does use the data we have and may offer some insight. When averaging across the three issues, 49 percent of voters said that Obama would do a better job, and 47 percent said Romney. This closely parallels the final vote. It does not mean voters actually decided in this way. It does imply that the balance of support on the issues was consistent with what we expected based on referendum judgments alone, however. Taking into account the choice between Romney and Obama on the set of three domestic issues seemingly did not make much difference.

The comparison of the candidates on international issues also may have mattered. The exit poll included a question about international crisis. Specifically, the question asked voters whether they would "trust [each candidate] to handle an international crisis." The results indicate a difference—57 percent said yes for Obama, and 50 percent did so for Romney. Some of the difference reflects uncertainty about the latter, given that 4 percent said they did not know about Romney and only 1 percent did not know about Obama. Among those offering an opinion, Obama held a real advantage, and one that is slightly larger than we saw on domestic issues. Even if it did matter on Election Day, however, the advantage on international affairs served mostly to reinforce referendum judgments of presidential performance.

Discussion: The Public and Presidential Elections

Presidential elections offer voters a choice. The decisions of most voters reflect their partisan predispositions. Of course, the result changes from election to election, given that the Democratic candidate wins in some years, the Republican in others. Even when the same party wins, the margin of victory can differ. This ebb and flow reflects changes in party identification and shifts in the behavior of floating voters, who are not attached to either of the parties. Referendum judgments drive the change from year to year. That is, floating voters decide to stay the course or change mostly based on presidential performance. This is true whether or not the incumbent is running for reelection. The economy is a big part of the story, but other aspects matter as well. In 2012, conditions gave President Obama a slight advantage, even on the economy but especially in other areas, particularly foreign affairs. The result matched the expectation: a close victory for Obama.

But as noted previously, presidential elections are not just referenda. The choice candidates offer also is important. The 1964 election often is considered a classic example, when incumbent Democrat Lyndon Johnson trounced the "too conservative" Republican Barry Goldwater. In 1972, incumbent Republican Richard Nixon won in a landslide over "too liberal" Democrat George McGovern. In 2000, Democrat Al Gore's positions may have hurt him on Election Day (Wlezien 2001). It is not clear that the choice was decisive in any of these years, however. The same is true in 2012. The public perceived a difference between the candidates to be sure, but it varied across measures and, on balance, reinforced the referendum-based judgment. That is, the comparison gave Obama a slight advantage. This is not to say that the choice was not important. After all, had Romney fared better in his comparison with Obama, the election would have been closer and might have turned out very differently.

The predictability of the 2012 election seems to imply that the campaign did not matter. That would not be right, however. We already have seen in earlier chapters that the events of the campaign did change preferences. This was true in previous elections (Shaw 1999). Of course, many events do not matter, and those that do may have temporary effects (Erikson and Wlezien 2012b).[7] Perhaps more important than the effects of events is that the campaign determines the impact of fundamental variables. That is, their impact does not happen magically (Holbrook 1996; J. Campbell 2000; Vavreck 2009; Erikson and Wlezien 2012b). In 2012, the campaign served to deliver the knowable fundamentals to voters. This is not always true—consider the 2000 election, when referendum indicators pointed to an easy Gore win. That it was true in 2012 helped make the election predictable well in advance.

NOTES

1. I am most grateful to Janet Box-Steffensmeier, Michael Hagen, and Steven Schier for helpful advice and comments; to Andreas Graefe for assembling and sharing the Pollyvote forecasting data; to James Stimson for updating and providing his mood series; and to John Sides for graciously letting me use his YouGov ideological placement data.
2. A lot of work combines polls and economic indicators to forecast the election—see, for example, *PS: Political Science and Politics* 45 (610–674), the 2012 forecasting issue. For research on pre-election polls (and poll projections) and election prediction markets, see Erikson and Wlezien (2008).
3. The emphasis on late economic change is universal in models of the presidential vote—see again *PS: Political Science and Politics* 45 (610–674), the publication's 2012 forecasting issue. This is true even for those scholars who take into account the full election cycle (Hibbs 1987; Erikson and Wlezien 2012a).
4. Similar results obtain when perceptions of "personal" conditions and also the broader Index of Consumer Sentiment are used (also see Erikson and Wlezien 2012b).
5. Also note that to the extent voters considered the economy to be in bad shape, the exit poll indicates that 53 percent of voters blamed former President George W. Bush, and only 38 percent blamed Obama.

6. It is worth noting research on the actual positions of the candidates, not public perceptions, some of which relies on measures of the liberalism–conservatism of the national party platforms from Budge et al. (2001). This research demonstrates that platform ideology works in conjunction with public mood to impact presidential election outcomes (Erikson, MacKuen, and Stimson 2002; also see Erikson and Wlezien 2012b). Unfortunately, as of this writing (December 8, 2012), platform ideology data for 2012 are not available.

7. The same may be true for political advertising (Gerber et al. 2011).

REFERENCES

Abramson, Paul R., John H. Aldrich, and David W. Rohde. 2007. *Change and Continuity in the 2004 and 2006 Elections.* Washington, DC: CQ Press.

Asher, Herbert. 1992. *Presidential Elections and American Politics since 1952.* Pacific Grove, CA: Brooks/Cole.

Bartels, Larry. 2000. "Partisanship and Voting Behavior, 1952–1996." *American Journal of Political Science* 44: 25–50.

Bartlett, Tom. 2012. "Poll Quants Won the Elections." *Chronicle of Higher Education.* http://chronicle.com/blogs/percolator/the-poll-quants-won-the-election/31722.

Brody, Richard, and Lee Sigelman. 1983. "Presidential Popularity and Presidential Elections: An Update and Extension." *Public Opinion Quarterly* 47: 325–328.

Budge, Ian, Hans-Dieter Klingemann, Andrea Volkens, Judith Bara, and Erik Tannenbaum. 2001. *Mapping Policy Preferences: Estimates for Parties, Elections, and Governments, 1945–1998.* Oxford: Oxford University Press.

Campbell, Angus, Philip E. Converse, Warren E. Miller, and Donald E. Stokes. 1960. *The American Voter.* New York: Wiley.

Campbell, James E. 2000. *The American Campaign: U.S. Presidential Campaigns and the National Vote.* College Station: Texas A&M University Press.

Campbell, James E. 2012. "Forecasting the Presidential and Congressional Elections: The Trial-Heat and Seats-in-Trouble Models." *PS: Political Science and Politics* 45: 630–634.

Claggett, William, and Byron Shafer. 2010. *The American Public Mind: The Issue Structure of Mass Politics in the Postwar United States.* Cambridge: Cambridge University Press.

Converse, Philip E. 1964. "The Nature of Belief Systems in Mass Publics." In *Ideology and Discontent,* ed. David E. Apter. New York: Free Press.

Downs, Anthony. 1957. *An Economic Theory of Democracy.* New York: Harper.

Ellis, Christopher, and James A. Stimson. 2012. *Ideology in America.* Cambridge: Cambridge University Press.

Erikson, Robert S., Michael MacKuen, and James A. Stimson. 2002. *The Macro Polity.* Cambridge: Cambridge University Press.

Erikson, Robert S., and Christopher Wlezien. 1999. "Presidential Polls as a Time Series: The Case of 1996." *Public Opinion Quarterly* 63: 163–177.

Erikson, Robert S., and Christopher Wlezien. 2008. "Are Markets Really Superior to Polls as Election Predictors?" *Public Opinion Quarterly* 72: 190–215.

Erikson, Robert S., and Christopher Wlezien. 2012a. "The Objective and Subjective Economy and the Presidential Vote." *PS: Political Science and Politics* 45 (4): 620–624.

Erikson, Robert S., and Christopher Wlezien. 2012b. *The Timeline of Presidential Elections: How Campaigns Do (and Do Not) Matter.* Chicago: University of Chicago Press.

Gelman, Andrew, and Gary King. 1993. "Why Are American Presidential Election Polls So Variable When Votes Are So Predictable?" *British Journal of Political Science* 23: 409–451.

Gerber, Alan, James G. Gimpel, Donald P. Green, and Daron R. Shaw. 2011. "The Influence of Television and Radio Advertising on Candidate Evaluation: Results from a Large-Scale Randomized Experiment." *American Political Science Review* 105: 135–150.

Hibbs, Douglas. 1987. *The American Political Economy.* Cambridge, MA: Harvard University Press.

Hillygus, D. Sunshine, and Todd G. Shields. 2008. *The Persuadable Voter: Wedge Issues in Presidential Election Campaigns.* Princeton: Princeton University Press.

Holbrook, Thomas. 1996. *Do Campaigns Matter?* Thousand Oaks, CA: Sage.

Jackman, Simon. 2005. "Pooling the Polls over an Election Campaign." *Australian Journal of Political Science* 40(4): 499–516.

Jessee, Stephen. 2012. *Ideology and Spatial Voting in Presidential Elections.* Cambridge: Cambridge University Press.

Lenz, Gabriel S. 2012. *Follow the Leader? How Voters Respond to Politicians' Policies and Performance.* Chicago: University of Chicago Press.

Salam, Reihan. 2012. "Why Romney Is Losing." CNN, August 10. http://www.cnn.com/2012/08/09/opinion/salam-romney-struggle/index.html.

Shaw, Daron R. 1999. "A Study of Presidential Campaign Event Effects from 1952 to 1992." *Journal of Politics* 6: 387–422.

Sides, John. 2012a. "It's Still Hard for People to Get the Fundamentals Right." *The Monkey Cage,* September 18. http://themonkeycage.org/blog/2012/09/18/its-still-hard-for-people-to-get-the-fundamentals-right/

Sides, John. 2012b. "Romney's Pivot to the Center Didn't Work (But It Didn't Need To)." *The Monkey Cage,* October 11. http://themonkeycage.org/blog/2012/10/11/romneys-pivot-to-the-center-hasnt-worked-but-it-didnt-need-to/.

Soroka, Stuart, and Christopher Wlezien. 2010. *Degrees of Democracy: Politics, Public Opinion, and Policy.* Cambridge: Cambridge University Press.

Stimson, James. 1999. *Public Opinion in America: Moods, Cycles and Swings.* 2nd ed. Boulder, CO: Westview Press.

Vavreck, Lynn. 2009. *The Message Matters: The Economy and Presidential Campaigns.* Princeton: Princeton University Press.

Wlezien, Christopher. 1995. "The Public as Thermostat: Dynamics of Preferences for Spending." *American Journal of Political Science* 39: 981–1000.

Wlezien, Christopher. 2001. "On Forecasting the Presidential Vote." *PS: Political Science and Politics* 34: 24–31.

Zaller, John. 1998. "Monica Lewinsky's Contribution to Political Science." *PS: Political Science and Politics* 31: 182–189.

Zaller, John. 2004. "Floating Voters in US Presidential Elections, 1948–2000." In *The Issue of Belief: Essays in the Intersection of Non-Attitudes and Attitude Change,* ed. Paul Sniderman and Willem Saris. Princeton: Princeton University Press.

9   Religion in the 2012 Election

James L. Guth and Leigh A. Bradberry

Religion has always played a vital role in American politics. Although electoral tides often rise or fall on economic events, foreign policy crises, or other "secular" concerns, contemporary partisan coalitions are characterized by remarkably stable religious alliances that shift only marginally from election to election. Those shifts do sometimes produce dramatically varied outcomes, with Republican victories in 2004 and 2010 and Democratic triumphs in 2006 and 2008. Although one journalist proclaimed that "God was remarkably absent" from the 2012 election, religion did in fact play a significant role in that contest.

This chapter considers that role. First, we outline two perspectives shaping expert interpretation of religious politics, the ethnoreligious and restructuring theories. Then we review the 2008 voting patterns that set the context both for President Obama's approach to faith groups in 2012 and for the electoral prospects of his GOP challengers. We then focus on the 2012 Republican nomination, examining the cast of candidates, their religious strategies, and the effectiveness of those strategies. Next, we turn briefly to Obama's approach, arguing that he reluctantly abandoned his 2008 ecumenical appeal as a result of first-term political controversies and shifted to an emphasis on the Democratic Party's core constituencies. Finally, we discuss "faith-based" mobilization in the general election campaign and look at the vote choices of religious groups.

Alternative Theories of Religious Coalitions

Two analytic approaches have long competed in professional analysis of religious voting: *ethnoreligious theory,* originally developed by historians, emphasizes the combined impact of ethnicity and religious affiliation on electoral choice (Kleppner 1979). Nineteenth-century parties were warring coalitions of ethnoreligious groups, with the GOP representing historically dominant mainline Protestants, such as Episcopalians, Presbyterians, and Methodists, whereas Democrats spoke for ethnoreligious minorities: Catholics, Jews,

and evangelical Protestants (especially in the South). These alignments survived New Deal class politics but by the 1980s had changed in composition;
as mainline Protestants dwindled in number, evangelicals joined the GOP,
Anglo-Catholics deserted the Democrats, and black Protestants became a
critical Democratic bloc, along with "new" minorities such as Muslims,
Hindus, Buddhists, and secular voters. Despite these changes, many pundits
still think in ethnoreligious terms, referring to the "evangelical," "Catholic,"
"Jewish," or "Muslim" vote.

Religious restructuring theory, formulated more recently by sociologists, sees a
crucial theological factionalism emerging *within* old ethnoreligious traditions:
the "orthodox" accept an external, definable, and transcendent authority and
adhere to traditional doctrines, whereas "progressives" create new religious
understandings based on experience or scientific rationality, joined by secular
Americans who have abandoned religion but see morality in the same way
(Hunter 1991, 44). The "God gap" beloved by journalists (between church-
attending Republicans and secular Democrats) is a crude indicator of these
divisions, given that the orthodox are more observant than the progressives,
but the factions are actually rooted in competing worldviews, not just religious behavior. These perspectives not only produce "culture wars" over
abortion, feminism, gay rights, and the role of faith in public life, but infuse
other policy attitudes as well (Layman 2001; Green 2007).

Both approaches can help explain the 2008 results, reported in Table 9.1,
which reports the results of a national random sample survey of voters in the
2008 election. The results are drawn from a total sample of 4,017 adults. The
survey has a margin of error of 1.5 percent. First, note that ethnoreligious
traditions differed dramatically. Latter-day Saints (Mormons) and evangelicals were overwhelmingly Republican in vote choice. Latino Protestants had
voted Republican in 2004, but four years later, they joined most other ethnoreligious "minorities," including Jews, black Protestants, Latino Catholics,
those of other non-Christian faiths, and the unaffiliated in the Democratic
camp. Mainline Protestants and Anglo-Catholics were "swing" groups,
almost evenly divided—a pattern present in the last several presidential races.
But theological divisions also mattered (rather than Hunter's dichotomy, we
prefer a threefold division of "traditionalist," "centrist," and "modernist" to
capture these tendencies). In 2008, evangelical, mainline, and Catholic traditionalists were far more Republican than their modernist co-parishioners,
many of whom were strongly Democratic. Indeed, each theological faction
resembled its counterparts in other traditions more than opposing factions
within its own, with McCain relying on traditionalists and Obama appealing
to modernists. Religiously unaffiliated voters were also Democratic, with
agnostics and atheists holding that preference most strongly.

Each party, then, had a distinct religious base. Despite a lack of personal
rapport with religious conservatives, McCain received four-tenths of his

Table 9.1 Religious Voting in the 2008 Presidential Election (in Percent)

Ethnoreligious tradition and theological faction	McCain vote	Obama vote	GOP vote coalition	Democratic vote coalition
Latter-day Saint (Mormon)	72	28	5	2
Evangelical Protestant	76	24	39	11
Traditionalist	*88*	*12*	*24*	*3*
Centrist	*68*	*32*	*12*	*5*
Modernist	*54*	*46*	*3*	*3*
Traditionalist-modernist	*+34*	*-34*	—	—
Mainline Protestant	50	50	20	18
Traditionalist	*68*	*32*	*7*	*3*
Centrist	*49*	*51*	*8*	*7*
Modernist	*39*	*61*	*5*	*7*
Traditionalist-modernist	*+29*	*-29*	—	—
Anglo-Catholic	51	49	23	20
Traditionalist	*58*	*42*	*8*	*6*
Centrist	*63*	*37*	*10*	*5*
Modernist	*34*	*66*	*5*	*9*
Traditionalist-modernist	*+24*	*-24*	—	—
Latino Protestant	33	67	1	2
Latino Catholic	27	73	2	4
Unaffiliated	27	73	7	16
Unaffiliated believer	*41*	*59*	*3*	*4*
Secular	*22*	*78*	*3*	*8*
Agnostic/atheist	*19*	*81*	*1*	*4*
Jewish	23	77	1	3
All others	19	81	1	4
Black Protestant	5	95	1	20
Total sample	46	54	100	100

Source: 2008 National Survey of Religion and Politics, University of Akron.

votes from evangelicals alone, mostly from traditionalists and centrists. Adding mainline and Anglo-Catholic traditionalists, Latter-day Saints, and Latino Protestants gave the GOP a solid traditionalist majority, holding conservative positions on social issues, foreign policy, and even economic issues (see Guth 2011). Of course, Republicans still needed votes from other ethnoreligious groups and unaffiliated voters to win a national election, but no GOP presidential aspirant in 2012 could ignore the party's traditionalist base.

The Democrats' strategic situation was more complex, given their greater religious diversity. In 2008 Barack Obama had doggedly pursued an "ecumenical" approach, appealing to religious groups outside the usual Democratic coalition, making marginal but crucial inroads among usually Republican religious blocs, such as Catholic and mainline traditionalists (for details, see Guth 2009). Nevertheless, Obama's largest single constituency was black Protestants, who supplied one-fifth of his total vote, matched by Anglo-Catholics and followed by mainline Protestants. In these latter two constituencies, Obama's support was strongest among religious modernists. Unaffiliated voters of various sorts added a slightly smaller 16 percent to his total. Obama's remaining votes came from a wide scattering of groups, including Latino Catholics and Protestants, Jews (an important financial and activist constituency), and a few evangelicals.

Changes in the American Religious Landscape

Candidate strategies in 2012 would be shaped not only by past electoral patterns but also by changes in the broader religious landscape, some of them dramatic. First, there was a continued ebbing in public receptiveness to religious appeals by politicians. In 2004 most Americans wanted a president with a strong religious faith, thought religious groups should speak out on issues, and felt that the campaign had about the right amount of religious involvement. By 2012 opinion was less positive about religious politics, although most still wanted the president to have a strong faith (Guth et al. 2006; Pew Forum on Religion and Public Life 2012b). Some attributed these changes in the political environment to disenchantment with the Christian right's politicization of religion, whereas others credited secularization, as religiously unaffiliated Americans grew steadily in number. Public sentiment had also liberalized on some religiously tinged issues such as same-sex marriage, civil unions, and stem cell research. Most important, perhaps, the national agenda was dominated by the financial crisis of 2008–2009, the economic recession, and controversies over the Affordable Care Act of 2010, concerns less immediately tied to religious faith.

On the Republican side, the party's Christian right allies were suffering from organizational problems, as their old leaders passed from the scene and financial woes mounted. Master evangelical strategist Ralph Reed was trying to replace the moribund Christian Coalition with a new Faith and Freedom Coalition, with uncertain results, and James Dobson had retired from Focus on the Family as it retrenched financially and as Jim Daly, its new leader, sought to return to a less political mission. Some evangelical denominations that had buttressed conservative politics, such as the Southern Baptist Convention and the Assemblies of God, were also turning inward to deal with institutional problems. Meanwhile, a few prominent evangelical leaders, such as Richard Cizik, Rick Warren, Bill Hybels, and Joel Hunter, were seeking to draw the community toward a broader agenda and more moderate policies, even cooperating at times with liberal groups, a strategy with some appeal among younger evangelicals (Seiple 2012). Despite all these challenging developments, however, conservative religious activists remained a formidable cadre within the GOP.

In 2008 the Democratic side had been bolstered by—and had cultivated—a new religious left, spearheaded by liberal evangelical Jim Wallis, founder of *Sojourners* magazine, whose appeals on poverty, disease, the environment, and international peace were reaching a broad audience (Wallis 2008). Wallis and his allies were welcomed by the aging forces of mainline Protestant liberalism as they sought to unite religious centrists and liberals into a political force, using the Internet to overcome old barriers among potential constituents (Kellstedt et al. 2007). Although Wallis formally eschewed partisanship, the movement's agenda and policy clearly tilted Democratic, allowing party leaders to create several auxiliary religious groups in 2008. And although the Obama administration had not always nurtured these allies as carefully as the Obama campaign had, most were still available for "remobilization" in 2012.

Developments in the large Catholic community were more ambiguous. The Church had a growing cadre of activist bishops eager to confront what they perceived as the moral evils of the era. Although this traditionalist bloc had previously focused on confronting pro-choice Democrats over abortion, in 2012 they added strong opposition to same-sex marriage to their agenda. Just as relevant to the presidential race, Catholic institutions were battling the Obama administration on several fronts, most notably the Health and Human Services Department's ruling that the Affordable Care Act required their health insurance plans to include free contraception. After failing to achieve satisfactory exceptions, Catholic institutions took the administration to court, and the National Conference of Catholic Bishops (NCCB) instituted a "religious freedom" campaign to inform parishioners on these issues, initiatives that drew some support from evangelical leaders and institutions as well. Many observers saw all these developments as a significant move toward the right, at least among the most vocal and influential prelates.

Although the bishops insisted that their protests were not designed to influence the 2012 election, liberal Catholic groups were not so sure. Based in the Church's extensive social welfare institutions, these organizations were preoccupied by prospective federal budget cuts for programs assisting the poor. Such sentiments were shared by many bishops and by the Church's growing Latino constituency but were especially strong in women's religious orders, always a "liberal" force in Catholic politics. Indeed, a national tour by a few sisters ("Nuns on the Bus") attracted extensive media coverage and was lauded by secular liberal groups. However, this action exacerbated the ongoing conflict between the religious orders and the NCCB on internal issues, rooted in the growing theological and ideological divisions in the Church, paralleling those in the larger religious world.

All these developments influenced partisan arguments over religious strategies. Although Obama had made aggressive appeals to religious traditionalists in 2008, other strategists still preferred to rely on a "new Democratic majority" based on ethnoreligious minorities, such as black Protestants and Latino Catholics, combined with secular Americans, concentrated in the highly educated and professional sectors of the electorate (Judis and Teixeira 2002; Teixeira 2010). Because all these groups were growing in size—as emphasized by several widely publicized surveys in 2012—this strategy would assure Democratic success. On the GOP side there was a parallel debate: some strategists saw victory based on effective mobilization of religious traditionalists and economic conservatives (groups with considerable overlap), whereas others, such as Karl Rove, hoped to attract socially traditionalist ethnoreligious minorities, such as Latino Protestants and Catholics, even if that necessitated ignoring Tea Party ethnocentrism and softening the harsh Republican line on immigration.

Winnowing the Field: Republican Candidates and Religious Strategies

The partisan religious alignments we have described are not confined to voters but also increasingly characterize party activists (Green, Guth, and Fraser 1991), national convention delegates (Green and Jackson 2007), and members of Congress (Guth 2007). The reshaping of the Republican religious coalition finally reached the pool of GOP presidential candidates in 2012. As columnist Ross Douthat noted, the long-term dominance of mainline Protestants ended, and considering both parties, the nation finally had "a presidential field that mirrors the diversity of American Christianity as a whole" (Douthat 2012). The initial GOP field did indeed reflect that party's contemporary religious coalition for the first time, but it also revealed potential fractures.[1]

The putative front-runner, former governor Mitt Romney of Massachusetts, was a member of the Church of Jesus Christ of Latter-day Saints. Indeed, Romney not only was a faithful Mormon but also had held leadership positions in the Church. As we saw in Table 9.1, Mormons rival evangelicals as the staunchest supporters of the GOP (and share many similar political views). Indeed, a 2012 study showed not only that Mormons and evangelicals were the most Republican religious groups (80 and 70 percent identifying or "leaning" Republican), but also that those preferences had intensified since 2008 (Pew Forum on Religion and Public Life 2012d). Despite similar politics, however, the two groups were religious antagonists: evangelicals often regard Mormonism as "a cult" and "not Christian." Such sentiments had influenced their response to Romney in the 2008 Republican contest, and polls still showed that a substantial minority of evangelicals would not vote for a Mormon in 2012—at least not in the GOP primaries (Pew Forum on Religion and Public Life 2011). Because evangelicals constituted a majority of GOP caucus and primary voters in many states and a substantial minority in others, this resistance presented a major problem for Romney.

In 2008 Romney hit those concerns head-on with a well-publicized speech on religion and politics, but in 2012 he ignored the religious issue, hoping that his attacks on Obama's economic policies would create common ground among all Republicans. Indeed, Romney's staff vigorously discouraged reporters' interest in his faith (Barbaro and Parker 2012; Horowitz 2012). Romney did profess conservative beliefs on social issues, but these commitments were still questioned by social conservatives who remembered his relative liberalism as governor of Massachusetts. Skepticism about Romney came into focus during the GOP debates. Although candidates such as Rick Santorum were eager to bring up family values, abortion, and traditional marriage, Romney was typically on the defensive when it came to these topics—when his conservative credentials were being questioned (Bradberry 2012). Romney did have a staff assistant for relations with evangelicals, but he made little effort to win their support during the primaries, preferring to rely on Mormon and business networks for fundraising and mainline Protestants and Anglo-Catholics for votes.

Not surprisingly, Romney's challengers included several evangelicals, emerging from the party's religious core. Congresswoman Michele Bachmann of Minnesota belonged to the traditionalist Wisconsin Evangelical Lutheran Synod (WELS), had attended law school at Oral Roberts University (rooted in Pentecostalism), and helped run her husband's "biblical worldview" counseling service. During her campaign she faced criticism on WELS's anti-Catholic posture, ultimately resigning her membership and joining the Eagle Brook Church, an evangelical megachurch. Her meteoric campaign drew avid support from evangelical pastors, parishioners, and social conservatives in Minnesota and Iowa, but her erratic pronouncements sapped her early momentum, and she withdrew from the race after a poor showing in the Iowa caucuses.

Former Minnesota governor Tim Pawlenty started with strong evangelical credentials, combined with a mainstream electoral appeal. Raised a Catholic, Pawlenty had converted to Evangelicalism in 1987 and was an active member in Eden Prairie's Wooddale Church, pastored by his friend Leith Anderson, president of the National Association of Evangelicals. Although Pawlenty was reliably conservative on abortion, same-sex marriage, and embryonic stem cell research, he joined Anderson in deviating for a time from Republican orthodoxy on global warming (and taxes), citing religious grounds. Although he later recanted, his campaign failed to catch fire, and after losing the Iowa straw poll in Ames to Bachmann, he withdrew from the race, soon endorsing Romney and serving as a surrogate for his campaign.

Two other GOP hopefuls shared Bachmann's experience of rising to front-runner status in the polls prior to the Iowa caucuses but quickly falling back to earth. Former Godfather's Pizza magnate Herman Cain briefly tickled Republicans' fancy with his personal charm and catchy Tea Party–inspired slogan on tax rates ("9-9-9"). Cain also claimed a strong religious connection, but one typically associated with Democrats. A longtime member of Atlanta's Antioch Baptist Church, part of the historically black National Baptist Convention USA, Cain was a licensed preacher and served as an associate minister, although he was often at odds with the congregation's political leanings. His campaign imploded when he was confronted with sexual harassment and infidelity charges.

Governor Rick Perry of Texas was the next hope of social conservatives, offering a candidacy appealing to business conservatives and the Tea Party as well. With an untarnished electoral record, Perry had stronger political credentials than many other contenders. After spending most of his life as a United Methodist, by 2010 he had migrated to the Lake Hills Church, a nondenominational evangelical congregation. Encouraged by Christian right leaders such as Richard Land of the Southern Baptist Convention, Tony Perkins of the Family Research Council, and Gary Bauer of American Values, Perry kicked off his campaign with a prayer rally in Houston's Reliant Stadium, drawing over 30,000 participants. Perry was unabashed about using religious appeals during his governorship and presidential campaign, but despite considerable fundraising prowess, his poor performances in debates and miserable showings in Iowa and New Hampshire forced him out of the race.

Perry's failure left religious conservatives without a candidate, at least one who shared their broad theological and social perspectives both, with evangelical voters in Iowa and New Hampshire having scattered their ballots among most of the contenders. Rick Santorum carried a plurality in Iowa, but Mitt Romney accomplished the same feat in New Hampshire, albeit among a smaller evangelical constituency. To stop Romney, social conservatives needed to unite behind a single champion, but which one? Although Representative Ron Paul of Texas was a committed Christian who attended both evangelical Free and Baptist churches, he was usually (though not always) adamant about keeping his faith out of the campaign. Paul did have evangelical supporters, but traditionalist leaders did not regard him as a serious possibility, doubting his electability and distrusting his libertarian streak. Two other GOP aspirants were not options for religious conservatives (or any other kind of conservatives). Former Utah governor Jon Huntsman was, like his relative Mitt Romney, a Mormon, but a nonobservant one with unsettled religious views, and former New Mexico governor Gary Johnson, a nominal Lutheran, had not practiced his faith since childhood and also had strong libertarian leanings.

That left two Catholics: former Pennsylvania senator Rick Santorum and former Speaker of the House Newt Gingrich. Both were religious "traditionalists," but Santorum was a lifelong Catholic by heritage and personal commitment, whereas Gingrich had converted from nominal Lutheranism as a youth and Southern Baptist affiliation as an adult. For social conservatives, each had liabilities. Although Santorum credited his adult recommitment to his faith to participation in a largely evangelical prayer group on Capitol Hill, not all evangelicals resonated with the candidacy of a very traditionalist Catholic, whose pronouncements on abortion, same-sex marriage, and related issues often seemed extreme even to them. Santorum's wooden campaign style was also compared unfavorably to that of Mike Huckabee, the 2008 evangelical favorite and Fox News talk show host. Gingrich's problems were different. For social conservatives his marital history and infidelities were indeed troublesome. Although he took the right stances on culture war issues, the former Speaker exhibited idiosyncratic tendencies on some questions and was not universally regarded as trustworthy. Even if Gingrich had written *Rediscovering God in America* (2006) and used religious language in speeches, most evangelicals and other traditionalists did not see him as a credible political spokesman for their concerns.

Still, social conservatives hoped to achieve agreement on a candidate before the often-critical South Carolina primary (Wallsten and Tumulty 2012). Meeting in Texas, 150 mostly evangelical leaders voted overwhelmingly (on the third ballot) to coalesce behind Santorum. Nevertheless, Gingrich vowed to stay in the race, his supporters arguing that the first ballot had been much closer, and the "overwhelming" vote came only after Christian right bigwigs James Dobson, Tony Perkins, and Gary Bauer argued strongly for a clear, single endorsement (Martin 2012). Whatever the degree of unity achieved, Santorum's anointing came too late for South Carolina, which was carried by Gingrich. It soon became evident, however, that the Georgian's appeal was limited outside the South, and Santorum gradually emerged as the alternative to Romney. None of the "anti-Romney" candidates were willing to drop out of the race, however, and the presence of Gingrich, Santorum, and Paul on the ballot continued to split the conservative vote and allowed Romney to emerge as the GOP nominee, although not before intramural bloodletting had drained party coffers and presented the Democrats with potent issues for the general election.

How did religious constituencies respond to the GOP primary campaign? With a look at the state exit polls for which religious measures are available (and taken before Santorum dropped out), it is clear that religious factors shaped the outcome. Santorum won the most frequent church-attenders (57 percent to Romney's 26 percent), whereas Romney prevailed among the least observant (48 percent to Santorum's 27 percent). Similarly, Santorum carried 49 percent of those who preferred a candidate who shared their faith, compared to 21 percent for Romney. Outside his home state and neighboring South Carolina, Gingrich did not do well among church-attenders or those to whom the candidate's religious views were important (Bradberry 2012).

The candidates also had quite different appeals to the GOP's major religious constituencies. State by state, Romney's vote share had a strong negative correlation with the size of evangelical presence in GOP primaries ($r = -.75$) but was strongly and positively correlated with the Catholic electorate ($r = .68$).[2] Santorum and Gingrich shared almost identical aggregate profiles, with a modest advantage in states with many evangelicals ($r = .40$ and .37, respectively) but no statistically significant advantage or disadvantage in heavily Catholic ones. The mean proportions of the evangelical and Catholic vote, however, provide a somewhat different angle. Santorum barely edged Romney among evangelical voters (35 to 32 percent), with Gingrich (22 percent) and Paul (9 percent) trailing. Among Catholics, Romney had a decisive advantage over Santorum in the 13 states where they were identified in the exit polls (Romney with 46 percent to Santorum's 25 percent).

Did these tendencies vary over the course of the campaign? To check this possibility, we simply correlated the candidates' evangelical and Catholic vote proportions with the chronological order of primaries. This exercise shows that Romney made some very slight gains among evangelicals as the campaign wore on and moved out of the South ($r = .25$), but Santorum's rise was more dramatic, as he markedly increased his vote among both evangelicals and Catholics in the later primaries ($r = .63$ and .72, respectively), largely at the expense of Gingrich and, to a much lesser extent, Ron Paul. Had social conservatives been able to focus their energies on one candidate prior to Iowa, then Romney might have had an even tougher time securing the GOP nomination. Although he did improve slightly on his 2008 performance among churchgoers and evangelicals, Romney clearly won the nomination without the full endorsement of all the party's core religious constituencies.

Securing the GOP Religious Base

Although Romney hoped that public reaction to the nation's economic and budgetary woes would sustain his campaign, social conservatives' lack of enthusiasm was still a concern. Having secured the nomination, Romney acted to propitiate this wing of the party. He gave the commencement address at Liberty University, founded by Jerry Falwell, stressing the common commitment to faith and conservative values among all the GOP's religious constituencies. His campaign organized "Catholics for Romney," headed by six former American envoys to the Holy See and buttressed by a candidate visit to Poland, the ancestral home of many Catholics in Midwestern battleground states. He also established a Jewish liaison body and traveled to Israel, appealing both to Jewish voters disgruntled by Obama's Mideast policy and to pro-Israel sentiment among evangelicals. And in a dramatic departure, Romney also put more emphasis on his life as a person of faith, even inviting reporters to join him at Sunday worship services—but not Sunday school (Barbaro and Parker 2012). He also attacked the Obama administration's "war on religion," arguing that church–state separation had been "taken by some well beyond its original meaning" (Swaine 2012).

Although these actions were welcomed by Christian conservatives, movement leaders held out for more, specifying that Romney's choice of running mate would influence their willingness to work for the ticket. The reputed short list for the post certainly ran the gamut of American religion. Tim Pawlenty would be an evangelical choice who might also appeal to Catholics. Senator Rob Portman of Ohio, a United Methodist, would reassure the "old" mainline GOP elite. Others would attract religious groups that were inclined toward the Democrats but were perhaps in play in 2012, such as minority Catholic governors Bobby Jindal of Louisiana or Susana Martinez of New Mexico. Senator Marco Rubio of Florida was not only Latino and a Tea Party favorite, but was also a serious religious person who had spent time in Catholic, evangelical, and Mormon churches. Former secretary of state Condoleezza Rice was a devout evangelical Presbyterian from the black Protestant tradition, if not quite pro-life enough for a GOP convention.

Romney's choice of Representative Paul Ryan of Wisconsin was initially seen as a gesture toward Tea Party enthusiasts and to other economic conservatives, but it was more than that. Although Ryan's fame rested on leadership of the House GOP on budget issues, he was also a staunch social conservative: pro-life and opposed to same-sex marriage and embryonic stem-cell research (Condon 2012). A devout Catholic, he participated regularly in a Wednesday morning congressional prayer group frequented by evangelicals. As a result, he had a strong appeal to social conservatives: Christian right leaders were universally enthusiastic about Ryan. Indeed, the warm welcome accorded an Irish Catholic by evangelical leaders (coming after their primary endorsement of Santorum) seemed to validate claims of culture war theorists that religious alignments in politics are now determined by theological traditionalism or modernism, not ethnoreligious affiliation.

Ryan's sudden prominence not only brought his controversial proposals for reforming social welfare entitlements to the forefront of debate, but also highlighted his social conservatism. Democratic strategists immediately attacked his "anti-woman" position on "choice" issues, as well as his opposition to same-sex marriage (although he had supported anti-employment discrimination legislation for gay citizens). This attack was soon augmented by the media furor over comments made by Ryan's House colleague Todd Akin, running for the Senate in Missouri (Akin asserted that in cases of "legitimate rape," there was little likelihood that the victim would become pregnant). Because Ryan's congressional votes on abortion closely matched Akin's, he was an easy target for Democratic critics. On the other side, Concerned Women for America (a Christian right powerhouse), the National Right to Life Committee, and other conservative organizations quickly sprang to his defense (Haberman, Shultheis, and Romano 2012).

Ryan's budget proposals also evoked religious criticism. He had already been targeted by religious left organizations and, perhaps more importantly, by some members of the Catholic Bishops Conference, who argued that his budget cuts would disproportionately harm the poor. Liberal Catholics asserted that Ryan's view of Catholic social teachings was warped by enthusiasm for the doctrines of libertarian thinker (and atheist) Ayn Rand (Sibley 2012). Ryan refuted this charge in addresses to Catholic audiences, claiming, "The work I do as a Catholic holding office conforms to the social doctrine as best as I can make of it." In this claim he was quickly supported by his own bishop and some others (Pew Forum on Religion and Public Life 2012c). He was unable, however, to fend off the "Nuns on the Bus," who made his budget proposals a prime target of their national tour. Indeed, his views soon became a cynosure of the debates between traditionalist and liberal Catholics, fought out in both the religious and the secular press (Davies and Antolin 2012).

Reverting to the Base: Barack Obama's Religious Strategy

The factors influencing Barack Obama's strategy were rather different from those confronting Romney, but they also resulted in a movement toward the religious base. In 2008 Obama had followed an "ecumenical" approach that reflected both his personal experience and Democratic political imperatives. Obama himself embodied a crucial Democratic ethnoreligious constituency—black Protestants—but his background was even broader. Raised in an agnostic home, Obama had grown up in contact with several traditions: his (absent) father and Indonesian stepfather were Muslim (leading to persistent rumors that he was too); he attended a Catholic school for a time; and he encountered the black Protestant tradition as a community organizer in Chicago (and was paid by a Catholic organization). Eventually he joined the Trinity United Church of Christ, a large politically active congregation affiliated with the predominantly white United Church of Christ, the most theologically and politically liberal mainline Protestant denomination (Pinckney 2008). Although Obama withdrew from that congregation in 2008 after controversial statements by Pastor Jeremiah Wright threatened his campaign, the episode did little to reduce his appeal to black Protestants. To round out his ethnoreligious profile, Obama even had an in-law who was an African American rabbi in Chicago.

Obama's religious strategy had been shaped by political imperatives when he was a presidential candidate as well. Concerned by the "God gap" favoring the Republicans, Obama was outspoken in welcoming people of faith into the Democratic Party while criticizing those who would restrict such access. During his 2008 campaign, Obama made strong overtures to normally Republican religious groups and leaders, including evangelicals and conservative mainline Protestants and Catholics, hoping to add members of these groups to the usual Democratic coalition of ethnoreligious minorities, modernists, and seculars. These appeals were often as much rhetorical as substantive, but he also pledged to find middle ground on culture war issues such as abortion, continued to oppose same-sex marriage, and supported a faith-based initiative not very different from that of the Bush administration. Indeed, few recent Democratic candidates have had a more impressive religious mobilization operation (Guth 2009). Even Obama's 2009 inauguration was a festival of religious ecumenism.

Once in office, however, Obama was unable to sustain this strategy, given that the imperatives of mobilizing partisan majorities for his signature policy initiatives ultimately evoked the very ethnoreligious and culture war cleavages that he had sought to overcome in his campaign. His administrative and judicial appointees almost exclusively reflected the Democrats' traditional ethnoreligious and secular constituencies, his health care proposals renewed traditionalists' fears about public funding for abortion, his push to eliminate the "don't ask, don't tell" policy on gays in the military angered traditionalists, and his overtures to the Muslim world and Middle East policies bothered some Jews and many evangelicals. Finally, his efforts to extend and clarify Bush's faith-based initiatives failed to satisfy conservatives—or religious liberals, for that matter. Even Obama's rhetoric and personal behavior took on a more secular mien; his use of religious language waned, and he rarely attended church once in office. In the 2010 congressional elections, Democrats gave back most of the gains Obama had made in 2008 among typically Republican religious groups (Guth 2011).

As the 2012 campaign approached, Obama abandoned any thought of reviving his broad-based appeal of 2008. Rather, his executive actions and campaign rhetoric stressed policies designed to maximize his margins and turnout among traditional Democratic ethnoreligious and culture war constituencies. Executive actions on immigration policy, contraception in health plans under the Affordable Care Act, and Justice Department briefs on the Defense of Marriage Act (and his own "evolved" position in favor of same-sex marriage) are just a few instances of a host of actions directed at ethnoreligious minorities, feminists, gay rights advocates, secular citizens, and other base Democratic constituencies. Democratic mobilization strategies sought to maximize the vote and turnout among these groups, rather than to renew the wider appeals of Obama's 2008 religious outreach.

As the general election loomed, then, the evolution of religious strategies for both Romney and Obama converged on the politics of core constituencies, despite the evident initial preferences of both nominees for a different sort of coalition-building: in Obama's case, for a sort of "grand coalition" of religious forces and in Romney's, for a focus on economic issues and management that would take attention away from issues more strongly shaped by religious alignments. The president's preferred strategy was negated by the political battles of his administration, and Romney's approach was defeated by the imperatives of Republican nominating politics. All this suggested that religious coalitions in 2012 would remain largely unchanged from those that have characterized American politics for the last three decades (Kellstedt and Guth 2012).

Conventions and the Campaign

The next task for both parties was to make sure any marginal changes in these coalitions favored their candidate. The Republican and Democratic conventions served both intentionally and inadvertently to solidify the parties' religious bases. In the Republican case, there was a major effort to assimilate Mitt Romney's religious experience to that of the GOP base through films and testimonials to his pastoral activities as head of the LDS stake in Boston and on his substantial financial contributions to church and charities. The Republican platform maintained its long-term commitment to conservative social policies on abortion, same-sex marriage, and other culture war issues. If the party's highlighting of minority members, such as Senator Rubio, Governor Martinez, and Secretary Rice, had an impact, it was often to emphasize the larger problem Republicans had attracting Latino and African American voters. Many convention speeches and the platform itself had substantial stretches of religious language. Finally, the choice of New York cardinal Timothy Dolan, a prominent traditionalist, to deliver the closing prayer was seen as a gesture to conservative Catholics worried about abortion, same-sex marriage, and the "religious liberty" issue (Goodstein 2012).

The Democratic convention sought to portray the party's commitment to both faith and ethnoreligious diversity. To some observers, the 2012 meeting seemed one of the most "accessible" to religious concerns in recent decades. The embrace of faith by convention planners and party leaders was on display with opening and closing prayers offered by leaders of many faiths, including Cardinal Dolan (who was hastily invited by the Democrats to offset any impact from his GOP appearance); delegate prayer meetings each morning; and gatherings of the Faith Caucus throughout the week. Speeches featured Sister Simone Campbell, one of the "Nuns on the Bus," who declared, "I am my sister's keeper" and repeated the assertion of some members of the Bishops Conference that Ryan's budget failed a basic moral test by harming poor families.

But the convention also inadvertently highlighted both the growing role of secular activists in the party and some interreligious conflict. The platform and convention speeches stressed repeatedly the Democrats' commitment to choice on abortion and legalization of same-sex marriage, issues with the greatest appeal to seculars and modernists, abandoning the more moderate language of the 2008 document. The platform committee had also removed a ritual reference to God in previous documents and omitted language recognizing Jerusalem as the capital of Israel, presumably in response to the sensitivities of Arab American and Muslim delegates, present in record numbers. Obama strategists quickly realized the negative potential of both deletions, as Republicans boasted that *their* platform included a dozen mentions of the deity *and* recognized Jerusalem.

To remedy this "oversight," former Ohio governor Ted Strickland offered an amendment on behalf of the Obama campaign to reinstate language that endorsed "government that stands up for the hopes, values and interests of working people and gives everyone willing to work hard the chance to make the most of their God-given potential." The amendment also recognized Jerusalem as the capital of Israel. As an ordained United Methodist minister, Strickland was there "to attest and affirm that our belief in God is central to the American story and informs the values we have expressed in our party's platform" (CSPAN 2012). But the amendment effort quickly ran into trouble: on three successive voice votes, the motion drew as many "nays" as "yeas." The presiding officer, Los Angeles mayor Antonio Villaraigosa, finally overcame his indecision and ruled that the amendment had passed with the required two-thirds majority, eliciting a loud chorus of boos (Markoe 2012). Although the jeers no doubt reflected varied objections—to the parliamentary procedure followed, to the commitment to Jerusalem as capital of Israel, and to the use of "God-language" in a party platform—the media had a brief frenzy with headlines such as "Democrats Boo God in Charlotte." Even a friendly academic observed that "the Democrats were not sure they wanted God in the campaign at all" (Worthen 2012).

Once the conventions had adjourned, attention returned to voter mobilization. Despite spotty media coverage of religious mobilization, there seems to have been a good bit going on. First, there was the usual raft of candidate endorsements by religious leaders. A long list of evangelical officials endorsed Romney, headlined by Billy Graham's clear imprimatur after a meeting with the GOP candidate, and a host of black Protestant leaders gave a similar thumbs-up to Obama, most notably Bishop Vashti McKenzie's "personal" endorsement following the First Lady's speech to the annual meeting of the African Methodist Episcopal Church. Both candidates highlighted endorsements or quasi-endorsements by prominent Catholics (Grant 2012; Kucinich 2012; McElwee 2012).

Second, each party sought assistance in religious mobilization. Evangelical groups such as the Faith and Freedom Coalition, the Family Research Council, and others promised to deliver millions of voter guides to conservative churches and make a comparable number of other contacts, but they were hardly alone in the field. A group called the Alliance Defending Freedom expanded earlier efforts to persuade conservative pastors to challenge IRS restrictions on church electioneering by endorsing candidates (i.e., Mitt Romney) from the pulpit—and sending transcripts of the offending sermons to the agency (Skeel 2012). The Romney campaign, however, was most focused on attracting white Catholic voters, critical in battleground states, by emphasizing "religious liberty" questions arising from the Health and Human Services contraception mandate. In this the campaign was assisted by Priests for Life, the EWTN network, CatholicVote.org, and several other conservative Catholic organizations, which produced Republican-friendly voter guides—at least online. And although the National Council of Catholic Bishops merely reissued its old 2007 election guide, several conservative prelates left little doubt about their preference for Romney (Gibson 2012).

Although Obama had staff dedicated to activating more liberal mainline Protestants and Catholics, the main focus was on mobilizing black Protestant churches. During the campaign there were numerous reports of voter registration drives in African American churches, followed by "Souls to the Polls" actions in which entire congregations would leave Sunday services, pile in church buses, and vote early in crucial states such as Florida and Ohio (despite futile attempts by state Republicans to limit voting on Sunday). Like some evangelical counterparts, more than a few African American clergy seemed ready to ignore the apparently moribund IRS prohibitions on pulpit endorsements, making clear their enthusiasm for President Obama's reelection (O'Keefe 2012; Nicholas 2012).

How many voters did such tactics reach? By some past markers, the religious mobilization was not terribly impressive (Pew Research Center 2012b, 2012c). Despite considerable outside encouragement, clerical endorsements from the pulpit remained rare: only 5 percent of regular churchgoers heard one, although this rose to 13 percent among Anglo-Catholics (all such endorsements were of Romney). Similarly, only 8 percent of voters reported being contacted by religious organizations, mostly on behalf of the GOP ticket. Nor were voter guides particularly abundant, with only 13 percent of regular churchgoers reporting their availability, half the number in 2004, although evangelicals and Anglo-Catholics reported slightly higher averages (16 and 17 percent, respectively). Of course, the paucity of contacts reported in national polls may well reflect the religious groups' decision to concentrate on only a few battleground states, certainly a rational use of limited resources.

Such measures of direct campaigning probably understate the amount of indirect activity transpiring in churches. A majority of churchgoers reported being urged by clergy to vote, especially those in the parties' core constituencies: black Protestants (79 percent) and evangelicals (52 percent). Many clergy also discussed the candidates explicitly, especially in black Protestant churches (40 percent) and Anglo-Catholic parishes (17 percent). Of those hearing such messages, only 3 out of 10 said the messages favored one candidate, but that favoritism followed predictable lines, with black Protestant clergy overwhelmingly favoring Obama and Anglo-Catholic priests and evangelical pastors supporting Romney. Of course, such pastoral preferences may not have had much impact: these clergy were preaching to the choir, backing the candidate already favored by most parishioners (see Jones, Cox, and Navarro-Rivera 2012).

Even less-direct political cues took the form of issue discussions. Not surprisingly, clergy were very likely to speak about hunger and poverty (74 percent), with Anglo-Catholics slightly more likely to hear about the topic. Abortion came in second, with 37 percent of churchgoers hearing of this issue, with Anglo-Catholics (58 percent) and evangelicals (40 percent) topping the list. Homosexuality was slightly less discussed, with evangelicals (40 percent) and black Protestants (37 percent) hearing the most. Finally, "religious liberty" discussions were heard by only 21 percent of churchgoers, but by an impressive 36 percent of Anglo-Catholics, perhaps explaining other poll findings that Catholic laity did tend to share their leadership's concerns on these issues (Pew Research Center 2012a). Interestingly, mainline Protestants, the old American religious elite, ranked lowest of all major groups on hearing issue discussions, receiving voting guides, reporting pulpit endorsements, and remembering any clerical discussion about the election.

Religious Voting in 2012

From the most important standpoint, Obama's strategy of solidifying his religious base produced an electoral victory. Nevertheless, most observers are hard-pressed to see dramatic changes in partisan religious alignments. As one first cut at the exit polls suggested, "the basic religious contours of the 2012 electorate resemble recent elections" at least as far back as 2000 (Pew Forum on Religion and Public Life 2012a). Indeed, looking at the crude religious measures available in the exit polls, what is remarkable is the absence of much change at all in the behavior of religious groups over the past four presidential races. Nor has there been any substantial modification of the "God gap," the difference in electoral choices of frequent churchgoers, more infrequent attenders, and the nonobservant (Pew Forum on Religion and Public Life 2012a).

With finer-grained measures, however, we can say a little more about some important, if subtle, shifts in religious voting and electoral coalitions. In Table 9.2 we report on religious voting using data from the preliminary pre-election poll of the University of Akron's National Survey of Religion and Politics (NSRP) for evangelicals, mainline Protestants, and Anglo-Catholics; this allows us to use the NSRP's rich battery of religious questions to classify respondents by theological orientation. For the smaller ethnoreligious

Table 9.2 Religious Voting in the 2012 Presidential Election (in Percent)

Ethnoreligious tradition and theological faction	GOP Romney vote	GOP Obama vote	Democratic gain/loss from 2008	vote coalition	vote coalition
Latter-day Saint (Mormon)*	78	21	+6	3	1
Evangelical Protestant	74	26	-2	36	12
Traditionalist	*86*	*14*	*-2*	*19*	*3*
Centrist	*71*	*29*	*-3*	*12*	*4*
Modernist	*52*	*48*	*+2*	*5*	*5*
Traditionalist-modernist	*+34*	*-34*	—	—	—
Mainline Protestant	55	45	+5	18	14
Traditionalist	*73*	*27*	*+5*	*7*	*2*
Centrist	*62*	*38*	*+13*	*7*	*4*
Modernist	*33*	*67*	*-6*	*4*	*8*
Traditionalist-modernist	*+40*	*-40*	—	—	—
Anglo-Catholic	62	38	+11	23	13
Traditionalist	*67*	*33*	*+9*	*7*	*3*
Centrist	*62*	*38*	*-1*	*11*	*6*
Modernist	*52*	*48*	*+18*	*5*	*4*
Traditionalist-modernist	*+15*	*-15*	—	—	—
Latino Protestant	40	60	+7	3	4
Latino Catholic*	21	75	-6	2	10
Unaffiliated	34	66	+7	11	19
Unaffiliated believer	*49*	*51*	*+8*	*3*	*3*
Secular	*32*	*68*	*+10*	*6*	*11*
Agnostic/atheist	*24*	*76*	*+5*	*2*	*5*
Jewish*	30	69	+7	1	2
All others*	23	74	+5	2	6
Black Protestant	5	95	0	1	21
Total sample	48	52	+2	100	100

Source: National Survey of Religion and Politics, University of Akron, 2010.

*Estimate from national exit polls (Pew Forum on Religion and Public Life 2012d).

groups, we draw on the preliminary findings of the network exit polls, to minimize errors from the smaller subsamples in the NSRP (Pew Forum on Religion and Public Life 2012b).

How did religious groups vote in 2012? Not surprisingly, Romney carried 78 percent of his fellow Mormons, a better performance than John McCain's in 2008, but he fell a little short of matching the Arizonan's totals among evangelicals, losing some ground among the large traditionalist coterie, while gaining a bit among the smaller contingent of modernists. Thus, although Romney's Mormon faith and questionable commitment to conservative social values did not produce major defections among the GOP's largest religious constituency, neither did they foster maximum commitment, despite the best efforts of many evangelical leaders and Christian right organizations.

As his performance in the primaries suggested, Romney was much more attractive to the old GOP religious elite in the shrinking ranks of mainline Protestants, doing better than McCain among traditionalists and especially among centrists, but losing ground to Obama among modernists. Thus, there was an enormous 40 point voting gap between mainline traditionalists and modernists, considerably larger than that between the bookend evangelical factions. This confirms the massive evidence from the religious press that mainline Protestantism is at the center of religious restructuring, as these churches struggle with internal conflict over theology, social values, and political choices. Once "the Republican Party at prayer," mainline Protestantism is now a religious and political battlefield.

Romney also gained ground on Obama among Anglo-Catholics, but here theological divisions were much reduced, as modernists actually gave Romney a slight majority, albeit a smaller one than their traditionalist co-parishioners did, with centrists standing pat on their solid GOP vote from 2008. Although restructuring influences are still evident among Anglo-Catholics, the results remind us that historic ethnoreligious loyalties and institutions can still create a modicum of group unity under the right conditions. Whether Romney's success among Catholics reflects the campaign's sustained outreach efforts, the Church's highly visible battle with the Obama administration over health care rules and other policies, or historically greater Catholic sensitivity to poor economic conditions is uncertain. As with mainline Protestants, however, Romney gained less than he hoped from this successful appeal to white Catholics, given their declining contribution to the electorate (Pew Forum on Religion and Public Life 2012a).

Romney also improved on McCain's performance among usually Democratic ethnoreligious groups, gaining modestly among Latino Protestants (something of a surprise), unaffiliated voters (even agnostics and atheists moved slightly toward the GOP), Jews, and "all other" faiths, although in each case he still won only a minority of the vote—sometimes a rather small one. President Obama, on the other hand, held on to virtually unanimous support among black Protestants and actually improved on his overwhelming 2008 margin among Latino Catholics, a gain fortified by a substantial increase in their turnout rate. On the whole, then, although the president lost some ground within many religious groups, he minimized losses in the Democratic Party's core religious constituencies and actually increased his vote in some.

A comparison of Tables 9.1 and 9.2 shows some changes in the significance of religious groups for the parties' electoral coalitions. Evangelical and mainline Protestants were a slightly smaller proportion of Romney's coalition than they were of McCain's (36 and 39 percent, respectively, for evangelicals; 18 and 20 percent for mainliners). This reflects a number of factors. Romney's stronger appeal to other groups diluted the total contribution of white Protestants, and the declining number of mainline voters also reduced their presence (evangelicals constituted about the same proportion of the electorate in 2012 as in 2008). Anglo-Catholics, on the other hand, retained their newer prominence in the GOP electorate, with almost a quarter of the vote. As many observers pointed out, these results meant that well over two-thirds of GOP voters were from the three large white Christian traditions, a proportion further augmented by Latter-day Saints, some Jews, and many unaffiliated voters. And a solid majority of GOP voters also came from traditionalist camps within the three largest ethnoreligious groups, augmented by social conservatives among Latter-day Saints, Latino Protestants, and a few other religious communities.

The Democratic coalition shifted further in the direction of its base ethnoreligious constituencies, drawing proportionately fewer mainline Protestants and Anglo-Catholics than in 2008 (14 percent mainline Protestants in 2012 versus 18 percent in 2008; 13 percent Anglo-Catholics in 2012 versus 20 percent in 2008) and larger proportions from among Latino Catholics (4 and 10 percent in 2008 and 2012, respectively), the unaffiliated (16 and 19 percent), other faiths (4 and 6 percent), and black Protestants (20 and 21 percent). And to the extent that the Democrats still attracted some voters in America's largest white religious traditions, their appeal was concentrated (perhaps increasingly) among religious modernists.[3]

Conclusion

After every presidential election the inevitable discussion begins about the long-term meaning of the results. Although political scientists are increasingly skeptical about applying a realignment model to electoral change, almost invariably some partisans on each side argue that the election has established a new, dominant electoral majority vindicating their strategy (if they are on the winning side) or requiring drastic changes in party policy and tactics (if they lost). Within hours of the 2012 election, some Democratic theorists were trumpeting the triumph of the "emerged Democratic majority," based on ethnoreligious minorities, such as black Protestants and Latino Catholics, young people, and the growing number of "secular" Americans with liberal social values (McArdle 2012). And Republicans debated whether their party was "too Christian," "too white," and "too traditionalist"—and if so, what to do about it (Ayres, McHenry, and Frans 2012).

Within a week or two, however, experienced political observers were cautioning against drawing long-term conclusions about party strength from any one contest (Kohut 2012). From the perspective of religious coalitions, indeed, what is remarkable about the 2012 election is how much it resembled the previous ones in this century. The Republican and Democratic parties consistently draw from a stable alignment of religious groups, with marginal changes in that support during any election cycle based on the traits of the candidates on offer, major political issues or events, and minor changes in the numbers and turnout of each group. But mostly, to quote political theorist Yogi Berra, "it's déjà vu all over again" when it comes to religious voting.

Nevertheless, there are significant if gradual changes transpiring in religious politics. First, the religious population is indeed shifting in directions that benefit the Democrats—assuming that the GOP fails to make inroads into growing population groups such as Latinos, where the party has had some success in the past. Second, the Republican and Democratic electoral coalitions are growing more distinct, experiencing a "big sort" along ethnoreligious and theological lines. Evangelical, mainline, and Anglo-Catholic traditionalists have become the core of the GOP, whereas ethnoreligious minorities, modernists, and secular citizens increasingly dominate the Democrats. In the past, mainline Protestants and Anglo-Catholics were major forces in both parties, but with their numerical decline (and theological sorting), these groups provide much less overlap and common ground between the parties.

In policy terms, this religious sorting has created—or at least reinforced—partisan divisions on a vast array of issues, from abortion and same-sex marriage to economic regulatory policy and foreign policy questions (Guth 2011). Indeed, some of the partisan acrimony evident in Washington reflects this religious sorting. And because the religious groups with more extreme ideological stances tend to produce more party activists, candidate selection reflects that dominance, sometimes to the party's disadvantage in general elections. In 2012 Romney was hindered in his quest for the presidency by the constraints imposed by his need to appeal to conservative GOP primary electorates, and Republicans also nominated several Senate candidates who were favored by their religious core but were unacceptable to general election voters. Democrats have not suffered as much recently from an analogous malady, but they will face such challenges in the future as their electoral base becomes ever more distinct religiously—and increasingly diverse as well.

NOTES

1. The candidate profiles in the following paragraphs are drawn from a wide variety of sources, but the single most useful compendium of information was the website of the Pew Forum on Religion and Public Life.

2. The Pearson product moment correlation (r) is a statistic that measures the strength and direction of a relationship between two variables. This statistic runs from 0 (no relationship) to $+/-$ 1.0 (a perfect relationship). In this case, one could predict the likelihood of Romney's success in a GOP primary by knowing the proportion of evangelicals in the state (a strong negative influence) and the proportion of Catholics (a strong positive influence).

3. We emphasize that the findings of all these studies are preliminary. When available, the NSRP post-election survey will provide final estimates for religious group voting. The exit poll results will also be subject to revision based on secondary analysis of the data with more accurate weighing of respondents (Pew Forum 2012a). For another insightful survey on religious voting and electoral coalitions, with estimates quite similar to ours, see Jones, Cox, and Navarro-Rivera (2012).

REFERENCES

Ayres, Whit, Jon McHenry, and Luke Frans. 2012. "2012: The Year Changing Demographics Caught Up with the Republican Party." *Resurgent Republic,* November 9. http://www.resurgentrepublic.com/research/2012-the-year-changing-demographics-caught-up-with-republicans (accessed December 1, 2012).

Barbaro, Michael, and Ashley Parker. 2012. "Scripture, Song and Six Grandchildren: Romneys Open Church Doors to Press." *New York Times,* August 19. http://www.nytimes.com/2012/08/20/us/politics/romneys-at-church-scripture-songs-and-six-grandchildren.html (accessed December 1, 2012).

Bradberry, Leigh A. 2012. "The Effect of Religion on Republican Primary Vote Choice." Presented at the annual meeting of the Midwest Political Science Association, Chicago, April 12–15.

Condon, Stephanie. 2012. "Paul Ryan's Anti-Abortion Rights Record a Target for Obama Camp." CBS News, August 15. http://www.cbsnews.com/8301–250_162-57493360/paul-ryans-anti-abortion-rights-record-a-target-for-obama-camp/?pageNum=2 (accessed December 1, 2012).

CSPAN. 2012. Democratic National Convention Hub. http://www.c-span.org/DNC/ (accessed February 1, 2013).

Davies, Antony, and Kristina Antolin. 2012. "Paul Ryan's Catholicism and the Poor." *Wall Street Journal,* August 18. http://online.wsj.com/article/SB10000872396390444375104577592892933747400.html (accessed December 1, 2012).

Douthat, Ross. 2012. "In 2012, No Religious Center Is Holding." *New York Times,* April 7. http://www.nytimes.com/2012/04/08/opinion/sunday/douthat-in-2012-no-religious-center-is-holding.html?pagewanted=all&_r=0 (accessed December 1, 2012).

Gibson, Ginger. 2012. "Catholic Voters Target of Aggressive Push." *Politico,* October 15. http://www.nytimes.com/2012/08/25/us/politics/cardinal-dolans-convention-role-shows-gops-push-for-catholic-vote.html (accessed December 1, 2012).

Gingrich, Newt. 2006. *Rediscovering God in America.* Nashville: Integrity House.

Goodstein, Laurie. 2012. "Invitation to Cardinal Shows G.O.P.'S Catholic Push." *New York Times,* August 24. http://www.nytimes.com/2012/08/25/us/politics/

cardinal-dolans-convention-role-shows-gops-push-for-catholic-vote.html (accessed December 1, 2012).

Grant, Tobin. 2012. "The Year of the Personal Endorsement." *Christianity Today* (web only), November 2. http://www.christianitytoday.com/ct/2012/november-web-only/year-of-personal-endorsement.html (accessed December 1, 2012).

Green, John C. 2007. *The Faith Factor: How Religion Influences American Elections.* Westport, CT: Praeger.

Green, John C., James L. Guth, and Cleveland R. Fraser. 1991. "Apostles and Apostates? Religion and Politics among Political Activists." In *The Bible and the Ballot Box,* ed. James L. Guth and John C. Green, 113–136. Boulder, CO: Westview.

Green, John C., and John S. Jackson. 2007. "Faithful Divides: Party Elites and Religion." In *A Matter of Faith: Religion in the 2004 Presidential Election,* ed. David E. Campbell, 37–62. Washington, DC: Brookings.

Guth, James L. 2007. "Religion and Roll Calls: Religious Influences on the U.S. House of Representatives, 1997–2002." Paper presented at the annual meeting of the American Political Science Association, Chicago, August 30–September 2.

Guth, James L. 2009. "Religion in the 2008 Election." In *The American Elections of 2008,* ed. Janet M. Box-Steffensmeier and Steven E. Schier, 117–136. Lanham, MD: Rowman & Littlefield.

Guth, James L. 2011. "Obama, Religious Politics and the Culture Wars." In *Transforming America: Barack Obama in the White House,* ed. Steven E. Schier, 77–100. Lanham, MD: Rowman & Littlefield.

Guth, James L., Lyman A. Kellstedt, Corwin E. Smidt, and John C. Green. 2006. "Religious Influences in the 2004 Presidential Election." *Presidential Studies Quarterly* 36 (2): 223–242.

Haberman, Maggie, Emily Shultheis, and Lois Romano. 2012. "Paul Ryan Targeted on Women's Issues." *Politico,* August 19. http://www.politico.com/news/stories/0812/79856.html (accessed December 1, 2012).

Horowitz, Jason. 2012. "Mitt Romney, as a Leader in Mormon Church, Became a Master of Many Keys." *Washington Post,* August 19. http://www.washingtonpost.com/politics/mitt-romney-as-a-leader-in-mormon-church-became-a-master-of-many-keys/2012/08/19/7c8fe1bc-cf89-11e1-8e56-dffbfbe1bd20_story.html (accessed December 1, 2012).

Hunter, James D. 1991. *Culture Wars: The Struggle to Define America.* New York: Basic Books.

Jones, Robert P., Daniel Cox, and Juhem Navarro-Rivera. 2012. *The 2012 Post-Election American Values Survey.* Washington, DC: Public Religion Research Institute. http://publicreligion.org/research/2012/11/american-values-post-election-survey-2012/ (accessed December 1, 2012).

Judis, John B., and Ruy Teixeira. 2002. *The Emerging Democratic Majority.* New York: Scribner.

Kellstedt, Lyman A., and James L. Guth. 2012. "Survey Research: Religion and Electoral Behavior in the United States, 1936–2008." In *Political Science Research in Practice,* ed. Akan Malici and Elizabeth Smith, 93–110. New York: Routledge.

Kellstedt, Lyman A., Corwin E. Smidt, John C. Green, and James L. Guth. 2007. "A Gentle Stream or a 'River Glorious'? The Religious Left in the 2004 Election." In *A Matter of Faith: Religion in the 2004 Presidential Election,* ed. David E. Campbell, 232–256. Washington, DC: Brookings.

Kleppner, Paul. 1979. *The Third Electoral System, 1853–1892: Parties, Voters, and Political Cultures.* Chapel Hill: University of North Carolina Press.

Kohut, Andrew. 2012. "Misreading Election 2012." *Wall Street Journal,* November 14, A15.

Kucinich, Jackie. 2012. "Evangelicals Mobilize for Romney/Ryan Campaign." *USA Today,* October 18, 4A.

Layman, Geoffrey. 2001. *The Great Divide: Religious and Cultural Conflict in American Party Politics.* New York: Columbia University Press.

Markoe, Lauren. 2012. "'God Talk' and the Democrats." *Christian Century,* October 3, 14–15.

Martin, Jonathan. 2012. "Social Conservatives Back Rick Santorum." *Politico,* January 14. http://www.politico.com/blogs/burns-haberman/2012/01/social-conservatives-back-santorum-110869.html (accessed December 1, 2012).

McArdle, Megan. 2012. "Is Demography Destiny?" *The Daily Beast,* November 7. http://www.thedailybeast.com/articles/2012/11/07/is-demography-destiny.html (accessed December 1, 2012).

McElwee, Joshua J. 2012. "Outspoken Bishops Step into Election Fray." *National Catholic Reporter,* October 12–25, 1.

Nicholas, Peter. 2012. "Sunday Sermons in Florida Push Early Voting." *Wall Street Journal,* October 29, A4.

O'Keefe, Ed. 2012. "'Souls to the Polls' Aims to Turn Out Early Voters in Ohio." *Washington Post,* November 4. http://www.washingtonpost.com/blogs/post-politics/wp/2012/11/04/souls-to-the-polls-aims-to-turn-out-early-voters-in-ohio/ (accessed December 1, 2012).

Pew Forum on Religion and Public Life. 2011. "Romney's Mormon Faith Likely a Factor in Primaries, Not in a General Election." November 23. http://www.pewforum.org/Politics-and-Elections/Romneys-Mormon-Faith-Likely-a-Factor-in-Primaries-Not-in-a-General-Election.aspx?src=prc=headline (accessed December 1, 2012).

Pew Forum on Religion and Public Life. 2012a. "How the Faithful Voted: 2012 Preliminary Analysis." November 7. http://www.pewforum.org/Politics-and-Elections/How-the-Faithful-Voted-2012-Preliminary-Exit-Poll-Analysis.aspx#rr (accessed December 1, 2012).

Pew Forum on Religion and Public Life. 2012b. "More See 'Too Much' Religious Talk by Politicians." March 21. http://www.pewforum.org/Politics-and-Elections/more-see-too-much-religious-talk-by-politicians.aspx (accessed December 1, 2012).

Pew Forum on Religion and Public Life. 2012c. "Paul Ryan." http://www.pewforum.org/rp2012/paul-ryan/ (accessed December 1, 2012).

Pew Forum on Religion and Public Life. 2012d. "Trends in the Party Identification of Religious Groups." February 2. http://www.pewforum.org/Politics-and-Elections/Trends-in-Party-Identification-of-Religious-Groups.aspx (accessed December 1, 2012).

Pew Research Center. 2012a. "Catholics Share Bishops Concerns about Religious Liberty." August 1. http://pewresearch.org/pubs/2317/catholic-bishop-obama-romney-religious-liberty-protest-voters-government-policies-abortion-contraceptive-churchgoers-church-observant-nuns-pope-leadership-gay-rights (accessed December 1, 2012).

Pew Research Center. 2012b. "In Deadlocked Race, Neither Side Has Ground Game Advantage." October 31. http://www.people-press.org/files/legacy-pdf/10-31-12%20Campaign%20Outreach%20Release.pdf (accessed December 1, 2012).

Pew Research Center. 2012c. "Voters Give Low Marks to 2012 Campaign." November 15. http://www.people-press.org/2012/11/15/section-3-the-voting-process-and-the-accuracy-of-the-vote/ (accessed December 1, 2012).

Pinckney, Darryl. 2008. "Obama and the Black Church." *New York Review of Books,* July 17, 18–21.

Seiple, Chris. 2012. "The Politics of Evangelicalism: How Washington Is Leaving the Faithful Behind." *Foreign Affairs Online.* http://www.foreignaffairs.com/print/134631.

Sibley, Angus. 2012. "Paul Ryan: Thomist or Randian?" *National Catholic Reporter,* September 14–27, 32.

Skeel, David. 2012. "Politicking from the Pulpit and the Tax Man." *Wall Street Journal,* November 23, A13. http://online.wsj.com/article/SB10001424127887323713104578133181817762710.html (accessed December 1, 2012).

Swaine, Jon. 2012. "Church and State Separation Gone Too Far, Says Romney." *The Telegraph,* August 21. http://www.telegraph.co.uk/news/worldnews/us-election/9490951/US-election-Church-and-State-separation-gone-too-far-says-Mitt-Romney.html (accessed December 1, 2012).

Teixeira, Ruy. 2010. "Demographic Change and the Future of the Parties." Center for American Progress Action Fund, June. http://www.americanprogressaction.org/issues/progressive-movement/report/2010/06/16/7953/demographic-change-and-the-future-of-the-parties/ (accessed December 1, 2012).

Wallsten, Peter, and Karen Tumulty. 2012. "Conservative Activists Scramble to Stop Mitt Romney." *Washington Post,* January 10. http://www.washingtonpost.com/politics/conservative-activists-scrambling-for-a-strategy-to-block-romney/2012/01/10/gIQAVFATpP_story.html (accessed December 1, 2012).

Wallis, Jim. 2008. *The Great Awakening: Reviving Faith and Politics in a Post-Religious Right America.* New York: HarperOne.

Worthen, Molly. 2012. "The Power of Political Communion." *New York Times,* September 16. http://www.nytimes.com/2012/09/16/opinion/sunday/catholics-and-the-power-of-political-communion.html?_r=0 (accessed December 1, 2012).

10 The Reaffirmation of the Post–Cold War Electoral Order

The Meaning of the 2012 Election

Nicol C. Rae

Since the end of the Cold War and the election of Bill Clinton to the presidency in 1992, the United States has experienced an era of highly competitive and close national elections between increasingly ideologically polarized national political parties (Theriault and Moeller 2013). This development is based on post–New Deal electoral alignments along racial-ethnic/cultural/religious lines (Layman 2001) and reinforced by clusters of "policy demanding" interests around each of the major parties (Cohen et al. 2008); by ideological networks of campaign contributors, grassroots activists, media, and think tanks (Fiorina 2006, 2009); and by the advent of new political media—cable news, talk radio, the Internet/blogs—that encourage political "narrowcasting" (Sunstein 2007). All of this has increased the costs of crossing party lines in Washington, DC, on any issue and has made the compromises needed to advance legislation in America's separated system of government much harder to achieve (except, perhaps, in the few months following the election of a new president). One result is wider public exasperation with "gridlock" and "political dysfunction" in the U.S. federal government (Brownstein 2008).

During the two decades between Bill Clinton's first inauguration and the second inauguration of Barack Obama, the Democrats controlled the presidency for 12 years to the Republicans' 8 years; the Republicans controlled the U.S. House of Representatives for 14 years to the Democrats' 6 years; and control of the U.S. Senate has been held by each party for 10 years in total. Elections during the period for both president and Congress were closely contested, although there appears to be a slight Democratic advantage in presidential elections and a slight Republican advantage in House elections, with Senate elections very evenly balanced.

Perhaps because of the increasing ideological polarization between the parties, there has been an unwholesome tendency for recent victorious presidents and congressional leaders (aided and abetted by excitable political commentators) to claim "mandates" for significant policy change, electoral realignment, or emergent durable partisan majorities following fairly narrow and inconclusive electoral victories. These claims rest on flimsy evidence and have been deleterious to the conduct of American government over the past decade. The last two presidents misinterpreted relatively narrow electoral victories to claim mandates from the electorate that, upon close examination of the electoral results, did not exist. The results were either failed presidential policy initiatives for want of public support or the implementation of such initiatives in close and bitterly contested votes in Congress with little regard to public opinion. In such circumstances, the resistance of the opposing party is enhanced, and policy stasis and rhetorical excess in Washington are exacerbated, to the detriment of public confidence in national governing institutions.

This chapter's central theme is that the 2012 election campaign and results reiterated the post-1992 pattern of highly contested and close elections between polarized national political parties in the United States. The claims of specific policy mandates from the election have little foundation, and the evidence that the 2012 election is a harbinger of a durable national Democratic Party majority is even more slender. I also take issue with the problematic assumption that such durable long-term policy mandates and partisan majorities can still be generated given the highly fluid nature of contemporary American politics, and I point out the pitfalls of the underlying theory of "realignment" for analysts and practitioners of American politics and government today. The chapter concludes by suggesting an alternative framework that may prove more fruitful in understanding current American electoral politics.

The "Emerging Democratic Majority" and the Obama Administration

John Judis and Ruy Teixeira's 2002 book *The Emerging Democratic Majority* has been one of the most influential works of political science in the past decade. *The Emerging Democratic Majority* has not only aroused controversy among political scientists and electoral analysts—see Sean Trende's recent *The Lost Majority* (2012)—but has also had an influence on Democratic electoral strategies and, perhaps indirectly, on the policies of the Obama administration. The core of Judis and Teixeira's argument is their correct identification of growing groups that are supportive of the modern-day Democratic Party. Specifically, racial minorities, younger "millennial" voters, single women, LGBT Americans, and secular highly educated professionals will constitute an increasing share of the American electorate in the first half of the twenty-first century, relative to the more religiously observant, middle- and working-class white voters on which the Republican Party has increasingly depended. Judis and Teixeira also note accurately that younger voters tend to hold liberal opinions on cultural issues such as same-sex marriage and marijuana legalization. In the long term this should also work to the Democrats' advantage electorally as older, more socially conservative, Republican-leaning voters become a progressively smaller component of the American electorate. In short, demographics and social change, Judis and Teixeira argue, are finally turning George McGovern's minority 1972 Democratic coalition into a new national governing majority: a coalition of the ascendant forces in twenty-first-century American society.

Judis and Teixeira's argument offered a plausible rationale for the nomination and election of Barack Obama in 2008 and a road map for keeping that majority in place. Obama's 53 percent of the national popular vote in 2008 was the highest for a Democratic presidential candidate since 1944 (with the exception of the freakish LBJ landslide in 1964). After the 2008 election, the Democrats enjoyed their largest House majority since 1994 and their largest Senate margin since the 1970s. The victorious Democratic electoral coalition of 2008 was indeed based on the "demographically ascendant" segments of the electorate cited by Judis and Teixeira—minority voters, younger voters, highly educated professionals, LGBT voters, and single women (Pew Research Center 2008). Many of those who rapidly wrote off American conservatism and the Republican Party in the wake of the 2008 results argued along the same lines as Judis and Teixeira. They held that the Republican party had gotten itself on the wrong side of the birth rate in national elections for some time to come and that Barack Obama's seven-point popular vote victory and Democratic gains in Congress indicated a new era of Democratic dominance and a mandate for a more interventionist federal government (Smith 2008; Tanenhaus 2009).

A closer examination of the 2008 election campaign and results indicates, however, that this conclusion was premature at best. After the 2008 Republican convention, Barack Obama was actually trailing John McCain in the general election polling, and the election turned decisively in Obama's direction only after the financial meltdown in late September. Even in the midst of two unpopular wars and an economic meltdown, Obama could summon only 53 percent of the popular vote against a palpably weak Republican candidate and with a very unpopular Republican incumbent in the White House. Exit polls in 2008 also showed that the percentage of Americans describing themselves as conservative (34 percent) or moderate (44 percent) still far outnumbered the 22 percent who described themselves as liberal (Zernike and Sussman 2008). The exit polls also indicated that Obama and the Democrats won the election because of the unpopularity of the George W. Bush administration and the financial meltdown of September 2008. Independent and moderate voters flocked to Obama to fix the economy, not to implement a twenty-first-century New Deal (Rae 2011).

This was borne out by the public reaction to the measures taken by the Obama administration in its first two years. The $787 billion economic stimulus package, the bailouts of General Motors and Chrysler, and the 2010 Affordable Care Act (health care reform) appeared to many voters to cater more to specific Democratic constituencies and Democratic base voters than to the interests of the country at large. Independents and moderates began to desert the president, and the worsening federal budget deficit only seemed to confirm their fears (Rae 2011).

For Republicans, demoralized after a failed Republican presidency and two successive election defeats, the Obama agenda proved to be a rallying point. Following CNBC commentator Rick Santelli's notorious rant on the floor of the Chicago Stock Exchange in February 2009, the Tea Party movement erupted (Rasmussen and Schoen 2010), reinvigorating the conservative grassroots and contributing significantly to the 2010 Republican resurgence with severe Democratic losses in Congress, state governorships, and state legislatures. At the same time, the president's approval ratings dropped from the stratospheric levels around the time of his inauguration to the fifties or below—dangerous territory for an incumbent. Significant national security achievements such as the killing of Osama Bin Laden, the defeat of the Gaddafi regime in Libya, and the withdrawal of U.S. forces from Iraq provided only temporary upticks in presidential approval. During the first three years of the Obama administration, the U.S. economy remained mired in slow growth, with relatively high unemployment, a barely revived housing market, and record budget deficits. Thus, as the Republican presidential nominating contest got underway in the summer of 2011, the emerging Democratic Majority seemed to have fizzled, and the Republicans fancied their chances of dislodging the Democratic incumbent and securing the four Senate seats needed to gain control of both chambers of Congress.

The Election Campaign

For all of President Obama's travails in mid-2011, it remains the case that incumbent presidents are hard to dislodge. They have about a 70 percent success rate in running for reelection. Election years that coincide with significant economic distress (1932, 1980, 1992), however, do tend to correlate with one-term presidencies. On the other hand, there were some signs of economic recovery during 2012 as the housing market and broader economic growth began to pick up and as the unemployment rate trickled down from 9 percent to 7.9 percent by Election Day. As Schier and Box-Steffensmeier chapter in this volume points out, various statistical models produced by political scientists—based largely on various economic indicators and poll ratings—pointed toward a close race, with Obama having a reasonable prospect of reelection (Schier and Box-Steffensmeier 2013). One significant Obama advantage was that unlike other recent one-term presidents (Ford, Carter, and George H. W. Bush), he was able to avoid a serious intraparty challenge for renomination. Unlike the one-term presidents, Obama remained extremely popular with the grassroots of his party. Even in his darkest days, Obama's approval rating never fell significantly below

45 percent, roughly equivalent to the core national Democratic vote in the electorate in recent decades.

In a polarized and partisan era, there seemed little reason for grassroots Democrats to give the other side a major advantage by undermining their party's incumbent president. Obama also had continuing advantages in terms of a formidable national organization and fundraising network left over from the 2008 campaign. The four incumbent presidents in the past half-century who endured serious challenges for renomination—Johnson, Ford, Carter, and George H. W. Bush—had all offended a major segment of their party's electoral base. Obama, in contrast, had done nothing to contravene the fundamental tenets of the contemporary Democratic Party while in office.

Even in an era when the Republican party has been generally perceived as moving to the right ideologically, there has been an uncanny GOP tendency in recent decades to nominate the perceived runner-up from the previous contested Republican nomination as its presidential candidate—Reagan in 1980, George H. W. Bush in 1988, Dole in 1996, McCain in 2008—or to put it another way, the party establishment candidate. By this standard the obvious front-runner for the 2012 Republican nomination was former Massachusetts governor Mitt Romney, who had seriously contested the 2008 GOP nomination (former Arkansas governor Mike Huckabee actually won more delegates than Romney in 2008, but he declined to run in 2012) and who was probably the most serious threat to the eventual nominee John McCain. The problem with Romney, however, given the increasing conservatism of the Republican primary electorate, was the very liberal (for a contemporary Republican) positions he had taken on abortion and gay rights to win the governorship of Massachusetts in 2002. Then there was the greatest Romney apostasy of all—his introduction of a universal health care plan in that state that served as a blueprint for the "individual mandate" at the center of the 2010 Obama health care reform (Brownstein 2012c).

Romney had the money, the organization, and the endorsements—all the attributes of a front-runner in contemporary presidential politics—and he was untainted by Washington experience. In securing the 2012 GOP nomination, Romney also had considerable luck. As Barbara Norrander's chapter points out, plausible alternative candidates—Jeb Bush, Sarah Palin, Mitch Daniels, Paul Ryan, Chris Christie, and Mike Huckabee—with strong GOP establishment or Tea Party credentials and fundraising potential passed on the race (Norrander 2013). The candidacies of potentially serious rivals who did enter the fray—former Minnesota governor Tim Pawlenty, businessman Herman Cain, Texas governor Rick Perry, and former House Speaker Newt Gingrich—all imploded for one reason or another. Candidates with limited appeal beyond certain narrow primary constituencies such as Minnesota congresswoman Michele Bachmann and the perennial libertarian gadfly and youth favorite Texas congressman Ron Paul stayed in the race and drained support from more plausible conservatives, to Romney's benefit. Romney's last serious remaining rival—former Pennsylvania senator Rick Santorum—was a strong social conservative with too narrow an appeal to win a presidential general election, as became evident when the media spotlight turned to Santorum's hard-line conservative positions on social and cultural issues such as contraception, abortion, and same-sex marriage.

Mitt Romney was effective in meeting many of the criteria of a successful primary candidate. He was steadfast, on-message, and effective at rebutting attacks, and his campaign demonstrated a capacity to pivot rapidly in response to events. In the primaries, Romney was a generally articulate and competent debater. The key to his nomination was a series of Midwestern primary victories over Santorum in Michigan, Ohio, Illinois, and Wisconsin, based on Romney's strong support from the upscale white suburbs of the major metropolitan areas of these states. In the 2012 Republican field, the former Massachusetts governor was the clear favorite of northern, traditional, high-income, business-oriented, suburban Republicans—the old-fashioned core of the party (Barone 2012b). Yet in order to allay the concerns of socially conservative voters, Romney's rhetoric in the primaries locked the former Massachusetts governor into a dangerously far-right position with regard to the general election—particularly with regard to immigration, a critical issue for the growing Hispanic electorate in the swing states of Nevada, Colorado, and Florida (MacGillis 2012).

The primary process did reveal that Romney had severe weaknesses among Republicans in the South, social conservatives, and small-town and rural voters (Cost 2012). In addition to receiving distrust from social conservatives on ideological grounds, Romney was also widely perceived as a wealthy, upper-status Republican at a time of economic stress (Heilemann 2012b). Some of Romney's campaign rhetoric, inadvertent or not, certainly reinforced this impression. In the Republican primaries—a more sympathetic audience to be sure—Romney was generally effective at deflating or deflecting attacks on his record as chief executive of the venture capital firm Bain Capital, his failure to disclose his tax returns, and his personal wealth. As Boatwright and Norrander point out in their chapters, Romney's hefty campaign war chest and that of his Super PAC also certainly helped (Norrander 2013; Boatwright 2013). The Romney campaign's inability to prove as effective in allaying concerns among the general electorate regarding these matters would be critical to the outcome of the fall campaign.

The seeds of Obama's victory in the general election were sown during the late spring and summer months after Romney had clinched the GOP nomination. The president's reelection campaign recreated the successful organization (and much of the same personnel) of 2008 with impressive national fundraising, a network of neighborhood offices in the swing states, and state-of-the-art techniques for reaching likely supporters (Dickerson

2012). A sluggish economy meant that running once more on the ideas of hope and change was unlikely to prove a successful formula for Obama 2012. Instead, the campaign focused on regenerating the enthusiasm of 2008 among the president's base electoral constituencies—African Americans, Hispanics, younger voters, gays and lesbians, and single, highly educated, professional women. Doing so would require rendering Romney such an unacceptable alternative for such voters that they would turn out in sufficient numbers to defeat the Republican (Heilemann 2012a).

To this end the Obama campaign and allied political action committees (PACs) ran hard-hitting negative TV advertisements prior to the conventions in the swing states, spending money officially raised for the nonexistent Democratic nominating process. Romney, in contrast, had spent all his primary funding winning the GOP nomination and by law could not spend his general election funds until after the GOP convention at the end of August (Boatwright 2013). Obama's ads relentlessly focused on Romney's personal wealth, upper-class upbringing, career as a venture capitalist, and reluctance to release his tax returns. A constant theme in the key auto industry state of Ohio was Romney's earlier opposition to the Obama administration's federal bailout of General Motors and Chrysler.

In tandem with the negative advertising, the administration announced a number of executive initiatives tailored to arouse enthusiasm among key constituencies in the Democratic electoral base. Hispanics got an executive order ending temporarily the threat of deportation for the "dreamers" (undocumented immigrants brought to the United States as children). Young voters received more generous terms for federal student loans. African American voters got Justice Department challenges to voter identification laws in several states. The president's announcement in a television interview that he had "evolved" to a supportive position on same-sex marriage coupled with administration-supported litigation against the 1996 Defense of Marriage Act was expected to enhance already strong support for the president among gay and lesbian voters (Kotkin 2012; Brownstein 2012b).

The Democratic convention, held in early September in Charlotte, North Carolina, enthused the Democratic base. The conclave served to highlight Romney's liabilities (most notably, the alleged war on women being waged by the GOP). It reemphasized what the president had done for the core Democratic electoral constituencies. Voters were reminded that—as Vice President Joe Biden put it in his convention speech—"Osama Bin Laden is dead, and GM is alive." The case against the Republicans and for a second Obama term was also made brilliantly by former president Bill Clinton in a prime-time speech directed at one of the electoral constituencies where the president remained highly vulnerable—lower-income white voters.

Romney made his situation worse with a series of unforced errors and missed opportunities during the summer and early fall campaign. A tour of the United

Kingdom, Israel, and Poland designed to enhance the nominee's foreign policy credentials resulted in an embarrassing series of missteps—especially Romney's implicit criticism of the organization of the London Olympics—and negative press coverage. Romney's vice presidential selection of Wisconsin congressman and House Budget Committee chairman Paul Ryan pleased conservatives with whom Ryan was a particular favorite. But in choosing Ryan, Romney passed up the opportunity to select a running mate from one of the arguably two most critical swing states—Senator Rob Portman of Ohio or Senator Marco Rubio of Florida (who also would have provided significant outreach to Hispanic voters). The GOP convention in Tampa proved to be a rather uninspiring affair that failed to set out clear themes for the fall campaign or provide voters with a convincing rationale for rejecting the incumbent (Schier and Box-Steffensmeier 2013). Romney's liabilities were reinforced by remarks secretly taped at a fundraiser where the GOP nominee speculated that 47 percent of the electorate would never support him because they were dependent on federal government benefits in some way (Hirsch 2012).

By late September, the consensus on the race was that Romney was a weak candidate up against a masterful Obama campaign, and the incumbent would win with margins equivalent to 2008. The Republicans received more bad news in the Senate races. Some uninspiring candidates contesting vulnerable Democratic-held seats and the vulnerabilities of Republican incumbents made it less likely that the GOP would be able to regain control of the chamber. The most conspicuous example was in the most winnable Democratic seat of all—Missouri—as the Republican nominee congressman Todd Akin expressed the outlandish view in a local television interview that rape was unlikely to result in pregnancy because women's bodies were less likely to conceive in such a circumstance. This not only ended GOP prospects of unseating highly vulnerable Democratic incumbent Claire McCaskill but also revived the Democrats' "war on women" theme at an opportune moment in the presidential election campaign.

The first presidential debate in Denver, however, changed the dynamic of the campaign. Romney benefited from appearing on the same stage as the president and from the incumbent's surprisingly lackluster performance (Nagourney et al. 2012). The Denver encounter reminded voters that Mitt Romney was a decent debater and a highly plausible presidential candidate and that the incumbent still had serious vulnerabilities on the economy and the still unpopular Affordable Care Act. Romney also used the opportunity to move toward the political center and sell himself as a president who could work with the opposite party based on his experience in heavily Democratic Massachusetts. With the sheen of Obama inevitability tarnished, despite the president's more robust performances in the two succeeding debates, the opinions polls closed nationally and in the swing states, but more so in the former than in the latter. In the key state of Ohio, the president held onto a lead of 2–5 percent while Romney moved narrowly ahead in some national polls. The Republicans remained optimistic heading into Election Day based on the widespread belief—shared by many commentators and pollsters—that the Democrats could not generate the same enthusiasm and turnout among minority voters and the young as in 2008, whereas Republicans were apparently markedly more enthusiastic than four years previously (Scheiber 2012).

During the last week of the campaign, however, the hurricane strike on New York and New Jersey suspended the campaign for a couple of days and allowed the incumbent to act presidentially in the face of a crisis. The final poll averages pointed to a very narrow Obama victory in the national popular vote and somewhat larger margins in enough swing states to guarantee reelection in the electoral college.

The Election Result: Status Quo

On November 6, President Obama won reelection with 332 electoral votes to Mitt Romney's 206. The president held all the states he had carried in 2008 except Missouri and North Carolina. Obama won by over 4.5 million votes (with some votes still being counted as of this writing), with 51.0 percent of the vote to 47.2 percent for Romney—a 3.8 percent margin, down 3.5 points from Obama's 7.3 percent edge over John McCain in 2008. Electoral turnout appears to have decreased somewhat from 2008, although the extent of the decline was not yet clear at this writing.

Obama's winning margin was somewhat larger than predicted by the average of national polls and the poll averages in most of the swing states. Analysis of the results and of the exit polls indicated that contrary to expectations of a decline in enthusiasm and turnout on the part of Democrats, the 2008 percentages of the electorate from the core Democratic electoral constituencies—African Americans, Hispanics, Asian Americans, single professional women, and younger voters—either increased or remained the same in 2012 (Calmes and Thee-Brenan 2012). African Americans maintained their share of the electorate at 13 percent, as in 2008, whereas the Hispanic share of the electorate grew from 9 to 10 percent, the share of Asian Americans from 2 to 3 percent, and the share of 18- to 29-year-old voters from 18 to 19 percent (Edison Research 2012). With the exception of younger voters (who were six points more Republican than in 2008), the president either sustained or increased his margins of victory among these groups. Most notably, Obama's margin among Hispanics grew from 67–31 percent in 2008 to 71–27 percent in 2012, and his margin among Asian Americans grew to 73–26 percent compared to 62–35 percent in 2008. This unexpected mobilization of the Democratic base was the key to Obama's reelection (Balz 2012).

Romney won 59 percent of the white vote—a 4 percent increase over 2008—but the white percentage of the electorate fell to 72 percent from 74 percent in 2008. Romney maintained the high Republican margins among male voters (4 percent over McCain), older voters (3 percent over McCain among voters over 65), evangelical Christians (4 percent over McCain), and the religiously observant in general, but this could not offset the president's mobilization of the Democratic base. Romney won 93 percent of Republican voters and carried independents 50–45, but in an election where Democrats were 38 percent of the electorate to the Republicans' 32 percent (a six-point Democratic advantage as compared to seven points in 2008), the president's huge margin among his own partisans (92 percent) was sufficient to carry him to reelection (Edison Research 2012). The GOP and many of its conservative media allies had anticipated a 2012 electorate more similar to 2004 (where the parties' share of the electorate was level) than 2008 in its partisan composition (Scheiber 2012)—hence their pre-election optimism that Romney could pull off a narrow victory.

The exit polls revealed some other factors in the president's victory. Romney won most voters who thought the economy was the most important issue, but by a very narrow margin (51–47 percent), and among the 40 percent of voters who thought the economy was improving, the president won 88 percent. Among exit poll respondents, 53 percent said that the president "was more in touch with people like them" (in comparison to 43 percent who said that Romney was) (Kohut 2012). In terms of ideology, the exit polls revealed an electorate composed of 41 percent moderates, 35 percent conservatives, and 25 percent liberals, with the president winning the moderates by 56–41 percent: a slight decrease from his 2008 margin (Edison Research 2012). Obama won convincingly on foreign policy, reflecting public approval of the elimination of Osama Bin Laden and the winding down of the Iraq and Afghan wars. The exit polls revealed that 64 percent of voters said the president's handling of Hurricane Sandy during the last week of the campaign was a factor in their vote, and over 70 percent of those who rated this as the most important issue (15 percent) supported the president (Calmes and Thee-Brenan 2012; Schier and Box-Steffensmeier 2013). Obama also received increased margins of victory over 2008 in the two states most badly affected by the storm—New York and New Jersey.

In terms of geography, the electoral map of 2008 was little altered. Obama's 71–27 margin among Hispanic voters was critical to winning the key swing states of Nevada, Colorado, and Florida (Kopicki and Irving 2012). The auto bailout surely was critical to his narrow victory in Ohio, where Republican margins among white male middle-class voters were lower than in other swing states (Brownstein 2012a) and where there was a pronounced surge in African American turnout from 11 to 15 percent of the electorate (Balz 2012). African American turnout also helped in Florida and the other critical swing state of Virginia. Concentration of advertising and voter targeting on the swing states helped the Obama campaign keep the reduction in the

Democratic presidential margin from 2008 to 2012 below the national figure in most of the battlegrounds. Democratic turnout held up well enough where it mattered to reelect the president despite the indifferent economy.

Romney increased Republican margins in the northern plains and in the Appalachian states. He did reduce Democratic margins over 2008 in the rustbelt states generally—most specifically, Wisconsin, Illinois, Michigan, and Pennsylvania. Despite having been governor of Massachusetts, Romney made no significant inroads in the Democratic bastions of New England, the middle Atlantic states (with the exception of Pennsylvania), and the Pacific coast states. Obama made advances over 2008 in Alaska (where the 2008 GOP victory margin was inflated by favorite daughter Sarah Palin's name on the 2008 GOP ticket) and in several Deep South states—South Carolina, Mississippi, and Louisiana—likely as a result of high African American turnout.

The Republicans also suffered disappointment in the Senate elections. Although the Democrats had considerably more Senate seats up for reelection, a combination of Obama coattails and weak Republican candidates led to the Democrats making a net gain of two seats and an increase in their Senate margin from 53–47 to 55–45 (the two independent senators will also caucus with the Democrats). The Democrats picked up Senate seats in their bastion of New England, with Democratic-leaning independent Angus King replacing retiring Republican senator Olympia Snowe and progressive icon Elizabeth Warren unseating moderate Republican Scott Brown in Massachusetts. They also gained veteran Republican Richard Lugar's seat in Indiana. Lugar lost the Republican primary to the more conservative Richard Mourdock, who then lost to Democratic congressman Joe Donnelly. Mourdock's extensive comments during a TV debate on his reasons for opposing abortion in incidences of rape played a key role in his defeat. The only Republican gain was in Nebraska, where Deborah Fisher won the seat of retiring Democrat Ben Nelson. Strong Republican pickup opportunities in typically red states such as Missouri, Montana, and North Dakota went begging in large part because of uninspiring Republican candidates (notably Todd Akin in Missouri). The GOP also suffered disappointments in Senate races in three purple states where they had initially been optimistic about success—Wisconsin, Florida, and Ohio. As Roger Davidson's chapter points out, for the second successive election, the Republicans forfeited control of the Senate due to the selection of weak candidates in a number of key Senate races (Davidson 2013).

The Republicans easily held onto control of the House of Representatives, however. Although the Democrats made a likely net gain of eight House seats and (as Davidson reminds us) actually secured a narrow plurality of the total national party vote for the House, the GOP maintained a somewhat comfortable 234–201 margin in the chamber. Davidson's chapter discusses how the GOP certainly benefited from control of the redistricting process, which allowed Republicans to protect their vulnerable freshman members from the 2010 Republican wave and even net a seat or two in key states such as Pennsylvania, Ohio, Wisconsin, Michigan, and North Carolina (Davidson 2013). On the other hand, the Democrats gained as many seats from control of the redistricting process in Illinois and a highly favorable outcome from a supposedly nonpartisan commission in California. The Democrats' more fundamental problem in House elections is the concentration of much of their national House vote in heavily minority urban districts as opposed to the more even distribution of the GOP vote (Davidson 2013; Barone 2012a). Perhaps surprisingly, given Congress's wretched approval ratings (generally below 20 percent), the 2012 election produced a status quo outcome on Capitol Hill.

In the 11 states that elect their governor in the presidential election year, the Republicans made a net gain of one seat by winning the governorship of North Carolina. The GOP also held onto much of its extensive state legislative gains from the 2010 midterms, although it did lose both legislative chambers in Minnesota and Maine and one house in Colorado, New Hampshire, New York, and Oregon. The Republican realignment in the South continued as the GOP gained control of both houses of the Arkansas legislature for the first time since Reconstruction and won back the Wisconsin Senate, lost in recall elections earlier in the year. After the election, the Republicans controlled the governorship and both legislative chambers in 25 states to the Democrats' 15, with the remainder having divided control. In terms of statewide initiatives and referendums, Maine, Washington, and Maryland became the first states to approve same-sex marriage by popular vote, an important advance for the gay rights movement. Minnesota rejected an attempt to place a bar on same-sex marriage in the state constitution. In California, Governor Jerry Brown won statewide approval for state income-tax raises on high earners in an effort to tackle the state's budget crisis.

Implications of the Election: Little Mandate, No Realignment (Again)

The tendency on the part of presidential election winners and political commentators to claim policy mandates from electoral victories—no matter how narrow—has become a quadrennial feature of post-election analysis. After losing the national popular vote in 2000, President George W. Bush still claimed a mandate for substantial reductions in income tax rates for higher earners and largely achieved it in Congress. These tax reductions in combination with the substantial increases in national security expenditure after September 11, 2001, created an escalating budget deficit in the United States during the following decade. After winning reelection in 2004, Bush claimed that he had "political capital" and embarked on a fruitless crusade for Social Security reform in 2005, though there was little indication of popular enthusiasm for it in his narrow 2004 election victory (Edwards 2007). Barack

Obama believed he had a mandate for a sweeping reform of health care in 2008, but though Obama was able to pass this reform through Congress, the American public was never won over, and this cost his party dearly in the 2010 midterms and almost cost Obama reelection in 2012 (Rae 2011).

The 2012 exit polls suggest that Obama won because voters preferred him to Mitt Romney as president rather than because of public endorsement of his policy agenda for the next four years (Sides 2012a). Though the auto bailout might have been decisive in Ohio, overall the electorate still indicated a deep skepticism regarding federal government interventionism (in the exit poll, 43 percent favored "an activist government" as compared to 52 percent in 2008) and still disapproved of Obamacare by a 49–44 percent margin (Kohut 2012).

The president's most decisive advantages were in "caring for people like us" and voter confidence that the fragile U.S. economy was indeed improving. These were the themes of Obama's singularly un-ideological reelection campaign, which offered few positive policy prescriptions for the second term (Kohut 2012; Cass 2012). In the post-election euphoria, many Democrats and their media allies seemed to forget that the president's pop-ular (and electoral vote) winning margin from 2008 had actually declined. Obama became the first reelected president since Andrew Jackson in 1832 whose percentage of the popular vote decreased between his first and sec-ond election—hardly a ringing endorsement, no matter how effectively the president mobilized his party's base vote. Democrats also appeared to forget that the GOP had maintained control of the U.S. House, thus making it unlikely that any significant measures could be passed in Obama's second term without Republican support on Capitol Hill.

If the evidence for an electoral policy mandate from the 2012 election was thin, I concur with Schier and Box-Steffensmeier (2013) that the evidence for an electoral realignment in favor of the Democrats was thinner still. In realigning elections, electoral coalitions should change significantly; the vic-torious party wins a sweeping victory (and policy mandate), and electoral turnout rises. In 2012, none of these conditions obtained (Sides 2012b). The reelected incumbent president actually lost support from the previous election, turnout fell, and the geographic and social contours of the party coalitions of the past 20 years were replicated in the election results (Theriault and Moeller 2013).

If we look at realignment from the point of view of long-term secular electoral change, we do see further evidence in the 2012 results of incremental electoral change along the lines predicted by Judis and Teixeira, particularly with regard to the implications of the changing racial/ethnic composition of the U.S. electorate for long-term partisan alignments. These changes—as we shall see in this chapter—do have potentially strong downsides for the Republican Party that were brought into sharp focus in the 2012 balloting.

The poor Romney performance among Hispanics was an ominous sign for the GOP, given the likely continued gradual growth of this segment of the electorate. Almost as ominous was the lackluster Republican performance among another fast-growing segment of American Society: Asian American voters. Although Romney did better than McCain among younger voters, he still lost them by a wide margin, and his gains were almost exclusively among white voters in this category. Recent polling by Pew has also revealed that younger voters are significantly more liberal and Democratic than the electorate as a whole (Pew Research Center 2012). All of these trends were brought into focus by the 2012 poll, but Judis and Teixeira had spotted them much earlier.

There can be no question that such trends are ominous for the GOP. But despite post-election handwringing on the right and the triumphalism of the left at the increased influence of their "coalition of the ascendant," the Republicans are in no worse a position than the Democrats were after their narrow presidential defeat in 2004. Indeed, the Republicans going into 2013 are in a better position since they control one house of Congress and most state governorships and state legislatures.

Romney's weaknesses as a candidate in appealing to middle-class voters regardless of race and ethnicity and his hard-line anti-immigration position in the primaries were critical to his defeat, but regardless of the demographic challenges faced by the party, there were plausible Republican nominees in 2012 who could have defeated Obama had they chosen to run (Hirsch 2012). The fact remains that American politics continues to be highly polarized and elections closely contested. There is no reason to think that the Republican Party is doomed inevitably to defeat and decline after their presidential candidate won 47 percent of the national popular vote and secured at least 45 percent of the vote in each of the swing states needed to win the presidency.

A Better Way to Interpret American Elections?

The failure of the realignment paradigm—at least in its "critical elections" version—to explain recent electoral trends in the United States leaves us searching for an alternative framework that might do a better job of interpreting contemporary political reality. Given the inherently fluid nature of electoral politics—the emergence of new issues that divide the parties in unanticipated ways, the efforts of defeated parties and candidates to embrace new electoral strategies and appeals in response to electoral defeats (such as the "New Democrats" of the early 1990s and George W. Bush's "compassionate conservatism" in the late 1990s), and continuous socioeconomic change—it is dangerous to see any electoral pattern or trend as inevitable, permanent, or "ascendant" (Trende 2012). However, we can discern certain patterns in electoral outcomes that may be more helpful in making sense of our current electoral era.

One thing we know, as Theriault and Moeller (2013) point out in their chapter, is that national elections in the United States since the early 1990s have been relatively close and that the parties and the electorate have become increasingly polarized. Based on electoral outcomes since 1992, we can discern a slight Democratic advantage in presidential elections (in large part based on the party's overwhelming advantages among minority voters, single professional women, and the very highly educated); a Republican advantage in U.S. House elections (in part because of the greater concentration of the Democratic vote in certain states and districts); and an evenly contested Senate with perhaps a slight Democratic edge.

In the early 1990s, Byron Shafer sought to explain the predominance of divided government in the 1970s and 1980s through the concept of an "electoral order" that related such electoral patterns to issues that had particular significance in electoral competition for control of the presidency, House, and Senate, respectively (Shafer 1991). In Shafer's electoral order, a conservative majority on foreign policy and cultural issues manifested itself in presidential elections to the benefit of the Republicans (who controlled the White House for 28 of the 40 years between 1952 and 1992). A persistent New Deal Democratic majority on economic and welfare issues manifested itself in U.S. House elections (Democrats held a majority in the chamber from 1954 to 1994). For much of the period (1954–1980), Senate elections paralleled the House, but the rising salience of cultural issues in the late 1970s and 1980s made the chamber more competitive.

The end of the Cold War, diminishing public support for cultural conservatism, and the long-term demographic changes already noted have led to a new electoral order, but with more finely balanced alignments, more competitive elections at each level, and a different mix of issues specific to each of the elected branches of the federal government. In presidential elections, cultural issues—reproductive rights, gay rights and later same-sex marriage, affirmative action, and immigration—have become more critical (perhaps due to presidential control of nominations to the body where these issues are generally resolved: the U.S. Supreme Court). There is a slight Democratic advantage reflecting the liberal tilt in public opinion on most of these issues since the early 1990s. The Democrats have secured a relatively small but persistent majority in the presidential popular vote in five of the last six presidential elections.

Further evidence for Democrats' slight advantage in presidential politics is that since 1992, Democratic presidential candidates have exceeded 300 electoral votes four times (including 2012), whereas no Republican candidate has exceeded that figure since 1988. In each of the last six presidential elections, the Democrats have also won 18 states totaling 242 of the 270 electoral college votes needed to win the presidency, including some of the largest, more demographically diverse, and most culturally liberal states—California, New York, Pennsylvania, and Illinois. This so-called Blue Wall of states gives Democrats an important structural advantage in current presidential politics because it forces the Republican candidate to run the table in the swing states to earn a narrow electoral college victory.

Given the Senate's role in confirming the Supreme Court nominations that determine the legal outcomes on cultural issues, the Democratic presidential alignment appears to have bled over into U.S. Senate elections. This was particularly evident in 2010 and 2012, when the Democrats were able to retain their Senate majority because of the extreme cultural conservatism of several Republican candidates in key states. The GOP retains its advantage in the House because of the better geographic distribution of the GOP vote mentioned earlier, but this advantage also perhaps reflects the continued fiscal conservatism of the U.S. electorate on economic issues and the lesser salience of cultural issues in that body. The 2012 election affirmed these patterns, but no party won a decisive enough advantage at any level to rule out control of all three institutions in a "perfect storm" scenario (such as the 2006 and 2008 elections for Democrats or 2004 for Republicans). By contrast, during the 1968–1992 period, partisan advantages at each level were strong enough to withstand presidential landslides such as those in 1972 and 1984. Perhaps it is in Congressional elections that the greater degree of ideological sorting and polarization among the electorate referred to by Theriault and Moeller has had its greatest impact (Theriault and Moeller 2013).

Implications for the Second Obama Term and American Government

President Obama won reelection through demonizing his opponent and through base mobilization in the swing states. It was a very similar pattern to that of Republican George W. Bush in 2004: a victory based on polarization. Bush then encountered embittered losing Democrats in Congress and domestic policy failures regarding Social Security reform and immigration (Kotkin 2012). We still live with the consequences of those failures today. One surefire recipe for disaster in the second Obama term would be for him to claim, as Bush did, that his victory provides him with "political capital": in Obama's case for a further expansion of federal government activity. Instead, the incumbent (like Bush in 2004) was reelected because he mobilized his base voters very effectively, and the sliver of undecided moderate voters found him more convincing on the biggest issue of the day in 2012—the economy (comparable to the issue of the war on terror for Bush in 2004)—than the relatively uninspiring alternative.

Obama has become an instant lame duck as the eyes of the "policy demander" elites (Cohen et al. 2008) who set the policy agenda in both parties turn toward 2016. Partly because of this factor, presidents do not tend to enjoy politically successful second terms (Rae 2011). Another reason for this is the hubris factor—the tendency of reelected presidents to overinterpret their mandate from the voters and overreach, not just politically, but also in terms of their actions and daily decision making. This also might explain why presidents appear to be particularly prone to scandal in their second terms, as they and their staffers invariably become increasingly overconfident, complacent, and careless. Moreover, as the next election approaches, there is less and less reason for members of Congress—even of the president's own party—to pay attention to a president who is becoming increasingly weak politically. This is reinforced by the tendency of the party of reelected presidents to suffer significant congressional losses in the sixth year, or second midterm election, of a two-term presidency. Thus, presidential second terms are generally bereft of significant legislative achievements except for relatively rare bipartisan breakthroughs such as immigration and tax reform in Ronald Reagan's second term and the Clinton-Gingrich budget deficit reduction plan in 1997 that contributed to the temporary budget surpluses and booming economy of the late 1990s. Of course, there is always the possibility of a second-term presidency that breaks the pattern as a result of unanticipated circumstances, and it also should be noted that in foreign and defense policy, where even lame-duck presidents can still more easily control the policy agenda, the record of second-term failure does not so clearly apply.

The outcome of the congressional elections was continued Republican control of the House and a closely divided Senate. This is not a scenario for the enactment of an ideological agenda by either side. The most pressing issue is whether some serious decisions regarding the future of the country—the expiration of the Bush tax cuts at the end of 2012 and the soaring budget deficit—can be addressed in a much-divided country and highly partisan atmosphere. The election result provides no mandate for further economic policy interventionism or expansion of the welfare state (Kohut 2012; Cass 2012). No Democratic policy priorities are likely to be enacted, at least with Democratic votes alone on Capitol Hill, as was the case with the 2009 economic stimulus package and the 2010 Affordable Care Act. There might be opportunities for bipartisan "grand bargains" on the budget deficit and comprehensive immigration policy because Obama no longer requires the solid support of congressional Democrats for renomination and reelection. But given the polarized ideological climate of current U.S. politics, it appears uncertain at best that the congressional GOP would be any more accommodating to a narrowly reelected Obama than the Democrats were to the narrowly reelected Bush in 2005–2006. Grand bargains or no, the Obama presidency is likely to become progressively weaker. Following past precedent, the Democrats will likely lose control of the Senate in 2014 and suffer further losses in the House.

Any grand bargain is thus more likely to occur before the 2014 midterm than after, given that the (already weak) incentives for Republicans to cooperate with Obama will decrease markedly as the 2016 election approaches. If the administration makes major compromises with the congressional Republicans on the budget or immigration, it is quite likely that serious party divisions could occur among Democrats, with minority and labor Democrats outraged at cuts in entitlement programs or an immigration compromise that includes a guest worker program. This outrage could provide a base of support for progressive 2016 presidential candidates. There should be little change in U.S. foreign policy, over which the president exercises more influence. Regardless of the course of events, grassroots Democrats are likely to become less enthusiastic as the Obama administration peters out.

Conclusion

The 2012 election reaffirmed America's post-1992 electoral order. Its key traits included close elections with slight advantages for each major party at different levels of government, the continuing electoral advantage to the Democratic party from the growth of the minority vote and the decline of the white percentage of the electorate, and continuing electoral skepticism regarding interventionist measures to deal with the economy, combined with concern over widening income levels. The post-2000 party coalitions remained broadly similar, but the Republicans face the challenge of appealing to minority, younger, and educated female voters alienated from the party by years of anti-immigration and culturally conservative rhetoric from Republican candidates. As social organisms seeking to secure political power, major political parties are compelled to adapt to such exigencies or keep losing elections. The lively post-election debate among Republicans regarding the future course of the party indicates that many in their younger generation of leaders—a surprising number of them Latino, Asian American, or female—understand the necessity of at least a change in the party's rhetorical tone over the next four years.

The challenge for Democrats is to maintain their top-bottom coalition through four years of economic uncertainty and in a post-Obama political universe. Can they easily find another presidential candidate with such simultaneous appeal to young voters, minorities, and the highly educated—the groups whose high turnout saved them in 2012? Can they withstand further House losses and the possible loss of the Senate in the "sixth year" midterm election of 2014? They also have to be wary of the typical second-term hubris that may lead them to assume they have a much greater policy mandate than is actually the case. Lacking control of Capitol Hill, the Obama administration will inevitably have to make deals with congressional Republicans that sacrifice some sacred party tenets regarding protection of entitlements, including the Obama health care reform due to come into full operation in 2014. Any compromise on immigration reform may also threaten some important Democratic constituencies, such as labor unions.

The second half of the first Obama administration provided evidence that the American political system, with its separated governing institutions and checks and balances, does not work well when national elections are highly competitive, control of the governmental branches is constantly at stake, and the major political parties are increasingly polarized culturally and ideologically. Given this set of circumstances, the usual policy outcome is legislative gridlock and policy stasis. The challenge for President Obama and the Republican congressional leadership over the next four years is to agree on effective measures that address the pressing economic and social concerns facing the United States.

REFERENCES

Balz, Dan. 2012. "Obama's Coalition, Campaign Deliver a Second Term." *Washington Post*. November 7. http://www.washingtonpost.com/politics/decision2012/obamas-coalition-campaign-deliver-a-second-term/2012/11/07/fb156970-2926-11e2-96b6-8e6a7524553f_story.html (accessed November 8, 2012).

Barone, Michael. 2012a. "Republicans Find Refuge in the House." *Wall Street Journal*. November 8. http://online.wsj.com/article/SB10001424127887324439804578106720953827886.html (accessed November 9, 2012).

Barone, Michael. 2012b. "Romney May Recapture Upscale Whites for the GOP." RealClearPolitics. March 12. http://www.realclearpolitics.com/articles/2012/03/12/romney_may_recapture_upscale_whites_for_the_gop_113433.html (accessed March 12, 2012).

Boatwright, Robert G. 2013. "Campaign Finance in the 2012 Election." In *The American Elections of 2012,* ed. Janet Box-Steffensmeier and Steven Schier. New York: Routledge.

Brownstein, Ronald. 2008. *The Second Civil War: How Extreme Partisanship Has Paralyzed Washington and Polarized America.* New York: Penguin.

Brownstein, Ronald. 2012a. "The American Electorate Has Changed and There's No Turning Back." November 8. *National Journal*. http://www.nationaljournal.com/magazine/the-american-electorate-has-changed-and-there-s-no-turning-back-20121108?print=true (accessed November 11, 2012).

Brownstein, Ronald. 2012b. "The Class Divide Deepens." *National Journal*. May 17. http://www.nationaljournal.com/blogs/decoded/2012/05/the-class-divide-deepens-17 (accessed May 18, 2012).

Brownstein, Ronald. 2012c. "Romney and the Right." *National Journal*. January 12. http://www.nationaljournal.com/magazine/romney-and-the-right-20120112 (accessed January 13, 2012).

Calmes, Jackie, and Megan Thee-Brenan. 2012. "Electorate Reverts to a Partisan Divide as Obama's Support Narrows." *New York Times*. November 7. http://www.nytimes.com/2012/11/07/us/politics/electorate-reverts-to-a-familiar-partisan-divide.html (accessed November 7, 2012).

Cass, Connie. 2012. "Exit Poll: Hint of Economic Optimism as Obama Wins." Associated Press. November 6. http://hosted2.ap.org/APDEFAULT/89ae8247abe8493fae24405546e9a1aa/Article_2012-11-06-Exit%20Polls/id-6038f159a7854fd4a5c85cc5f6cc6864 (accessed November 8, 2012).

Cohen, Marty, David Karol, Hans Noel, and John R Zaller. 2008. *The Party Decides: Presidential Nominations before and after Reform.* Chicago: University of Chicago Press.

Cost, Jay. 2012. "Morning Jay: Ideology Isn't Everything in GOP Race." *Weekly Standard*. March 7. http://www.weeklystandard.com/blogs/morning-jay-ideology-isn-t-everything-gop-race_633265.html (accessed March 7, 2012).

Davidson, Roger H. 2013. "Congressional Elections 2012." In *The American Elections of 2012,* ed. Janet Box-Steffensmeier and Steven Schier. New York: Routledge.

Dickerson, John. 2012. "How to Run a Killer Campaign." *Slate*. November 15. http://www.slate.com/articles/news_and_politics/politics/2012/11/jim_messina_offers_his_tips_on_how_barack_obama_s_campaign_team_beat_mitt.html (accessed November 16, 2012).

Edison Research. 2012. "Exit Polls: How the Votes Are Shifting." *Washington Post*. November 7. http://www.washingtonpost.com/wp-srv/special/politics/2012-exit-polls/ (accessed November 7, 2012).

Edwards, George C., III. 2007. *Governing by Campaigning: The Politics of the Bush Presidency.* New York: Pearson Longman.

Fiorina, Morris P. 2006. *Culture War? The Myth of a Polarized America.* 2nd ed. New York: Pearson Longman.

Fiorina, Morris P. 2009. *The Breakdown of Representation in American Politics.* Norman: University of Oklahoma Press.

Heilemann, John. 2012a. "Hope: The Sequel." *New York Magazine.* May 27. http://nymag.com/news/features/barack-obama-2012-6/ (accessed May 29, 2012).

Heilemann, John. 2012b. "The Lost Party." *New York Magazine.* February 25. http://nymag.com/news/features/gop-primary-heilemann-2012-3/ (accessed February 25, 2012).

Hirsch, Michael. 2012. "Mitt Romney Had Every Chance to Win—But He Blew It." *National Journal.* November 8. http://www.nationaljournal.com/magazine/mitt-romney-had-every-chance-to-win-but-he-blew-it-20121108 (accessed November 9, 2012).

Judis, John B., and Ruy Teixeira. 2002. *The Emerging Democratic Majority.* New York: Scribner.

Kohut, Andrew. 2012. "Misreading Election 2012." *Wall Street Journal.* November 13. http://online.wsj.com/article/SB10001424127887323894704578113231375465160.html (accessed November 15, 2012).

Kopicki, Alison, and Will Irving. 2012. "Assessing How Pivotal the Hispanic Vote Was to Obama's Victory." *New York Times.* November 20. http://thecaucus.blogs.nytimes.com/2012/11/20/assessing-how-pivotal-the-hispanic-vote-was-to-obamas-victory/?pagewanted=print (accessed November 22, 2012).

Kotkin, Joel. 2012. "The Tribal Election: Barack Obama Turns to the Karl Rove Playbook." *The Daily Beast.* July 24. http://www.thedailybeast.com/articles/2012/07/24/the-tribal-election-barack-obama-turns-to-the-karl-rove-playbook.html (accessed July 26, 2012).

Layman, Geoffrey. 2001. *The Great Divide: Religious and Cultural Conflict in American Party Politics.* New York: Columbia University Press.

MacGillis, Alec. 2012. "How Rick Perry—Mr. 'Oops'—Helped Kill the Romney Campaign." *The New Republic.* November 7. http://www.tnr.com/blog/plank/109905/the-revenge-rick-perry (accessed November 8, 2012).

Nagourney, Adam, Ashley Parker, Jim Rutenberg, and Jeff Zeleny. 2012. "How a Race in the Balance Went to Obama." *New York Times.* November 8. http://www.

nytimes.com/2012/11/08/us/politics/obama-campaign-clawed-back-after-a-dismal-debate.html?pagewanted=all (accessed November 8, 2012).

Norrander, Barbara. 2013. "Fighting Off Challengers: The 2012 Nomination of Mitt Romney." In *The American Elections of 2012,* ed. Janet Box-Steffensmeier and Steven Schier. New York: Routledge.

Pew Research Center. 2008. "Inside Obama's Sweeping Victory." November 5. http://pewresearch.org/pubs/1023/exit-poll-analysis-2008 (accessed November 9, 2008).

Pew Research Center. 2012. "Young Voters Supported Obama Less, but May Have Mattered More." November 26. http://www.people-press.org/2012/11/26/young-voters-supported-obama-less-but-may-have-mattered-more/ (accessed November 28, 2012).

Rae, Nicol C. 2011. "From Reconstruction to Recession: The Historical Context of the First Phase of the Obama Presidency." In *A Transformational Presidency? Barack Obama in the White House,* ed. Steven E. Schier. Lanham, MD: Rowman & Littlefield.

Rasmussen, Scott, and Doug Schoen. 2010. *Mad as Hell: How the Tea Party Movement Is Fundamentally Remaking Our Two-Party System.* New York: HarperCollins.

Scheiber, Noam. 2012. "Exclusive: The Internal Polls That Made Mitt Romney Think He'd Win." *The New Republic.* November 30. http://www.tnr.com/blog/plank/110597/exclusive-the-polls-made-mitt-romney-think-hed-win (accessed November 30, 2012).

Schier, Steven E. and Janet Box-Steffenmeier. 2013. "The General Election Campaign." In *The American Elections of 2012,* ed. Janet Box-Steffensmeier and Steven Schier. New York: Routledge.

Shafer, Byron E. 1991. "The Notion of an Electoral Order: The Structure of Electoral Politics at the Accession of George Bush." In The *End of Realignment: Interpreting Electoral Eras,* ed. Byron E. Shafer. Madison: University of Wisconsin Press.

Sides, John. 2012a. "The 2012 Election Was Not a Mandate." *The Monkey Cage.* November 7. http://themonkeycage.org/blog/2012/11/07/the-2012-election-was-not-a-mandate/ (accessed November 8, 2012).

Sides, John. 2012b. "The Perils of Democrats' Euphoria, or Why the 2012 Election Is Not a Realignment." *The Monkey Cage.* November 12. http://themonkeycage.org/blog/2012/11/12/the-perils-of-democrats-euphoria-or-why-the-2012-election-is-not-a-realignment/ (accessed November 14, 2012).

Smith, Richard Norton. 2008. "The Official End of the Reagan Era." *Time.* November 5. http://www.time.com/time/magazine/article/0,9171,1857001-1,00.html (accessed November 30, 2008).

Sunstein, Cass R. 2007. *Republic.com 2.0.* Princeton: Princeton University Press.

Tanenhaus, Sam. 2009. *The Death of Conservatism.* New York: Random House.

Theriault, Sean M., and Megan M. Moeller. 2013. "The Effect of the 2012 Elections on Party Polarization." In *The American Elections of 2012,* ed. Janet Box-Steffensmeier and Steven Schier. New York: Routledge.

Trende, Sean. 2012. *The Lost Majority: Why the Future of Government Is Up for Grabs— and Who Will Take It.* New York: Palgrave.

Zernike, Kate, and Dalia Sussman. 2008. "For Pollsters, the Racial Effect That Wasn't." *New York Times,* November 6.